Street Culture 2.0
An Epistemology of Street-dependent Youth

JT (Jerry) Fest

Copyright © 2013 JT (Jerry) Fest

All rights reserved.

ISBN-13: 978-1490949628
ISBN-10: 1490949623

DEDICATION

I am extremely grateful to the thousands of young people I've had the honor of meeting in over 40 years of work street-dependent youth. The strength and dignity that they show while surviving situations that few of us would be able to cope with has provided me with a priceless education, and shown me a remarkable demonstration of the resiliency of the human spirit.

This book is dedicated to the loving memory of Gail Loose.

TABLE OF CONTENTS

1	Preface	1
2	Introduction	9
3	Concepts Related to Bonding Needs: Part One	18
4	Concepts Related to Bonding Needs: Part Two	34
5	Codes of the Street	42
6	Concepts of Time	75
7	Time-related Behaviors	105
8	Concepts Related to Identity	138
9	Economic Concepts	155
10	Concepts of Property and Ownership	171
11	Inter-cultural Relationships	186
Appendix	An Introduction to the Positive Youth Development Approach	204

*"I can imagine that someday we will regard our children
not as creatures to manipulate or to change but rather as messengers
from a world we once deeply knew . . .
who can reveal to us more about the true secrets of life, and also our
own lives, than our parents were ever able to."*

~ Alice Miller

Preface

Author's Note -- 2.0 Edition:

This new release of *Street Culture* contains additional commentary following the "Key Points" section at the end of each chapter. This commentary provides further consideration/perspectives on the material, highlights changes that have occurred on the streets since the original 1998 release, and provides more in-depth recommendations concerning interventions and youth worker skills. The material and "Key Points" in the beginning of each chapter remain essentially unchanged from the first publication as a training manual in 1998.

    I am reluctant to call this an "update" of the material. *Street Culture* has showed steady sales over the years and continues to be used as a training aid in many programs for street-dependent youth[1], as well as an informational resource for parents, teachers, law enforcement officers, medical personnel, and many others interested in better understanding young people, particularly those surviving on our streets. Some may wonder if material that is well over a decade old is still relevant. My response would be to first clarify that *Street Culture* is considerably older than that.

    The earliest version of the *Street Culture* material appeared in the *Project LUCK Training Curriculum: A Practical Guide to Working with Street Youth* published by the Tri-County Youth Services Consortium in Portland, Oregon, in 1984. Four years later, the material appeared in *In and Out of Street Life: A Reader on Interventions with Street Youth*, edited by Debra Boyer, Ph.D. Prior to either of these publications I was presenting *Street Culture* as a live presentation for staff and volunteers after implementing Portland's first streetwork/outreach program in 1982[2]. There have, of course, been

---

[1] The term "street-dependent" youth is used throughout this book as a generic term encompassing all of the many labels that are used to describe the population, including but not limited to *runaway and homeless youth, unaccompanied youth*, and *street kids*. *Street-dependent* indicates that physical and social needs, as well as psycho-emotional development, has become less dependent on or fulfilled by traditional social structures/supports due to abuse, neglect, abandonment or systemic failure.

[2] This was a federal CETA (Comprehensive Employment and Training Act) funded program that

minor updates and changes over the years, but the core concepts have been presented in one form or another for over *30 years*. Yet even today organizations are ordering and utilizing *Street Culture* in their program designs and to train their staff. Why has *Street Culture* stood the test of time?

The times we live in may change. The environments we create certainly change. Our beliefs and our understanding of things change. But one thing that doesn't change is our basic humanity. We are "hard wired" to respond and react in certain ways. We have a will to survive; that's part of our make-up, not our environment. We are innately resilient. Research supporting a Positive Youth Development[3] approach demonstrates the human capacity for resilience, and new research into adolescent brain development supports the conclusion that human beings have certain neurobiological responses to our environment. *Street Culture* speaks to the way young people respond and the beliefs and behaviors that they will demonstrate in certain situations. The material in *Street Culture* has never been about the language of the streets or the current drugs of choice, or dress, or any of the other external trappings of street life. Indeed, I have long resisted all requests to develop a street-lingo "dictionary" out of the conviction that it would be obsolete as soon as it was written and probably not transferable to different communities[4]. The "look" of street life may change over time, and certainly different issues cycle through depending on local circumstances and community changes. What does not change, however, is how an adolescent responds to unstable or non-existent living situations, disconnection from healthy relationships and supports, and inadequate access to basic needs. It is these concepts that *Street Culture* speaks to, and these concepts are truths not confined to time or location.

In training, I often read an article from a local Portland newspaper[5]. The article is about a program for street-dependent young women, and I ask my audience if they see much difference between what was discussed in the Portland paper, and what they see in their own communities. The title of the article is: *Shelter Serves as Lone Escape for Abused Runaways*. It is sub-titled; *Girls fleeing brutal homes find a haven that helps them avoid lives of drugs, crime and prostitution*. Below are some of the quotes from the article that I share:

- For years, [we] chose to ignore the problem of … runaway youth. But as more and more children have taken to the streets and fallen prey to prostitution, crime and addiction … [we've] had no choice but to act.
- "Divorce, addiction, [and] poverty … are the main causes of runaways,"

ended when CETA was replaced by the Job Training Partnership Act. Outreach was re-established in Portland in 1984 when I founded *Yellow Brick Road*, which is still in operation.

[3] A brief overview of the Positive Youth Development approach is contained in the appendix.
[4] The Internet has enabled others to attempt such projects; for example, http://www.urbandictionary.com.
[5] The Sunday Oregonian, November 5, 2000

said the 30-year-old manager of ... the shelter ... "[t]here are parents who force their children to steal money for their heroin addiction. There are parents who brutally beat their children."
- [The shelter houses] 24 girls, ages 12 to 17.
- Their stories came spilling out ... and they documented some of the social ills ... divorce, parental abandonment, addiction, child abuse, unemployment.

Without exception, audiences throughout the United States and Canada have agreed that there is little difference between this Portland article and an article that could have been written about a shelter for girls in their own communities. It is only after I receive this confirmation that I let the audience know that, while the article appeared in a Portland *newspaper*, it is not about a *Portland* program. The true title of the article is: *Shelter Serves as Lone Escape for Abused* Iranian *Runaways*. The shelter program discussed is located in Tehran, Iran, which at the time of this writing is a fundamentalist Islamic republic that couldn't be more culturally different from the west. Yet, even there, when young people leave home and start surviving on the streets, their experience is similar to street-dependent youth everywhere and the concepts discussed in *Street Culture* apply.

Street Culture has been sold all over the United States, as well as in Canada, Guam, Israel, South Korea, Turkey, Norway, and Australia, among other international communities. Whenever a sale is made outside of the United States I conduct a follow-up evaluation to see if the material is applicable to them. While I sometimes receive feedback that the US-centric references are not relevant in their part of the world, they confirm that the basic concepts apply directly to *their kids*.

This is the reason for *Street Culture's* longevity, as well as its applicability to different locations and environments. It is not about the external "look" of the culture of the streets, which may change over time or from place to place. It is about the response to the environment exhibited by adolescents that underlies that culture. Because of this, and because much of the concepts are the result of *adolescent* thinking and behavior (as opposed to *homeless* thinking and behavior), much of the material has application even outside of the context of programming for and working with young people actually surviving on our streets. Since the material is focused on a "street" population, particularly in the original material, you may need to "translate" a bit to your particular young person or situation. But if you are challenged by youth behavior in any capacity, including parenting, you may recognize the challenges in the pages that follow and find tips that will help you become more effective with, and a better resource for, young people.

Thank you for purchasing *Street Culture*. The original 1998 preface follows.

JT (Jerry) Fest
Portland, Oregon, 2013

The reader should be aware that this book contains language that some may find objectionable. The inclusion of such language is intentional, for several reasons. One of them is a desire to remain true to the depiction of real-life events that are used as support for the material. But a more important reason is out of recognition that most of you will be applying this material to some form of direct service work with youth on the streets. Anyone in that position will be exposed to language much worse than anything contained herein. The usefulness of using graphic language here is to give you an opportunity to test your reaction to it. If, as it turns out, my choice of a particular word has you paying more attention to the way I am presenting something than to the content of what I am saying, then you are going to have a very difficult time working with street-dependent youth. The challenge for you will be to develop the ability to temporarily suspend your judgment about, and your reaction to, a youth's language in order to be able to understand and address the content of their message.

I strongly encourage you to pay close attention to all of your personal responses as you absorb this material. It is not possible to talk about the lives and lifestyles of youth on the streets without touching on subjects that are both controversial and sensitive. You may know people who have been touched by these issues, and some of you are likely to have had personal experience in these areas. At the very least you will have strong personal opinions on some of the topics. One of the difficult things about working with young people is learning how to keep our issues from becoming enmeshed in theirs. Dealing with our issues and getting our needs met through the young people we work with is both inappropriate, and a disservice. Your personal reactions to this material will be very useful in helping you to begin to identify your own feelings in order to develop coping strategies that will allow you to take care of yourself as you do this work.

Realize also that, in light of the controversial nature of the topics presented, it is possible that you may not agree with all of the perspectives and conclusions. That's only to be expected. Thomas Paine wrote that *"No two (people) think alike, who think at all,"* and my only request is that you approach this material as a student. That is, accept and learn from the material as it is presented, giving yourself the opportunity to try it on for size, or kick the tires a little bit (depending on which metaphor you prefer). Later you can compare it to your own beliefs and values and adapt it to your base of knowledge keeping what makes sense to you and discarding the rest.

The information in this book is intended to be broadly applicable both for programs working directly with street-dependent youth, as well as for organizations or individuals who encounter street-dependent youth in their work, such as doctors, lawyers, security and police personnel, teachers, and many others. The reader should be aware that there are many sub-groupings and special-needs populations that are not specifically addressed (some examples would be sexual minority youth, undocumented youth, and parenting youth, to name but a few). While the information in this book is applicable to these populations, it is not the final word on their unique and specific issues.

One final caution: it is often difficult to avoid the trap of getting so caught up in the lives of, and issues faced by, youth on the streets, and getting so focused on the outcomes that we wish for them, that you forget to enjoy them as human beings. Underneath the anger, the pain, the behaviors, and the needs, there is a wonderful young person who can play, laugh, and be a teacher and a source of knowledge for both you and your program. As you work with them, do not forget to enjoy them.

Key Points - Preface

- Graphic language is included in this book in order to remain true to the depiction of real-life events, and to give the reader an opportunity to gauge their personal reactions to content that is graphically presented.
- Issues related to street-dependent youth are both controversial and sensitive. It is a challenge to keep our issues from becoming enmeshed in theirs. It is also unlikely that you will agree with all of the perspectives and conclusions contained in this book.
- Do not get so involved in the issues and problems faced by street-dependent youth that you forget to enjoy them, play with them, and benefit from their knowledge.

2.0 Commentary:

As described in the original preface I intentionally incorporated graphic language into the material in order to give people the opportunity to gauge their reaction. A barrier to productive interaction is some adults' inability to get beyond the way a youth is *talking* in order to hear what a youth is *saying*. Communication on the streets is heavily peppered with language that many adults find objectionable, and that objection seems to increase when such language comes from the mouths of adolescents. Many consider use of such language not only objectionable, but *disrespectful*, as well. The result is that often we miss *what* a youth is saying because of our response to the *way* it is being said.

This isn't just something that happens on the street between young people and adults. It is a very human response (and one that we must and should work on and attempt to overcome) to pass judgment on and react to our preconceived beliefs about the way others speak. You could have an extremely intelligent person making a very valid point, but if their command of language is weak and they speak with a thick southern drawl, some may dismiss them as being stupid and irrelevant; just as one who speaks with a proper British accent may be dismissed as being snobby and out of touch. We do ourselves and others a disservice when we react more to *how* people talk than to *what* they are trying to say.

What was missing in the original material was an explanation for the language. Are youth just trying to be offensive? Have they learned from adults that talking this way has power? And what about non-street populations of youth? Street kids certainly haven't cornered the market on offensive language; many youth populations slip into graphic exhortations ... much to the frustration of many adults.

But if there is any single message contained in these pages it is that we need to consider *culture* when we examine youth behavior. Is it possible that graphic, offensive language is not simply a mimicking of adult talk or an attempt to offend? Is it possible that offensive language serves a helpful purpose? It's not only possible ... it actually has research behind it.

In 2009 British psychologists conducted a study[6] that had college students hold their hand in a bucket of ice water for several minutes and recorded how long they could endure the pain. The catch was this; half the subjects were only allowed to utter a neutral control word in response to the pain, while the other half was encouraged to curse up a storm. The findings? The cursing half was able to endure the pain nearly twice as long, and their cursing also reduced their perception of the pain intensity. The funny thing is that this is the exact opposite of what the study set out to prove. The experiment was inspired by anecdotal evidence from pain researchers that proposed that swearing was a maladaptive behavior that served to make things worse. But after conducting the study, the researchers concluded that *swearing actually increases a person's tolerance for pain.*

Let's apply this lesson to youth behavior. I think most people would agree that, generally speaking, the more well-adjusted, happy, and supported a young person is, the less likely they are to communicate with expletive-laden language. As we begin to encounter young people who are troubled, neglected, abused, etc., we begin to experience a much more graphic form of communication. Again, we can interpret this as simply "bad" behavior by "bad" kids ... or even an aggressive form of communication intended to

---

[6] NeuroReport, Volume 20, Issue 12, August 5, 2009, Swearing as a Response to Pain.

offend and make us uncomfortable. But, as helping professionals, we will benefit young people far more if we consider that such language may be expressive rather than aggressive. It's possible that the greater the psycho-emotional pain a young person is experiencing, the more graphic their language will be … *because swearing increases pain tolerance.* Instead of taking offense, maybe we should take notice. And instead of removing their coping mechanisms by restricting or banning their language, maybe we should remove the motivation for the language by looking past it and addressing the source of their pain. When young people are cursing at us they are trying to communicate a message … the question is whether or not we are able to hear the message that they are communicating. Instead of denigrating them for their language, maybe we should be grateful that they trust us enough to show us their pain.

I have seen this concern over language begin to mix with the next concern I highlighted back in 1998; our ability to keep our issues from becoming enmeshed in a young person's issues. As our culture, particularly the culture of social services, becomes more and more influenced by "political correctness," I have witnessed increasing conflicts between young people and youth workers that are caused, not by the youth's issues, but by adults' emotional reactions to words and dialog, or by the issues that adults may associate with certain language. Let me give you an example.

A young man received a text message containing a joke. He found it funny and wanted to share it with the staff; his only intention being that he thought it was a harmless, funny joke and wanted staff to enjoy it. While it was not by any means a "dirty" joke, it did contain a reference to female body parts. An argument can be made that the joke was inappropriate, but his intent in telling it was innocent and simply an effort to have a humorous exchange with the staff. Instead of responding to his innocent intent, the response was that he was being inappropriately sexist and misogynistic, creating an unsafe environment and violating the program's rules against hate speech. The young man was caught completely off guard by their response and began to escalate in defense of his intent. The incident eventually spiraled to where the young man was asked to leave the program.

The response was about staff's issues, not his, based on how they *perceived* the joke, not on his *intention* in telling it. If it was inappropriate there are many ways that the staff could have communicated it to him without challenging his *intent*. Instead, a kid trying to share a humorous moment was vilified as a sexist misogynist attempting to make the program unsafe. His integrity was called into question (see the chapter on Codes of the Street) and the escalation that followed was absolutely predictable.

There are all kinds of language issues with which we struggle; from two African-Americans calling each other "nigger" to various beliefs and expressions that we may consider hateful. But when dealing with a different culture, as you are when working with street-dependent youth, you can't always judge *their* behavior by *our* values. Things can deteriorate quickly when we are unable to recognize what is their issue and what is *ours*.

The greatest downside of failing to separate out our own issues is that it makes it really difficult to follow through on the reminder I gave at the close of the preface: *As you work with them, do not forget to enjoy them.* Street-dependent youth come wrapped in a protective suit of anger, distrust, and survival behavior, but the child that the suit protects will often be one of the most amazing human beings you have ever met in your life. Don't let their, or *your*, issues prevent you from meeting that amazing human being.

> *You are enrolling in a university from which there is no graduation, and every youth you meet will be a learning experience for you.*

Introduction

They're manipulative. They're unmotivated. They're aggressive. They're dishonest. Sound familiar?

These are just some of the labels commonly applied to youth on the streets. To complete the list simply think of any negative label and it will have been used somewhere to describe street-dependent youth. As a group, they have been traditionally seen as an extremely "undesirable" client population; one with little potential for successful outcomes, and one that is difficult at best to work with. This belief and reputation has fueled a steady trend towards early intervention, which is commendable in its own right. However, early intervention is often discussed in the absence of intervention strategies for adolescents who are already entrenched in street life, resulting in a response that often seems willing to throw an entire generation away in the hopes of preventing a new generation of youth on our streets. That attitude can only be justified if the premise is correct. So the questions must be; are these labels appropriate for street-dependent youth, and is it true that successful outcomes are unlikely and that working with street-dependent youth is difficult and unrewarding?

The interesting thing is that the answer to these questions can be either "yes'" or "no" depending on the actions that we take. Working with street-dependent youth is just like any other job in the world in that the degree of difficulty you will have is directly related to whether or not you are using the right tools.

You were forewarned that this book contains some graphic and possibly objectionable language. It would be less than honest of me, however, to allow you to believe that I was introduced to such language working with street-dependent youth. The truth is that I learned most of the graphic language I know while working on cars. The task that taught me the most vocabulary was the relatively simple job of changing the oil. Simple, except for removing the oil filter. I still believe that there is a team of sadistic engineers in Detroit who lay awake at night trying to design the most difficult, inaccessible spots to place the filter. Then, one day as I was changing the oil unceremoniously hammering a screwdriver through the filter in order to wrench it off, a friend came by and asked me why I wasn't using an oil filter wrench? The reason, of course, was that I had never heard of an oil filter wrench. I went down to the nearest auto parts store, spent a buck sixty-nine, and immediately discovered that the job wasn't as difficult as I had thought. It was the same job, and the oil filter was in the same ridiculous place. The difference was that I was now using the proper tool.

Metaphorically speaking, this book is designed to provide you with a variety of "oil filter wrenches" that you can use in your work with youth on the streets. The information is aimed at both helping you to better understand who street-dependent youth are, as well as preparing you with proven techniques that can make your interventions more effective. The next time you encounter a situation that may seem difficult or confusing to you, thinking back on the material presented here may help you to find a better "tool" that you can use to make the job easier.

If you use the right tools, and if you allow yourself to relax and enjoy the young people you have the privilege of meeting, you will find that working with street-dependent youth can be both gratifying and rewarding. The old negative labels that at first glance seemed to make sense will become harder to apply. New, more positive labels will start to show through, like mental toughness and resiliency. Recklessness will turn into a willingness to take risks. Failure to seek help will turn into independence. Stubbornness will turn into perseverance. You will discover that the potential for successful outcomes is much higher than commonly believed, if you are willing to look at long-term results. There is no overnight fix with street-dependent youth. Experience has shown me that to transition a youth from street life to a point where we feel that the youth will be successful, and that does not mean that all of their issues are resolved, is generally a two to three year process. You cannot expect that an adolescent who is recovering from more than a decade of abuse and neglect is going to be healthy and stable overnight. This means that any work with youth in shorter terms, whether it be short-term programs, or short-term involvement such as volunteer work, will often be frustrating and appear to yield few results. It takes an understanding that you are involved in a long-term process, and that you may not see the results of the seeds that you are planting today, to keep most people from giving up. Short-term involvement, however, does not mean that the work you are doing is unimportant, and a lack of short-term results does not mean that youth are unlikely to succeed. It only means that positive change often takes time and that people change at their own pace.

The Culture of the Streets

This book is titled *Street Culture* due to the fact that this information is based upon a specific premise. That premise is that when you are working with street-dependent youth you are doing cross-cultural work. Once a youth becomes entrenched in street life and alienated from traditional structures such as family and school, they have to all intents and purposes become acclimated to a different cultural perspective. That being the case, it is important for us to understand the mores, values, and belief systems contained in that culture in order for us to be effective. This is probably the single biggest mistake that traditional services have made in trying to reach out to street-dependent youth. While we spend a considerable amount of time looking at their issues and needs, we approach those issues from the perspective of our cultural biases and beliefs and fail to consider the cross-cultural nature of the work that we are doing. The result is that our services have often not worked very well with these youth, contributing to the belief that street-dependent youth have limited potential for success.

One of the reasons that we have been slow to recognize that services to street-dependent youth involve cross-cultural work is that street culture may not be readily apparent. If you were training to work with a more defined cultural group, such as southeast Asian refugees, for example, you would expect to study the culture in order to properly assess and understand your client's behaviors. Street-dependent youth, however, tend to be thought of as simply children of the dominant culture, and cultural considerations beyond race and ethnicity tend to go unrecognized. It is the lack of recognition for the unique cultural aspects of street life that is responsible for most of the mistakes that are made when working with street-dependent youth, and the reason why so many attempts to serve this population fail.

If you accept the premise that this is cross-cultural work then it is easy to see why street-dependent youth have developed a reputation for being difficult to work with. Without addressing a person's culture your services, at best, lack effectiveness and, at worst, potentially do harm. I have seen good-hearted people with nothing but the best of intentions make disasters out of situations simply because they were making cultural mistakes; the same type of mistakes that can be seen daily wherever two cultures misunderstand each other.

I read an excellent example of this in the paper not too long ago. A German tourist who was a very nervous flyer was returning home. His way of coping with his nervousness was to drink several beers before getting on the plane. Shortly after take-off, while the plane was still climbing and passengers were expected to remain in their seats, he stood up and started to walk down the aisle. When a flight attendant asked him to return to his seat, he turned to her and stated; *the roof is going to blow*. The flight attendant reported this to the pilot, who then turned the aircraft around and landed back in the United States. The tourist was promptly arrested and jailed for making a bomb threat on the aircraft. He was finally released when it was determined that *the roof is going to blow* is German slang for *I have to go to the bathroom real bad*. All this gentleman was trying to do was to tell the flight attendant that he had to go to the bathroom, and because she was not familiar with his culture it was interpreted as a bomb threat. Real harm was done to this tourist's life as a result of a cultural misunderstanding.

I have a friend who was able to avoid a tragedy like this because she was familiar with a person's culture. She was working as part of a mental health crisis team, and their job was to do crisis mental health assessments in the community. This team had the authority to involuntarily commit a person for a ten day observation period in a psychiatric hospital. One night they were responding to a call from a downtown hotel where a woman appeared to be having mental health problems. When they arrived they observed a woman from the Philippines who did not speak very much English, but in the broken English that she did speak she was hysterically talking about supernatural phenomena, demons, and other things that, in our culture, are sometimes indicative of a psychotic break. My friend's partner suggested involuntary commitment but, fortunately for this woman, my friend was married to a Filipino. She knew from her experience with her husband and his family that the types of things this woman was saying represented Filipino cultural beliefs and they did not mean the same things that they may have meant had someone from dominant American culture been saying them. As it turned out, the woman was lost and alone in a country that she didn't understand, unable to speak the language, and therefore unable to communicate what she needed. The proper intervention was an interpreter, not a psychiatrist. The team contacted a Filipino interpreter and the situation was resolved. Mental health intervention was not appropriate or necessary, but the woman was very nearly committed to a psychiatric hospital simply because a person with good intentions who was trying to help lacked an understanding of her culture.

These are the types of mistakes that can and do happen with street-dependent youth. Too often we make decisions and judgments that are rooted in our values and beliefs with the result being that we misjudge the situation and our decisions are in error. Without an understanding of the youth's culture, the possibility exists for our interventions to do more harm than good.

Defining "On the Street"

One of the most important things to do when communicating information is to define your terms. Throughout this book I will be referring to the phrase *on the street*. Often, when using this term, people assume that we are discussing an environmental circumstance or a socio-economic condition. This belief has lead to the labels *street-dependent youth* and *homeless youth* being used interchangeably, leading some to conclude that the underlying need to be met is housing.

I truly wish that being on the street were simply a matter of an environmental circumstance. If all that was needed to help young people exit street life was the ability to provide food, clothing, and shelter, we would be demonstrating a much greater level of success with our programs. While it may be true that resources are scarce, it is also true that a large amount of resources have been directed to this population, and that resources available have increased, not decreased, over the past twenty years. The federal Runaway and Homeless Youth Act has pumped millions into services for homeless youth, but the problem remains and is growing. The reality is that tangible concerns such as "homelessness" and similar needs are not the real issue. Technically speaking, the day a youth moves into a transitional living facility, that youth is "off the street;" fed, sheltered and clothed. But it generally doesn't take much more than a few minutes at such a program for an observer to conclude that the residents are far from *off the street* in terms of attitude and behaviors.

What I am referring to when I speak of being "on the street" is a belief system. It is a way of viewing yourself and your role in the world. Being "on the street" is a way of relating to the world around you through specific values and beliefs that are different from a person that we would consider "off the street." The need-based services that we offer, such as food, clothing, shelter, and education, are not what make the difference between a young person who is "on the street" and a young person who is "off the street." These are nothing more than the tools that we use to address the real issues, which are contained in a youth's belief and value systems. Helping a youth transition "off the street" is about helping them make *conceptual*, not physical, changes. Until a youth begins to change their concepts, they will remain "on the street" regardless of their environmental circumstance.

Since being on the street is a conceptual condition, this book presents the primary concepts that you will encounter when working with street-dependent youth. The goal is to give you an opportunity to view the world through a street-dependent youth's eyes, and to help you to understand the behaviors and responses that street-dependent youth exhibit. The format includes true-life examples of these concepts based on my personal experiences with youth, as well as suggestions for how to modify your approach when encountering these concepts in order to maximize the effectiveness of your interventions. One word of caution, however; when describing the concepts held by street-dependent youth, we are speaking in very general terms. It doesn't take much time with young people to realize that they are each a unique individual. This is one of the more challenging aspects of this field, because it doesn't really matter how much experience you have. Each new youth that you meet turns you into a rookie. If you are going to work with street-dependent youth, you are enrolling in a university from which there is no graduation, and every youth you meet will be a learning experience for you. This can be another area of difficulty for programs which are by their nature designed for populations, but applied to individuals. An example of what can happen can be seen in an early experience we had at a transitional living group home. As part of our effort to meet a perceived need for independent living skills in the area of cooking and nutrition, we implemented staff-guided cooking and nutrition education. The only flaw in our plan was that our staff at that time had difficulty boiling water, and one of our residents was a gourmet cook. This experience rather dramatically highlighted the need for flexible and personalized case planning.

The intervention strategies suggested in this book are tools, and it takes time, patience, and practice to learn what to do with tools and how to use them effectively. If you are able to approach this information from that perspective, and to include these tools in the bag of strategies that you already possess, working with street-dependent youth can be as easy as changing your oil, and far more enjoyable.

Key Points - Introduction

- Street-dependent youth are generally characterized by negative labels, seen as a population that is difficult to work with, and one that has little potential for success. This reputation is undeserved and the result of our lack of knowledge about what techniques and interventions are appropriate for youth who are surviving on the streets.
- Positive changes in street-dependent youth can often take time. Short-term interventions may not yield short-term results, but can be positive influences in long-term change.
- When working with street-dependent youth we are doing cross-cultural work, as youth on the streets form a culture that is separate from our dominant culture. Not understanding and addressing cultural differences is responsible for the failure of some services and the primary cause of most mistakes that are made when working with street-dependent youth.
- The term *on the street* does not refer to a socio-economic condition or an environmental circumstance. Rather, it describes a belief system and a conceptual perspective. Helping youth to transition off of the streets involves changing the way they view themselves and the world around them.
- Each new youth that you meet will be an individual with different strengths and needs. Services will need to be flexible enough to address these differences.

2.0 Commentary:

Perhaps the most obvious difference from the original text to what I would write today has to do with the statement *resources available have increased, not decreased.* Today we are still feeling the effects of one of the worst recessions in my lifetime and the entire system of services for street-dependent youth is extraordinarily strained. While acknowledging the different economic climate in which we work today, I'll reiterate the point I was trying to make; a street-dependent youth's ability to *transition out of street life* is impacted more by their personal belief systems and conceptual view of the world than by economic conditions. Economics may directly affect our ability to influence conceptual change, but if we were able to wave an economic magic wand and meet all of a youth's physical and financial needs, they would *still* be part of and impacted by street culture and behavior *unless* and *until* they develop different beliefs and conceptual views. As I pointed out, a few minutes at any youth program working with street-entrenched youth will confirm this premise.

When I began to re-read *Street Culture* in preparation for adding comments for the 2.0 release, I wasn't expecting what I found. The truth is that I hadn't really read *Street Culture* since shortly after it was first published in 1998. Over the years I've presented parts of the material, and I've certainly referenced particular techniques and sections both in my own work and in helping others respond to situations, but this was my first sit down, cover-to-cover read of the original text in years.

I expected that the material would still be relevant. As I described in the preface, the focus is on underlying rather than transient concerns and the steady sales of the original release demonstrated that it was still useful enough to be in demand by people and programs. But what I was not prepared for and, frankly, what I was disappointed by, was how little has changed in terms of our response to youth on our streets and how, where there has been change, things may have gotten worse.

Take, for example, a statement I make early in the introduction. I describe how street-dependent youth are often characterized by negative labels and viewed as an "undesirable" client population. While there are many of us in the field that do not share this belief, we equally must admit that we all know people in the field; *today*, years later; who *do* view them as "bad kids" at best. And it is unarguable that their media image and reputation in our communities is little if any improved since *Street Culture* was first published. But where we may have even lost ground can be seen when I say *this belief and reputation has fueled a steady trend towards early intervention ... discussed in the absence of intervention strategies for adolescents who are already entrenched in street life, resulting in a response that often seems willing to throw an entire generation away in the hopes of preventing a new generation of youth on our streets.* I had no way of predicting back then that I would remember that "absence of intervention strategies" almost nostalgically, as the trend toward intervention with this population has been along decidedly punitive lines.

Some may disagree with my assessment pointing to the rise of Positive Youth Development as an intervention philosophy among runaway and homeless youth services. However, the rise of Positive Youth Development has been fueled primarily by funding requirements as opposed to programs and services embracing the philosophy at a grassroots level. This has too often resulted in agencies adopting Positive Youth Development *language* with little if any real change in structure and services. At the same time there has been a drift away from the grassroots services that developed to meet the needs of street-dependent youth and toward established and accredited youth agencies; not a bad thing in and of itself, but this drift has sometimes resulted in losing touch with the reality of the lives of young people on our streets. Nowhere is this more apparent than in the disassociation of street youth services from the survival sex[7] industry that continues to be a major part of the street subculture. In researcher Debra Boyer's 2008 study "Who Pays the Price? Youth Involvement in Prostitution in Seattle[8]" an assessment of service gaps features as its second point "Key services directed toward street youth and other youth populations at high risk for sexual exploitation readily acknowledge their need for training to be more effective with the sexually exploited youth population." Yet it was specifically the issue of juveniles involved in prostitution that was the catalyst for the creation of most street-based services back in the early 1980's. The original system of services I worked with in Portland, Oregon (Project LUCK) was the result of a task force looking into juvenile *prostitution*, not youth *homelessness*. Over the years the manner in which marginalized youth are commercially sexualized has changed, strongly impacted as Boyer points out by technology and the internet, but it has not ceased to be an issue. Yet the issue has moved from an area of our expertise to one where we "readily acknowledge" a need for greater training and effectiveness. Additionally, with a few notable exceptions, research over the past decade has all but ignored the street-dependent youth population. There has been little in the way of new research offering us insight into the changing population demographics or the interventions and approaches that may hold promise[9]. While I strongly believe in the theories I express and the approaches I promote; all of which are the result of decades of my personal direct service experience; many are

---

[7] The current trend in survival sex responses refers to youth as "CSEC" youth; the Commercial Sexual Exploitation of Children.
[8] http://www.seattle.gov/humanservices/domesticviolence/Report_YouthInProstitution.pdf
[9] A notable exception being *The Midwest Longitudinal Study of Homeless and Runaway Adolescents*, detailed in the book Mental Health and Emerging Adulthood among Homeless Young People, by Les B. Whitbeck; Psychology Press; 1 edition (April 16, 2009).

still "unproven" in terms of a rigorous evaluation or research model. I can only hope that, perhaps in light of the current "cultural shock" over the sexual exploitation of children and youth in our communities, we will see renewed research interest.

Generally speaking, our approach to street-dependent youth remains a spectrum that runs from "damaged kids who need to have their problems fixed" (the kid is defined by *their problem*) on the one side to "out-of-control kids who need to be corrected and controlled" (the kid *is* the problem) on the other. Simultaneously there is a continuing trend toward incarceration[10] in this country that has resulted in a growing number of juveniles being tried as adults (despite the fact that the overall rate of juvenile crime has been decreasing since the mid-1990's), as well as more authoritarian responses to runaway and homeless youth such as Washington State's Becca Bill, which established "secure crisis residential centers" for runaway youth and authorized law enforcement officials to detain any youth found in "dangerous circumstances" in one of these centers.

I don't disrespect the intended ends of these approaches. I understand that the goal is to ensure safety for young people and provide alternatives to the streets. In fact, one of my greatest complaints is that we, as a culture, accept the fact that we have young people ... *kids* ... surviving on our streets through crime and sexual exploitation, being victimized and used by unscrupulous adults. We go about our daily lives fully aware of these conditions, but somehow we justify it all by thinking of them as "street kids" and once so labeled the whole situation seems easier to tolerate; safely distanced from our outrage. So it's not the ends that I challenge, it's the means. We need to move beyond viewing street-dependent youth as problems or threats and start seeing them for what they are; kids who have been dealt a really bad hand and are playing it as best they can. Only then will we be able to come up with creative approaches that offer young people what they really need, and what they find on the streets ... a place to belong.

---

[10] Interestingly, at the time of this writing, this trend is beginning to shift toward non-detention responses. This shift, however, is not driven by a change in attitude toward young people, but rather by financial considerations, as the continuing impact of the recession is straining State budgets to the breaking point and incarceration alternatives are proving extremely expensive. Without an attitudinal change, we can expect the punitive/detention response to re-emerge if economic conditions improve.

> *Surviving on the streets -- a lifestyle that can best be characterized as endless hours of excruciating boredom, punctuated by moments of extreme terror -- is not attractive to young people who have established a healthy bond with their family and are getting their needs met at home.*

Concepts Related to Bonding Needs: Part One

Concept of Family

Perhaps the most obvious street-developed concept is a street-dependent youth's concept of family. Family is a concept that we all have, and, as you will see, it's not that street-dependent youth have different concepts than the rest of us, but they often have dramatically different interpretations of those concepts.

Our concept of family is one of the earliest concepts that we develop and is where we get many of the needs that we have to bond to other human beings met. As much as we are individuals, we are also social beings and have some very strong drives to bond with others and groups of others. It is in the grouping we call "family" that we find the basis for long-term support, acceptance, and a sense of "connectedness." While it is traditional that the members of this grouping are related biologically, it is by no means a mandate. Individuals who are not biologically related to each other often form family groupings. This may be supported by religious and legal sanction, such as marriage or adoption, but not always.

It is important to understand that the concept of family is one of the most critical aspects of working with street-dependent youth that we as service providers need to come to terms with. This issue will challenge our own concepts and belief systems and, if we are not careful, set us and the young people we work with up for failure and disillusionment as we try to mold the reality of their world into a likeness of the ideal that we would like to see. The result is often one of two extremes; we are either too quick to place blame, or too quick to discount the fact that the youth's family of origin may not always be the best option for them.

Family of Origin

When we see the manner in which these youth survive, and when we look at not only what they are experiencing now on the streets but also at what they have often experienced at home and the dynamics of the families that they've come from, it's very easy for us to get angry and begin to place blame. When we do that, at least in the United States, we tend to unconsciously fall into an American cultural norm for dealing with problems. That norm, what I would call *'The American Way of Problem Solving,'* goes something like this:

- First: Ignore the problem for as long as possible.
- Second: When the problem reaches crisis proportions and can no longer be ignored, determine who is to blame.
- Third: Throw money at it until it goes away, or is able to be ignored again.

This is exactly what we have done with street-dependent youth. For years we simply did not acknowledge that there was a problem, and now that the problem is of such great proportions that it can no longer be ignored we're desperately trying to determine whose fault it is. One of the manifestations of this is the deluge of statistics that we are exposed to concerning street-dependent youth. As a prime example we can look at the statistics concerning sexual abuse. It is generally accepted that upwards of 80% of adolescents involved in prostitution have been sexually abused[11], and I don't argue with this statistic. In fact, the abuse that many street-dependent youth have been exposed to is often beyond belief. One of the challenges we've had to face in doing public education is simply getting the general public to believe the types of life experiences that these youth have had, because the abuse and situations that they've come from are often so hideous that they are literally unbelievable. It's difficult to imagine that anyone would treat another human being that way, let alone a child, let alone that the child is treated that way in the hands of their own parent. But, at the same time, I don't find statistics very helpful. Even if we all agree that 80% of adolescents who are involved in prostitution have been sexually abused, what we still don't know is why the other 20% are out there. We also don't know why so many young people who are sexually abused do not become involved in prostitution. Issues such as these may give us insight into a particular youth's challenges and needs, but they do little in terms of identifying why an entire culture of alienated young people exists in our communities.

When we allow ourselves to be seduced by these tangible, single focus issues, we dilute our effectiveness. Unfortunately, this seduction is often difficult to avoid. Faced with the image of children living under bridges and prostituting themselves to survive, we are prone to feelings of helplessness and strong personal needs to see the results of our efforts. So we focus on things that we can see. It is difficult to see if a youth is feeling better about

---

[11] Anecdotal and professional studies report wide ranges of sexual abuse/incest, from a low of 65% to a high of 90%.

themselves as a human being, but easier to see if they've stopped using drugs. Drugs, then, become our focus and a clean and sober youth our goal. It is difficult to see if a youth is developing boundaries around their sexuality, but easy to see if they've stopped selling themselves on the street. Prostitution, then, becomes our focus, and a legally employed youth our goal. Meanwhile, our sense of helplessness and frustration continues to grow because there are always more youth, and always more issues, and so many failures. So we blame some more.

Who better to blame than the youth's families? We see children out on the streets, many not yet at the age of majority, some not yet in puberty. They are living like animals, dying, malnourished, and selling themselves as sexual toys for adults. The love, consistency, and security that most of us took for granted in our own adolescence is nothing more than a cruel joke for these youth; *children without a childhood*. Where are their parents? Shouldn't they be doing something? Isn't it their fault?

Evidence supports our position. We examine the family histories of the youth that we work with and find unbelievable abuse, severe neglect, and outright abandonment. Finally, we really have figured out who is to blame. But before we even get to feel secure in our indignation, we run into a youth who blows our theory. This is the youth who is as alienated, as damaged, as hurt, as angry, and in as much need of our services as any other youth on the street. The problem is we can't find the abuse. As near as we can tell, this youth was cared for as a child. We see an intact family somewhere who appears to love the youth, and is in pain over the youth's involvement on the streets. Who do we blame now? The answer, of course, is that we begin to blame the youth.

Now our goal is re-uniting them with their families. Obviously these youth are just "acting out." What they need is family structure and parental control. So find their family and get them home. Our job is done; they're off the streets and safe.

It's important to clarify that there is a difference between runaway youth and street-dependent youth. Runaway behavior often calls attention to a family problem that may benefit from intervention, but the family remains viable and the youth is bonded to their family. Often runaway behavior is simply an experiment in independence, but, again, the family bond is healthy and the return home is viable. Youth in this category are quick to seek services, often terrified by their street experiences, and generally not accepted by street-dependent youth. This lack of acceptance can take the form of either rejection and victimization, or protection and assistance with seeking services. But nothing angers a street-dependent youth more than a *weekend warrior,* or a *mommy and daddy kid* being out on the streets. If, however, you are working with a truly street-dependent youth, before you rush to a goal of family reunification consider the following premise.

Surviving on the streets, a lifestyle that can best be characterized as endless hours of excruciating boredom, punctuated by moments of extreme terror, is not attractive to young people who have established a healthy bond with their family and are getting their needs met at home. In most cases the situation is so complex that there really is no clear villain, and in terms of the immediacy of a street-dependent youth's needs, it really doesn't matter who, if anyone, is to blame. Whether or not we are able to easily identify the family dysfunction, it is obvious by the youth's choices that the dysfunction exists. What's important for us to understand is that, for whatever reason, a healthy family bond in which the youth was able to get their developmental needs met failed to be established in this family, and that's the only reason that the streets are attractive. Our work is not about blame or simple solutions to long-term, complex problems. It's about facing hard realities and understanding what street-dependent youth really need to turn their lives around.

The Seduction of Bonding

If you accept this premise then when we are talking about street-dependent youth we are talking about young people who have never had some very critical bonding needs adequately met. This condition is exasperated in many street-dependent youth by issues such as sexual and physical abuse. Abused children often feel that they are the only ones that this is happening to, resulting in feelings of alienation from their peers as well as from their families. This leaves them extremely susceptible to almost any type of connection to other human beings who are willing to accept them as they are, and they begin to establish bonds with groups of similar youth in similar situations. It is the same type of bonding that you see when gangs are formed, with the gang becoming the primary bonding structure and acting as a replacement "family" for its members. As young people begin to distance more and more from family and traditional structures they come into contact with the established culture of street-dependent youth in their community and suddenly find themselves interacting with a group of people with similar issues and similar outlooks on life. A sense of "connection" begins to develop. That feeling of kinship, and the ability to begin to forge a bond with other human beings, is extremely seductive to a youth who has not had these needs met. The result is that they begin to form and become part of a "family" of street-dependent youth.

Dynamics of the "Street Family"

This bond that street-dependent youth feel with each other will be referred to by them in terms of a family unit. You'll hear them talking about their brothers on the street, and their sisters on the street, and even, mothers, fathers, and other relations. Without an understanding of what they're talking about, it's easy to think; *My God, the entire family is on the street!* But in most cases, they are not referring to biological or custodial family structures. They are talking about other street-dependent youth.

This is often where we make our first cross-cultural error. We look at the peer groups to which they belong and perceive them as "bad influences." It's an easy perception to have, considering the activities that youth on the streets are involved in. They are breaking into cars, stealing, selling and taking drugs, prostituting; all of which are activities that we wouldn't exactly consider healthy, viable life choices. We react to this by attempting to influence the youth away from their peer group, usually by some form of denigration of their peers. We tell them that they are being dragged down, held back, and negatively influenced by the people that they are involved with, and that if they are serious about making changes they will need to break away from these influences. The reality is that there is truth in this position. A young person who is going to successfully make the transition out of street life will, at some point, need to let go of their bonds to street families and begin to develop a new peer group. But there are also aspects of this position that are not true. An objective look at a street-dependent youth's life experience will reveal that the street family may have provided some of the more positive experiences and influences in their life. Certainly by our standards these positive influences may not have been very positive at all, but by the youth's standards they may have been the only positive influences that they have so far experienced.

It also may be a misinterpretation to say that they are negatively influencing each other to stay on the streets. We often see a youth attempting to do well who is apparently being held back by his or her peer group, resulting in a process characterized by tiny steps forward and major slides backward. What is actually occurring, however, may be far different from the conclusion that we leap to.

What we may misperceive as "holding each other back" is best described by an analogy. I am originally from the East Coast, and that, combined with my love of lobster, would take me to Maine for the best lobster in the world. On the Atlantic shore, where I would go to get the freshest lobster, I was often fascinated by these huge wicker baskets that were used to contain the lobsters after they were taken out of the traps. The thing that was so interesting to me was that they never put lids on the baskets, yet they weren't concerned about any of the lobsters escaping. As I watched I noticed that every time a lobster would start to climb out of the basket, all the other lobsters would try to climb out with it: the result being that they'd all fall back into the basket where the escape attempts would start all over again.

Street-dependent youth are in a sense like lobsters in a basket. It's not that they're trying to hold each other back; it's that they're all trying to get out at the same time. One youth will get a job and a place to stay, and in a week there're 20 other youth living there. Then the youth starts showing up late for work because there's too much confusion in the living arrangement and they end up losing their job, getting kicked out of the place to live, and soon they're all back out on the streets again. It's not that they're trying to hold each other back, however, it's that they have few resources and they all want to get out of the situation they're in. The minute one youth starts to succeed, their street family attempts to utilize the resources as well, overwhelming those resources and creating failure instead of success. But this admittedly negative result is not the same as youth being "bad influences" on each other or deliberately trying to hold each other back.

Group Identification

Above and beyond the issue of whether or not we are accurately judging peer influences on the street, there are some very practical reasons not to approach them from the "bad influence" perspective. The best reason of all is that this approach simply does not achieve our desired outcome. To understand why, all you have to do is realize that youth on the streets do not identify with you. They identify with each other. This being the case, everything you are communicating about their peers on the street is being interpreted by the youth as applying to them. If your position is that their peers are bad people, bad influences, not likely to succeed, and holding them back, the youth is hearing you say; *you're a bad person, you're a bad influence, you are not likely to succeed.* The practical result of an intervention such as this is to shame the youth and to reinforce their already poor self-esteem.

Even with an awareness of this, however, sometimes the temptation is almost irresistible. This is particularly true when witnessing relationships that are difficult for us. We may be working with a youth who is involved in a relationship that, by our standards, is a negative, unhealthy, or even abusive one. Our greatest hope for the youth is that they just dump the jerk and get on with their life. Then one day the youth comes to you, upset, angry, and talking about what an asshole this person is. Immediately we think; *all right, finally a glimmer of sanity!* We enthusiastically agree with them, confirming that the youth deserves better and that the jerk is no good. Suddenly, before you've even had a chance to unload all the unspoken frustrations that you've been bottling up, the youth is angry with you and defending the person who was an "asshole" only moments before. What happened?

Actually, what happened is something all of us can understand. If I had an argument with my family and was venting with you, I may get really rude and say some negative, hurtful things about them. You, however, better not say a word. They're my family, and I can say whatever I want to about them. The second you start badmouthing them, however, I'm going to jump to their defense and you become the enemy.

This does not mean that you just have to sit there and shut-up. Opportunities like these are excellent for helping a youth explore their needs, determine what outcomes they are looking for, and examine relationships in their life. It is a serious mistake, however, to go beyond neutral topics such as needs, desires, and relationships, and to begin to discuss and project judgments on specific people. At that point you achieve the exact opposite of your desired goal by placing the youth in a position to defend, and therefore strengthen, their relationships.

Sometimes problems are created by our failure to acknowledge the street family. Take, for example, an experience with a youth who had made an appointment through her case manager to get a welfare medical card. This appointment was a very important part of her transition plan, but the day of the appointment her street sister got into some kind of trouble. The youth missed the appointment in order to take care of her street sister's needs. When she went to see her case manager the next day to make amends for missing the appointment and to set a new time, she was surprised by his angry and frustrated response. In his mind she had been irresponsible, missing the appointment because she had allowed herself to get caught up in some pointless drama on the streets. This was a reaction that she couldn't understand because, just over a week earlier, this same case manager had canceled an appointment with her when his sister was in a car accident. She was having a great deal of difficulty trying to understand why it was acceptable for him to miss appointments to deal with his family, but not acceptable for her to do the same thing. The reason is, of course, because we don't acknowledge the reality or importance of the street family. The fact is, however, that the street family is every bit as real to them as your biological family is to you.

Sibling Rivalry

Keeping this concept of family in mind can often be difficult as we watch how youth deal with each other. They can be loud and aggressive, fights break out, they steal from each other, and it appears that, far from being a caring family, they are actually out for themselves at each other's expense. What we witness in their relationships is often not even close to what we would describe as a supportive, bonded family. Unless, of course, you happen to have experience with any family that has teenagers. I can tell you from my personal experience raising an adolescent step-son and daughter that I was often in awe at what they could find to fight about. I actually witnessed one very heated argument over whether or not they argued too much, and these are what you would describe as "normal" healthy teenagers. Psychology even has a term for it. It's called *sibling rivalry*.

If you apply the concept of sibling rivalry to a group of angry teenagers with poor impulse control who are in emotional pain and on drugs, then what you are seeing is really not that much different from the type of sibling rivalry that you will see with any other adolescent family group. No doubt it will be more dramatic and expressed with greater intensity than what you might see in a "normal" home, and certainly the consequences are often more severe, but those differences do not mean that street-dependent youth don't care about each other. It is a serious mistake to allow the intensity of the behavior to let you forget that they see themselves as a family, for if you take an action against the family unit they will not hesitate to show you how bonded they really are.

For example, a situation developed at a drop-in center where a baby was being cared for by her mother and her street family. Care for the child was being transferred from youth to youth and, in the youth's defense, they really were doing the best they could to care for and nurture the baby. Unfortunately, their "best" translates into; they weren't doing a very good job at all. When it reached the point where the baby's health and well-being was clearly in jeopardy, we were obligated to contact Children's Protective Services and have the baby taken into custody. This occurred on a very hot night where, earlier in the evening, it was literally all we could do to keep fights from breaking out. When we called CPS, however, and had the baby taken into custody, all of the petty conflicts that we had been witnessing evaporated. Suddenly, we were facing a tight-knit group of united young people. At one point the youth were explaining their reaction to us, and one of them stated; *You know, you gotta' understand, we're all family down here. We take care of each other.* Instantly, all the other youth began confirming that statement with a chorus of *Yeah, You bet,* and, *100%!* Despite what the appearance of how they deal with each other may lead you to believe, don't ever think that there isn't a strong family bond among street-dependent youth.

Nuclear versus Extended Family

There is a final aspect of street families that can be confusing for service providers. This has to do with the presentation of relationships, which tend to be described in traditional nuclear family terms. Most commonly you will hear talk of sisters and brothers, but you will also hear of mothers, fathers, and other nuclear family concepts. In practice, however, the relationships more closely resemble an extended family. Street-dependent youth will tend to create roles for people in their life, but the individual who fills that role may change from day to day. What this means for you is that when a youth talks to you about their street sister today and then comes back tomorrow and talks about their street sister, they may not be talking about the same person. This is complicated by the fact that relationships on the street develop and dissipate very quickly. You may see two youth who are so completely bonded that they are ready to fight and die for each other, and then discover that they only met an hour ago. It is not wise, therefore, to make assumptions about relationships on the street as youth may discuss the same relationship with you over time but may not necessarily be talking about the same person. This gets further complicated by the inconsistently defined nature of street relationships. A youth's "sister" today may be their "lover" tomorrow and an hour from now the relationship could be something else. A youth's "street mom" may be younger than they are and may even be male. In fact, the roles sometimes co-exist, with a person's street "brother" also being their boyfriend. The descriptions of the relationships will remain consistent, but the *nature* of the relationship, and the *person* in that role, can, and often does, change.

The question then becomes; how do you ever figure out who they're talking about? A quick answer is to pay more attention to the content; names used, situations described; than to actual references to the relationship. You'll find, however, that it's often not very important to determine identities. Most of the time the nature of the intervention has to do with how people and events are impacting the youth being worked with and what feelings that youth is experiencing as a result. If clear identification does become necessary, there is nothing wrong with verifying your assumptions through the conversation. Mistakes are made, however, when you make assumptions about relationships and identities and act on those assumptions without checking them out.

As a conclusion to this section I want to share something that was written by a 17 year old female who entered an essay contest we held for street-dependent and institutionalized youth. The following quote is from the 1st place winning essay and is this youth's description of the concept of street families.

"Even if I didn't have my natural family, I have brothers and sisters down here that mean a lot to me and who I love a lot. I read an article in the paper about street life that said the street kids have families, and they put it down and said that we don't care about each other in reality. This is really a bunch of shit and makes me mad. Because I know I have friends I have helped out and I know their family wouldn't do it for them. And I've never asked for nothing back. I've gotten ripped off by people and used and been through a lot, but its all been worth it because I've gained some true friends from it, who I know would help me out anytime or give me the protection I need. The people down here that are my family are my reality family, because they can understand my lifestyle, because they live the same way."

Key Points - Concept of Family

- Street-dependent youth have unformed or damaged bonds to their family of origin. This leaves them extremely susceptible to forming bonds with other street-dependent youth, creating "families" on the street that have the same psycho-emotional attachments and family dynamics as a biological family.
- Street-dependent youth are like "lobsters in a basket." What we may interpret as negative peer influences are often the consequences of young people overwhelming resources as they all try to change their lives.
- Many of the mistakes that youth-workers make are attributable to our failure to recognize the dynamics of "street families." These mistakes can include speaking negatively about other youth, or underestimating the bond between peers.
- Much of the violent, aggressive behavior between street-dependent youth is the result of a form of "sibling rivalry" and should not be interpreted as evidence that they don't care about each other.
- While "street families" will be described in nuclear family terms, they more closely resemble an extended family in practice.

2.0 Commentary:

If there is one point the original text I did not make clearly enough it would be that there is no such thing as working with "one" youth. Because of the depth of the interpersonal bonds that are created on the streets, as well as the interdependent nature of street life, every youth represents but a single point in an interconnected network of relationships upon which they depend and upon which depends on them. Most case management and intervention services have a strong individual bias, looking at the young person's issues, needs, and situation as though they existed in isolation of other relationship influences. The one area where relationships may be considered is in family of origin, which more often than not with this population represents damaged, dormant, harmful, or non-existent relationships in terms of current daily influences.

In my consultation work this is a situation that workers discuss with me over and over. From the "we finally got them a living situation but his/her girlfriend/boyfriend/friend-friend(s) crashed the place and blew it for them" to the "we caught him/her sneaking his/her girlfriend/boyfriend/friend-friend(s) into the program or stealing for them from the program" to all manner of similar situations where a youth's progress is "sabotaged" by their relationships with other youth; I am constantly presented with questions about *why* it happens and what to *do* about it.

The "why" it happens has two simple explanations. First, youth on the streets are bonded to an interconnected and interdependent network of relationships that either have strong peer influences, or upon which they place great value. In terms of the peer influences, one should never underestimate their power. We often, from our adult perspective, discount or ridicule the influence of peers, but it's a serious mistake to allow our attitudes to ignore the coercive power that such influence holds. Many, if not most, young people would quite literally risk *death* rather than do something that they perceive as losing face in front of their peers.

I can give you an example from my own childhood, and you may be able to think of similar situations in your childhood, that will help you to remember the reality of this truth. For me, the situation was that a small group of my friends and I were riding our bikes through the woods. We came across an area where the path dipped down and then came back up, making a place where we could gain speed going downhill and then "hop" our bikes at the top of the rise on the other side of the dip. We were having a lot of fun doing that until one of us picked up a broken tree branch and got a *great* idea. Two of us could face off over the dip, each with a tree branch, then charge down the dip on our bikes and have a kind of jousting match like the knights of old! This whole idea seemed really cool to me and I enthusiastically grabbed a branch and positioned my bike at the top of one of the rises. As I gazed out across the dip at my friend with his tree branch on the other side, and my other friends watching us as we prepared to joust, I was struck with a sudden moment of clarity. For some reason it just hit me that this great idea was *really stupid*, and I knew … *knew* … that if I went through with it I was going to die. Understand this; I didn't *think* I was going to be *injured*; I *knew* I was going to *die*. The choice before me as I believed it was to get off my bike and wimp out in front of my friends … or *die*. I lifted my branch and peddled down the hill.

Obviously I didn't die; I think we both sort of wimped out as we each dropped our bikes before we got near each other with the resulting cuts and scrapes putting an end to that particular grand idea; but the point is that I was willing to act against what I *knew* was my own best interest rather than to lose face in front of my friends. Even adults do this to some degree, but in childhood and adolescence this type of peer influence is *extremely* strong[12] and often self-imposed, as was the case in my situation. No one was making me joust; I just didn't want to do anything that I would perceive as looking weak in front of my friends. We set ourselves and the young people we work with up for failure when we discount how powerful this influence is.

---

[12] Complicated by the fact that impulse control has not yet fully developed in the brain.

But even if it's not direct peer influence we often overlook the value youth may place on street relationships. Imagine for a moment that you are in a survival situation. Every day you struggle for food and shelter; the basic necessities of life. Now imagine further that someone you care deeply about; your sibling, your spouse, your child, or someone to whom you owe a deep debt of gratitude; is in that situation with you. Suddenly you stumble upon an opportunity for shelter, for safety, for food; but this is an opportunity only for *you*. What do you do? From your place of deep need, do you turn that opportunity down? Do you accept the opportunity and abandon those you care about, those who have been there for you, to continue in the survival situation that you are now able to escape? Or do you accept the opportunity and clandestinely assist the important relationships in your life; stealing and manipulating to meet their needs, sneaking them into safety, risking your own benefits to benefit *them*?

If you're honest you know what you'd do, and it's the same choice street-dependent youth make. They will either turn the opportunity down (not accepting shelter or services because it is not available to their friend, or even their animal) or they will accept the help and, to the best of their ability, clandestinely assist their friends. It's not that they're ungrateful manipulators who are breaking the rules and don't want the help, it's that they're engaging in the same type of behavior that *you* or *I* would engage in if we were in similar circumstances.

Where this becomes a problem has to do with the second explanation of "why" it happens. We as helping adults *fail to recognize* that we are not working with an individual; we are working with an interconnected and interdependent network of relationships. We create options and plans for young people that do not take into account the impact that these plans will have on those relationships and the influences that those relationships will have on the young people we are attempting to assist. Without such accounting we are unable to develop *workable* plans for young people and we should expect that our plans will be challenged if not sabotaged by peer influences and loyalties.

So, what do we do about it? The first thing is that we *don't wait until it happens* to figure that out. Rather, we *anticipate* and *acknowledge* that the young person will *of course* be influenced by and consider their street relationships and we use this awareness to consider these relationships in any and all plans we make for the young person. As we work with the young person we remain aware that every choice, action, and decision that they make or take will be *influenced by* or *in consideration of* their current bonded relationships. Good or bad, it is simply a fact that we must take into consideration. Armed with this awareness, we then develop our interventions and plans for the young person in consideration of this reality[13].

Such consideration may take a variety of forms. It may mean not offering certain services at this time. If you are aware that this young person has strongly influential relationships to which they feel responsible and with which they are not able to set limits, maybe now is not a good time to place them into an independent living apartment that requires them to say no to friends who also need shelter; because you know that they're not going to say no, so why set them up for failure and your program up for dealing with that problem? It may mean that developing plans for *their friends* can be as important to this youth's success as the plans you develop for *them*. If you know that they have relationships on the streets that depend on them, you may want to address replacing that dependence as the young person transitions. It may mean setting up reasonable and agreed upon consequences for anticipated situations. Rather than trying to figure out what to do when a youth sneaks a boyfriend into the apartment, negotiate *in advance* acceptable behaviors and reasonable consequences and stick to them when and if it happens. It may mean helping youth learn to set limits with their friends or creating situations where we are able to *set limits for them*.

For example, in one program I directed we experienced problems with the guests of residents. While we had guest curfew, it was very difficult to get the guests to leave or to have residents take responsibility for asking their guests to leave. We experimented with several agreements by which residents were held responsible for their guests not staying past the curfew, but all we created was a series of staff/resident conflicts. In trying to negotiate resolution with the residents we came to learn that residents felt incapable of setting that boundary with their friends. Either the influence of the relationship was such that setting the limit risked repercussions outside of the program, or the emotional cost of sending someone they cared about away from safety and out into the streets was one they couldn't surmount. What finally worked was the realization that the curfew was not the wishes of the *residents*; it was the wishes of the *program*, so why were we making the residents responsible for its enforcement? A new agreement was implemented that took the entire matter out of the resident's hand. If a guest remained beyond guest curfew the program would no longer consider them a guest; they would be considered a trespasser and be given a choice of leaving or being removed by the police. This took the focus off of the resident and interestingly empowered them to work with their guests to leave by curfew in order to avoid consequences over which they had no control. As an aside, we also learned that our staff was as challenged by enforcing the curfew as our residents had been, resulting in implementation of a policy that staff would be issued a written warning that could jeopardize their employment if they failed to enforce curfew per policy.

---

[13] Eco-mapping is a highly recommended tool for helping us to understand these relationships.

This gave them the same "out" in terms of enforcement as our residents now had, resulting in increased ability on the part of staff to enforce curfew without damaging relationships.

If you want to improve the success of the individuals you work with, the first and most important step is to realize that you are *not working with individuals*. Unless and until you anticipate and plan for relational influences you will find the individual you are trying to assist being constantly "sabotaged" by other youth.

Having clarified that point, I should acknowledge that the nature of "street families" represents one area where there have been changes in the years since *Street Culture* was first published. The changes have been more in the form of evolution and addition, not replacing information I presented in the original text, but rather adding to it in terms of structure and how the "families" sometimes appear and play out. While everything I described still exists on the streets and within the culture, there has also been a decidedly darker trend affecting the formation of street families that can be traced to two primary influences; the impact of incarceration on the population and the beliefs about family structure and dynamics that youth bring with them to the streets.

As I referenced in the introduction, we have experienced a growing trend toward punitive responses and incarceration as an intervention approach. While in some cases this is justifiable, as in response to street violence where bodily harm or death is a result, in other cases incarceration is utilized as an attempt to protect or a means of dealing with survival behaviors. In either case, incarceration rarely reforms behavior or promotes development and more often than not simply layers *prison culture* on top of *street culture*. An unintended consequence is that we are seeing growing numbers of young people being released after serving their time with little change in their socio-economic or environmental circumstance, and negative change in their cultural perspectives and beliefs. While they may biologically be adults ranging from their 20's to 30's, they are *developmentally* and *conceptually* street-dependent adolescents with a prison acculturation.

Released back into their old environments they re-associate with the street scene, except that now they wield considerably more status and power becoming the "dads" and the "moms" representing "old school" street culture and positioning themselves as mentors and protectors of younger youth new to the streets. Their orientation is prison culture, so these newly formed "families," while still maintaining the "extended family" structure described in the original text, act in practice much closer to "mini-gangs" with the younger youth expected to carry out criminal activities in support of the family[14]. This can result in cultural phenomenon such as

---

[14] For a more in-depth insight into these newer, more violent street families, read *All God's Children:*

"taxing[15]" being taken to extreme levels where severe beatings and even murder may result (again, the influence of prison culture, where physical violence is a primary response). Younger youth who become enmeshed in these types of street families are often victimized and brutalized and used by the family to victimize and brutalize others.

What often sets these younger youth up for such victimization is the second influence I referenced; the beliefs about family structure and dynamics that youth bring with them to the streets. Rarely have these youth had positive, healthy family experiences, and what we often see in street families are extreme representations of abusive family structures that youth may have experienced prior to leaving home, or abusive institutional experiences where youth were victimized in foster homes or other systems. They are *might makes right* structures where rules are strict and consequences are severe; which can be really difficult for helping adults to understand. The same young person who won't stay in a shelter program because the "rules" are too "strict" will be part of a street family where they may be beaten, starved, imprisoned, or raped for relatively minor infractions of arbitrary rules.

This becomes easier to understand when you realize that many youth on the streets have learned in childhood to confuse physical and psycho-emotional punishment with caring and love; even to the point where they are uncomfortable with a lack of punishment and feel a need to provoke it in order to *feel* loved. Listen to the words of a 17 year-old female during a taped therapy session. In response to exploration about the physically abusive relationship she was in with her boyfriend/pimp, she explained it as follows:

"*Like, when we fight, everybody says he shouldn't hit you and stuff, but I do a lot of things to start those fights. I mean, I start the fights in a lot of ways. In a way I want him to hit me, because it makes me feel loved, for him to hit me. Because, there again, my father used to hit me. That's how I know he loved me. So when [my boyfriend] hits me, I know he loves me.*"

When this young woman felt unloved and needed intimacy, she would *provoke* situations that we would interpret as her being violently abused … but the truth is that she had as much control in those situations as her abuser.

Youth on the streets have been deprived of and are desperately seeking intimacy, affection, and support, but their life experience may have taught them to confuse such feelings with punishment, violence, and control, making them extremely susceptible to street "family" structures that utilize

---

Inside the Dark and Violent World of Street Families, by Rene Denfeld (PublicAffairs, January, 2007)

[15] "Taxing" is a culturally accepted practice on the streets in response to perceived or real disrespect or offense. If I feel you have wronged me I may *tax* you for your property or even your body, such as sexual acts or cutting your hair.

such methods as well as related relationships such as pimping and trafficking. This is why they may prefer violent families on the streets to the safety of youth programs, because they don't feel "cared" about in youth programs; at least not until their concepts related to being cared about and loved are challenged and begin to change. This, in my mind, underscores the importance of interventions that are voluntary and do *not* rely on punitive measures. Punitive, mandated approaches only serve to strengthen the confusion between force and caring; a street-reinforced concept that must be *challenged* if a young person is going to transition out of street life.

As a final thought I'd like to reference a statement I made at the beginning of these comments; that the one area where relationships may be considered is in family of origin, which more often than not with this population represents damaged, dormant, harmful, or non-existent relationships in terms of current daily influences. I want to be clear that this statement is not intended to discount considering family of origin when working with youth; in fact, I feel that we do not consider family of origin enough. Due to the nature of many of the youth's families, my observation has been that the field has become somewhat "family avoidant." The family may be viewed as the source of many of the youth's problems resulting in a tendency to "protect from" rather than "include in" where the family is concerned. While I totally support maintaining an awareness of the potential harm that some families may represent, I also support maintaining an awareness of the fact that many youth's families remain part of that interconnected and interdependent web of relationships within which we need to work. Additionally, I feel we are sometimes "nuclear-centric" in our view of families, dismissing the network of people that a family represents due to the harm we may perceive in the most dominant family relationships. It is possible that, beyond the damaged or abusive relationships that we see, there may be extended family members; aunts, uncles, grandparents, cousins, even family friends; who may be resources or healthy connections for this young person. We do young people a disservice if we fail to explore these opportunities based on a belief that family has been the "problem."

The business of services for at-risk youth is probably the strangest business in the world, in that it's the only business that I know of where the ultimate goal is to put ourselves out of business.

Concepts Related to Bonding Needs: Part Two

Necessity

The concept of "necessity" is related to "family" in that it also addresses bonding needs, but at a deeper level. In addition to simply identifying with and belonging to a group, we also have a need to feel as though we have a special role and that there is something unique about the contribution we are making that would be missed if we were gone. The catch is that whatever it is that meets this need must be something that has a positive effect on our self-esteem otherwise we will be left feeling empty and unfulfilled.

As adults, most of us have a variety of options for getting this need met. These include our work and home life, continuing education, social clubs and recreational activities in which we are involved. Youth on the street, however, have virtually no untainted options for feeling needed. It may be true that a youth involved in prostitution may feel "needed" by their customers or "dates," but this is hardly an option that increases self-esteem. Youth who develop "regulars" (customers who return to them specifically) may feel a somewhat greater sense of being needed, but this again is not an option that could be considered "untainted." The result is that the lifestyle of the streets does not provide for a key, important human bonding need.

The "My Friend Needs Help" Syndrome

Youth on the streets, being survivors with an impressive ability to adapt to their environment, have developed a cultural response that allows them to meet this need. This response is what I have termed the *My Friend Needs Help* syndrome. This syndrome may be seen in the way in which youth on the streets present themselves. This is the "tough" exterior that demonstrates an attitude of; *I've been through it all, I've seen it all, I can take care of myself, I don't need nothing or nobody*. That same youth, however, when given the opportunity, will just as quickly point out two or three friends who *really need help*. They'll express with genuine concern that their friends don't have a place to sleep, or that they're not getting enough food, or that they need clothes, or that they need to stop using drugs. As true as any of that may be, we can't help but notice that the problems they are identifying in their friends' lives are blatant problems in the youth's own life. A youth will talk about their friend who is shooting crank and killing herself with her abuse of drugs, and we observe the needle marks on this youth's own arms and have seen them tweaked out of their brain almost every day. How we respond in these situations depends on how we interpret the behavior we are seeing.

Denial
The traditional interpretation that has developed in social services is that the youth is "in denial" of their own problems. This is particularly related to any issue concerning the use of drugs. The accepted response is to ignore the youth's concerns about their friends' issues and to confront them about their own problems. However, if you choose to use that type of intervention in a setting such as street outreach, a drop-in service, or any other voluntary program, you should be prepared to lose contact with that youth. A confrontational response in these situations will almost always result in the youth withdrawing from services.

It is important to understand that this withdrawal from services is not because the youth can't handle facing their own issues. Rather, it is due to our misinterpretation of the situation and our failure to provide the service that the youth is seeking. The *My Friend Needs Help* syndrome does not signify that the youth is in denial about their issues. Instead, this syndrome indicates a youth who is asking you to help them meet a conceptual need; that need being a way to make a positive contribution to their peers and thereby enhance their self-esteem. When we refuse to help them do that and instead confront them with their own issues, we are actually denying them the service that they are requesting. It is little wonder that they then choose to take their business elsewhere.

Helping Youth Help Themselves
There are several ideas to keep in mind when you run into the *My Friend Needs Help* syndrome. The first and foremost is that they are actually requesting a service for themselves in that they are asking you to help them create a circumstance where they can make a positive contribution by helping someone else. The benefits of this approach, however, go beyond simply providing the requested service. When you work with a youth to help them address a friend's issues, that youth is absorbing everything you're saying. You are, in effect, educating both of the youth with information and problem solving skills. This type of education is probably the single most important focus of intervention with street-dependent youth. It is sometimes difficult to maintain this perspective, but it is not our role to "help" these youth, at least, not in terms of solving their problems for them. Our purpose is to serve as a resource that street-dependent youth

can use to help themselves, and our goal is to teach them how to deal with their own problems. If a youth comes to us with a problem and we solve it for them, all we've done is teach them that the solution to their problems is to bring them to us and by so doing we have failed. To teach them that we are the solution to their problems is a disservice because there will come a time when we are not there. Our programs may be defunded, or the youth may age out of eligibility for our services. Who will solve their problem for them then? Every time a youth brings a problem to us our goal should be to have them leave better able to cope with that problem without our intervention when they encounter a similar issue later. The truth is that the business of services for at-risk youth is probably the strangest business in the world in that it's the only business that I know of where the ultimate goal is to put ourselves out of business. *We don't want street-dependent youth to need us*, and we want our programs to be obsolete because there are no youth on the streets.

The *My Friend Needs Help* syndrome is one of the key concepts that makes youth involvement in programs such a successful approach to service delivery. Peer intervention models, or programs designed to include young people as partners in the resolution of their issues, are widely recognized as effective intervention strategies. It is also widely recognized, however, that the peers and partners are often helped as much as *or more than* the young people who receive the services. The reason for this effect is that, through involvement in the delivery of services, youth peers and partners are given the opportunity to fully address the concept of "necessity."

The Issue of Trust

There is an additional purpose that may be served by the *My Friend Needs Help* syndrome. It must be remembered that trust, particularly where adults are concerned, is a major issue for street-dependent youth. When you begin to learn about their life experience, the fact that they are distrustful of adults should come as no surprise and may even be a reason why they're still alive. The *My Friend Needs Help* syndrome can often be a method by which a youth is attempting to establish some level of trust with you by watching how you deal with someone else's issues before they are willing to trust you with their own. In some cases you may even find that the "friend" does not exist and that you are actually dealing with a third party account of the youth's own problems. This "third party" presentation may feel safer for them until they are comfortable. It leaves them with an "out" and limits our ability to betray their trust. I have had many experiences with street-dependent youth where we begin discussing a "friend's" issue and, at some point in the conversation, we end up talking in the first person. The conversation never would have taken place, however, if I began with forcing them to confront their issues.

In short, when you see the *My Friend Needs Help* syndrome my advice is that you do not try to focus in on the youth's own problems. Trust that they'll deal with them when it's safe for them to do so. By working with youth to assist them in helping each other you will be building trust, teaching problem solving skills, and utilizing the power of youth partnership and peers helping peers. You will also be providing the true service that they are requesting, which is a way to feel needed and useful; a concept that is vital to a person's self-esteem. In addition to all of that, there is one more advantage to this approach. You will be reaching greater numbers of young people with your services. The reality is that you could have the best outreach program in the world and still be limited in the numbers of youth with whom you are able to build relationships. Once you get one youth to truly trust you, however, they will bring youth into your services at a rate that you will barely be able to keep up with. The benefits of helping street-dependent youth help each other far outweigh any potential gains from a more confrontational approach.

Key Points - Necessity

- Street-dependent youth will be far more willing to seek help for their friends than they will for themselves. This is not "denial" in the traditional sense, but rather their attempt to create a situation where they can feel needed and valued.
- Interventions can be more successful by helping youth to help their friends, rather than confronting youth about their own issues.
- It is the concept of "necessity" that explains the success of peer counseling and youth partnership approaches to services.
- Trust is a major barrier to services for street-dependent youth. Third-person presentation of problems is one way a distrustful youth can access services and begin to develop relationships.

2.0 Commentary:

One of the primary justifications I make for a non-confrontational approach to street-dependent youth has to do with earning the trust of young people on the streets. While I identify that the *my friend needs help* syndrome is often a service request (asking you to help them feel positively about themselves) I also identify it as a safety coping skill, allowing them to take advantage of your assistance without great risk; in effect, being able to get *assistance* from you without having to *trust you*. Here and in several others places in *Street Culture* I reference the issue of trust and offer techniques that will help street-dependent youth learn to trust you as you *earn* their trust. As I've presented *Street Culture* over the years, though, I have often encountered questions about the other side of that coin; what about *us* trusting *them*, and when can we expect them to earn *our* trust?

I'm going to make a statement that some might find hard to believe. I have never met or worked with a young person on the streets that I did not *fully trust without reservation*. Before you discount or misinterpret what I'm saying, let me talk about the nature of trust.

When you look at definitions of trust you learn that it is generally defined as *to be confident in* or *to have certainty about*. It means that you are able to anticipate with reasonable certainty what other people will do and what situations are likely to occur as a result of your interactions with them. This is why I can say without hesitation or qualification that I have never met a street-dependent youth that I didn't trust, because my trusting them is not based on an expectation that they will be anything other than who they are or behave in ways beyond their level of development and conceptual perception of the world. If I leave money out where there are youth who are surviving on the streets with whom I have little or no relationship, I *absolutely trust* that one of them likely will take it. When they do, they do not betray my trust by doing so; I betrayed *them* by allowing a situation where I knew, *or should have known*, that they would act out of survival needs in a manner that doesn't serve them well.

Street-dependent youth do not need to earn our trust because we have never been betrayed by them. They are behaving in a manner that is consistent with their life experience, and the reason why they don't trust *us* is because we represent the systems and values that have failed *them*. In fact, those of us in this field who follow stories related to homeless and street-dependent youth are aware that even the systems designed to help in their current situation are often guilty of perpetuating exploitation and abuse. Documentation of young people being physically and sexually abused in foster homes, detention and residential centers are sadly common. The 2007-8 "Cash for Kids" corruption scandal in the Pennsylvania juvenile justice system is a recent example of systemic abuse, and exploitive individuals pepper the systems designed to help. Consider the recent case of a Los Angeles probation officer assigned to the Department of Children and Family Services' Transitional Housing Program; a program that works with youth transitioning out of foster care. This particular probation officer worked for 3 years before he died of a heart attack. It was only then, when his cases were being transferred to another officer, that it was discovered that he had stolen as much as $15,000 from the homeless youth on his caseload[16]. Those of us who have worked within the youth service field for

---

[16] DCFS money scandal: Homeless youths' earnings pocketed -- Daily News, Los Angeles, 6/2/11

any length of time at all have more than likely had their own brushes with staff exploitation or abuse of the young people in their care, and stories of such abuse are regularly reported in the media.

Of course, that doesn't mean that we *all* have failed them, and for every instance of abuse and exploitation there are countless examples of caring and support. As young people learn that there are people who are different from what their life experience has taught them, we will begin to earn their trust and they will begin to act differently toward us. But that's going to take time and effort on our part, which is why the burden is on us to earn *their* trust. The key to us trusting *them* is to understand where the young person is at in terms of their development and conceptual view of the world, as well as understanding our relationship with them. If they "betray our trust" it is because *we* misunderstood one of these measures and expected behavior from them that they were not ready or able to offer. The bottom line is; *we* are the professionals and *we* are the adults. It is *our* responsibility to earn and maintain trust, *not theirs*.

One of the most important factors in earning trust is consistency. Remember, trust means being able to predict what other people will do and what situations will occur. One of the reasons why street-dependent youth don't trust adult helpers is because they don't feel that they can predict what we will do or what will happen as a result of interacting with us. Trust is earned as we become more predictable, and we become predictable by being consistent. I have been in the field long enough now to have had many experiences of being contacted by young (and even not-so-young) adults who I had worked with when they were adolescents, years after I worked with them. There was one young man who I worked with at a drop-in center; though "worked with" feels a little like an exaggeration. The truth is that all of my interactions with this young man were around setting limits. All I remember about him is that whenever he was in the center my time was spent intervening around boundaries and setting limits, constantly responding to nearly out-of-control behavior. That's why I was so surprised when he called me several years later. Our conversation went something like this:

"Hey Jerry, it's [so-and-so]. I'm doing really good these days. I'm in school and have a job, and I'm living in [a different city] in student housing. I just wanted to check in and see how you're doing, and to thank you for all the help you gave me."

To say that I was surprised is an understatement. I never really thought that we had much of a relationship at all, let alone one where he'd felt that I'd *helped* him. I pretty much said so in my response:

"It's great to hear that you're doing so well, but I have to admit you're one of the last people I ever thought I'd hear from. My memory of our relationship was that we pretty much butted heads all of the time."

His response spoke volumes and really drove home to me the

importance of consistency. I wrote it down when he said it, so what follows is an exact quote:

"Yeah, but ... Jerry, I always knew what to expect from you."

It was then that I realized that our "butting heads" provided him with exactly the service he was seeking from me. In a later chapter (see Concepts of Time) I speak about the importance of consistency and identify the street-developed concept that the world is random. By engaging in behaviors that provoked consistent responses from me this young man was able to structure a level of predictability into his life that didn't exist elsewhere. It may have been an odd way to do it, and I can think of about a hundred better ways that we could have achieved the same end, but this was *his* way and the only reason it worked for him was my commitment to *respond consistently*; neither ignoring his behavior due to being worn down nor overreacting to his behavior due to being frustrated or angry; and my consistency in responding to him resulted in his memory of me as someone who he could *trust* and someone who had *helped*.

It's actually very easy to be consistent and to earn the trust of street-dependent youth if you follow a very simple rule; *be trustworthy*. In all of your dealings with a youth be absolutely honest and reliable. Say what you mean, mean what you say, and do what you say you're going to do. This doesn't mean that a young person will always agree with or *like* what you say or do, but if you want to earn their trust they need to learn that you *are* what you claim to be.

In Positive Youth Development terms, the main point I make in this chapter; that the *my friend needs help* syndrome is really about positive impact on self-esteem; is supported by our knowledge of the importance of environmental Protective Factors and their relationship to fostering innate resilience. One of those Protective Factors; Meaningful Participation; is often misunderstood as giving youth "voice" and allowing youth input into governing structures. What Meaningful Participation is really about, or, more accurately, what its purpose is, is allowing each young person to experience a measure of control and "connectedness." Through the experience of active participation a young person develops a sense of belonging and value, therefore Meaningful Participation is a purposeful means of enhancing self-esteem and positively impacting an individual's mental health and wellbeing.

Obviously, what we want to do is to create as many opportunities for Meaningful Participation as we can, and we want to ensure that these opportunities meet the 3 qualifications for a successful strategy of participation. Those qualifications are *clarity* (the opportunity must be understood and free of ambiguity); *legitimacy* (the opportunity must be real and not oversold); and *relevance* (the opportunity must be relevant to youth *from the youth's point of view*). We are often challenged in creating Meaningful

Participation strategies that meet these 3 qualifications, so it makes complete sense from a Positive Youth Development perspective that we should not overlook or fail to take advantage of the strategies that young people create themselves, such as those that occur as a result of the *my friend needs help* syndrome. Here we have a ready-made strategy for addressing self-esteem and helping youth to experience a sense of control and connectedness that could not be *clearer*, more *legitimate*, or more *relevant* to them. To ignore that strategy in favor of challenging perceived "denial" makes little sense from a cultural perspective.

You cannot survive as a drug-impaired, unemployed, homeless adolescent, living outside of traditional society and the law, by being stupid and incapable

Codes of the Street

If it is true that a culture exists on the streets, then it is also true that, as with any other culture, the member's behaviors and decisions will be governed by a discernible code of mores and values. This code, or the cultures' "rules and regulations," will be the identifiable guidelines that mandate the conduct of the individuals within the cultural group. Most people when observing the interactions of youth on the streets for the first time believe that they are witnessing a completely unregulated environment where behaviors occur at random and "anything goes." Nothing could be further from the truth. There are in fact some defined, rather rigid, and clearly structured codes of conduct that youth on the streets live by. Our failure to recognize and understand these codes is one of the reasons that negative labels are often inappropriately applied. When street-dependent youth exhibit behaviors that we don't understand, we interpret those behaviors according to our cultural norms rather than seeing them as a rational response to the cultural norms of the streets. It is also important to understand that violation of street codes can have serious consequences for a youth; in some cases up to and including death.

An in-depth study of all of the codes and subtle variations of the rules and regulations on the street is beyond the scope of this book. There are 3, however, that have the distinction of being both important and areas where we as service providers seem to have difficulties. Hopefully, having an understanding of these 3 codes will sensitize you to the existence of other codes. With that perspective, you may be able to avoid misinterpreting behaviors that appear bizarre or unexplainable by realizing that the youth may be reacting to a governing structure with which you are not yet familiar.

Code One: Survive

This code is not only number 1 in order of appearance in this book, it is by far the primary code on the streets; *do what you need to do to survive.* When speaking of this code of survival it needs to be made clear that I am not talking about where they're going to sleep tonight or where their next meal is coming from or where are they going to get their clothes cleaned. Those are all aspects of day-to-day *living* on the streets. When I speak of the code of survival, I am talking literally about *not dying*. I am talking about being alive when morning comes. The sad truth of the matter is that death on the streets is a reality. Here is a promise to you, uncomfortable though it may be. If you work with street-dependent youth for any significant length of time, you will know a young person who dies. It simply comes with the territory and there is nothing unusual about it. In a single year in Portland, 15 of the youth I personally knew died, and I by no means knew every youth in Portland. Most youth on the streets know someone who died, or have been touched by death in some way. They are murdered, they die of exposure and accidents, and they die of drug overdoses. You name the manner in which a human body can cease to function and the potential for that occurrence exists on the streets.

Street-dependent youth are fully aware of these dangers and realize that they are in a life-threatening situation. It is not unique to street-dependent youth that people in life-threatening situations change the criteria by which they make judgments. Most of us judge behaviors and actions based on either a moral code or a legal code, usually some combination of the two, but street-dependent youth use different criteria. Legal codes and moral codes have no meaning. All that matters to them when making choices is how they answer the following question; *does this action help me to not die?* If you are able to accept that street-dependent youth truly are in a life-threatening situation, then their behaviors, decisions, and values begin to make sense. Regardless of the legal or moral implications, if the answer to the question of whether something helps them to not die is "yes," then the choice or action is justified.

The Lesson of History

History is littered with sociological examples of this phenomenon. Moral, righteous, upstanding individuals are thrust into a life-threatening situation; a natural disaster, or war, or some other catastrophe; and these nice, normal, law-abiding citizens suddenly start lying, stealing, killing, and doing whatever they need to do to stay alive. This is what you are seeing on the streets. Street-dependent youth are not "bad kids," they are young people who are trying to not die. In their desperate effort to survive they exhibit behaviors that we, viewing them from the safety and comfort of our non-life-threatening legal and moral codes, judge as "criminal," "delinquent," and "incorrigible." The problem is that street-dependent youth are not living within the safety of our legal and moral guidelines; they are living in a life-threatening world on our streets.

There is another quote from the essay I used earlier that addresses this issue:

"I'm a very open person and take people for what's inside, not what they do. I know guys who pull dates, but I'm close enough to them to know that they do it for

survival. I have a close friend who I seen catching dates and he had a girlfriend who he could have put out to do the same. But he cared about her enough to do it himself, and did not enjoy it. And he started to explain what he was doing, and I said -- hey, I'm your friend. Everyone has to survive somehow. I care about you, not how you get your money."

Attitudes on Prostitution

Clearly, the attitude expressed in this quote is that the legality or morality of the behavior is irrelevant. Her friend is doing what he needs to do to survive and as such his actions are not a reflection on him as a person. Before we move on, however, I would like to digress slightly and call attention to another attitude that is expressed in this quote. I feel it is important because I sometimes speak to groups in the community who are of the opinion that street-dependent youth enjoy prostitution, and that they are attracted to the perceived "glamour" and "excitement" of the lifestyle. Youth sometimes perpetuate this perspective by the way they present themselves and describe their experiences. Believing this is a serious mistake. When you are able to get past the youth's defenses, and get to their true feelings about prostitution, you will discover that prostitution is viewed as vile, degrading, and disgusting. Read carefully the following line in that quote:

"... he had a girlfriend who he could have put out to do the same. But he cared about her enough to do it himself, and did not enjoy it."

On the streets, prostitution is something that you protect your loved ones from.

Corollary

There is an important corollary to the code of survival; *don't interfere with someone's survival.* This is especially important to understand if you are going to be doing streetwork. You may develop a close relationship with a particular youth and it will tear at your heartstrings to see them getting into that car to pull a date. You'll be tempted to go up and intervene somehow. Resist the temptation. Not only will the youth not appreciate your intervention, but you may place yourself at risk. Your status in our dominant culture will not protect you on the streets.

In the early days of my career I was involved with a streetwork program that, in retrospect, was a demonstration project for what not to do. One evening we fielded a streetwork team consisting of two rather macho football players. Not too long into their shift, they came across a pimp who was beating the crap out of one of his girls. Without hesitation they decided to put on their superman suits and rescue this fair maiden in distress. They took the pimp down and before they were able to realize what was happening, the victim they were defending was beating them over the head with spiked heels trying to protect her man.

There are people in our communities who are paid to intervene in situations like this. We call them "police." If you witness something like this on the street, your job is to contact the people whose job it is to deal with these situations. It is not your job to intervene yourself. Your position as a streetworker trying to help the poor homeless youth will carry no status when intervening in street-survival situations, *so don't do it*. When working on the streets, it is wise to keep in mind the First Rule of Crisis Intervention; *Don't Die*.

Code Two: Don't Rat

This code could actually be known by any number of names. I settled on *Don't Rat* to make it self-explanatory to anyone who has ever seen an old James Cagney movie. It's a pretty straight forward concept. You don't "rat" on your people. You don't discuss what's happening inside of the culture with someone from outside of the culture. This is one of the "capital offenses," if you will, on the streets, and it is one strike you're out. The absolutely worst thing you can be known as on the streets is a "snitch," and if you get identified as such your life *will* be in jeopardy. Violation of the *Don't Rat* code carries the death penalty.

Inter-cultural Conflict

Unfortunately, this creates one of the biggest conflicts that street-dependent youth have in co-existing with our dominant culture. It is also one of the primary reasons that street-dependent youth so often get labeled "unmotivated." The conflict, and the behavior that results in the "unmotivated" label, is created by the relationship between the *My Friend Needs Help* syndrome and the *Don't Rat* code. Consider that youth on the street are surviving without resources, outside of the law, on drugs, dealing with a spectrum of abuse issues, and facing daily trauma. Sleep deprived and undernourished, they are faced with the same range of problems and issues that overwhelms us as adult service providers. Now consider that their self-esteem is largely invested in being able to assist their friends; the *My Friend Needs Help* syndrome. The reality is that they are virtually powerless to actually do something about their friends' issues without enlisting the aid of people from outside of the street culture. In order to survive emotionally, psychologically, and in some cases, physically, they need to go outside of their culture for assistance. The minute they do that, however, they risk violating, or being perceived as violating, the *Don't Rat* code.

The Need for Documentation

The nature of our services increases this risk. We are generally not profit-oriented businesses. Rather, we are funded by public and private institutions that require various levels of documentation in return for the funding we receive. They want to know what types of youth we're serving, how we are serving them, their issues and the nature of the problems they face, and what their histories are.

This documentation can sometimes be extensive. Programs funded under the federal Runaway and Homeless Youth Act are familiar with the information collection system known as the RHYMIS, or Runaway and Homeless Youth Management Information System. This is a national database of client information that includes 9 pages of questions that vary in their level of intrusiveness; from whether or not they're pregnant, to how many cigarettes they've smoked[17].

This, then, is how the scenario plays out. Youth on the streets attempt to deal with issues to the best of their abilities until the need for services overwhelms them. At that time they need to enlist the help of people outside of their culture and they come to our agencies for assistance. Once there it's possible that the first thing that happens is that they experience a barrage of questions. Many times the questions we ask are so innocent in our culture that we don't even consider the implications. How many times each day do we encounter a situation where we are giving our name, address, and phone number? Whenever we apply for a credit card, enter a store contest, order something from a catalog, sign in at a meeting or a presentation, and I could think of dozens of more examples, we give up our name, address, and phone number. Would you be so at ease giving up your name if you didn't trust who you were giving it to and were unsure as to whether or not you had a run report or warrant out on you, due to the fact that your lifestyle is largely illegal? Would you be comfortable giving up your address if you were trespassing in an abandoned building or sleeping in the homes of the customers to whom you prostitute yourself? How would you feel being asked for your phone number, when you don't have a phone, even though everyone else in the world has a phone? Questions that mean nothing to us can often be both terrifying and humiliating to street-dependent youth.

Creation of an Ethical Dilemma
As we continue to seek information from the youth, they begin to think; *can I trust these people? Why do they need this information? What are they going to do with it?* Eventually our need for information begins to include questions about the youth's lifestyle, including their activities on the street and information concerning their friends and drug use. Now the question in the youth's mind is; *am I snitching? I'm not going to be a snitch!* They get scared and they

---

[17] The nature of RHYMIS has changed since the 1998 release, as described later in the 2.0 commentary.

leave our agency. Once back out on the streets it isn't long before the need for service overwhelms them again and, needing help, they return to our agency. We ask more questions about what they're doing and what their friends are doing, and they get scared and leave again. The need for service overwhelms them and they come back. We ask more questions and they leave. We observe this back and forth behavior and we decide that the youth is "unmotivated." We're wrong. Street-dependent youth are not unmotivated; they are caught by an ethical dilemma.

Asking Questions

It's our challenge as service providers to recognize conflicts that exist for our clients and to find ways to address those conflicts as youth access our services. The good news is that, in this case, it's not that difficult to do. The difficulty comes in remembering to do it. The first step is simply a matter of awareness on our part. At all times when working with street-dependent youth we need to maintain an awareness of the dynamics created by their need for our services, our need for information and documentation, and the '*Don't Rat*' code of the streets. Anytime you ask a question, and it doesn't matter what the question is or how innocent it may seem to you, you are creating a potentially threatening circumstance for street-dependent youth. It may not always be the case, but any question has the potential to place a youth in a serious ethical dilemma. Simply maintaining an awareness of this will go a long way in helping you to develop sensitivity when questioning street-dependent youth.

There are also some practical steps that you can take. The first is to consciously reduce the number of questions that you are asking. The fact that a youth has come to our agency for service does not mean that we now have permission to know every little detail about their life. I have a personal rule that I will recommend to you. The rule is that, before I ask any question of any youth, I first silently ask a question of myself; *why do I need to know this information?* I have often found my answer to this question to be almost embarrassing, because the truth is that street-dependent youth are involved in a culture and lifestyle that is unique and different enough from what we normally experience to be fascinating to us. Look at how many TV shows, movies, and books are somehow built around street life and the culture of drugs and prostitution. Those of us outside of that culture are intrigued by it, and our curiosity finds it very seductive to have someone who is involved in that lifestyle sitting in front of us. When I ask myself my silent question, and I'm willing to answer it honestly, I find that a surprising amount of the time my answer is; *because I'm curious*. If that's my answer, I don't ask the question. My curiosity is not a sufficient reason to create a potential conflict for the young person I am trying to assist.

If, however, my answer justifies asking the question, such as; *I need this information to help this young person obtain a service;* or, *in order to give informed feedback to the issue or concern they have;* or even, *because I am required to obtain this documentation;* then I will present the question. My presentation of the question, however, will include some clearly defined elements.

- First, I inform them that I need to ask a question.
- Second, I explain to them what the question is.
- Third, I clarify why I need the information.
- Fourth -- **and this is the most important step** -- *I tell them what I will be doing with the information, how it will be shared, and the level of confidentiality that they can expect.*
- Finally, I ask their permission to ask the question.

It is not necessary to follow this as a rigid step-by-step process for each individual question you ask. Rather, this is the environment that you will want to create when asking questions. Each of us will develop our own technique for how we are comfortable creating this environment, but if these five conditions don't exist, you are running the risk of alienating the youth with your questions. Note that step number five; asking their permission to ask the question; requires that they give that permission. If they refuse permission and you ask the question anyway, the previous four steps are pointless. If a youth says *"no"* to your request to ask a question, drop it and don't pursue it any further at that time. Granted, this may result in your inability to provide a service, but if you are setting up a situation where you are asking permission, you must be willing to have that permission refused.

Confidentiality

I stated that step four, the step concerning confidentiality, was the most important step. Betrayal of confidence will destroy whatever delicate trust you have established with the young person, making intervention by others that much more difficult, and it is also the area where youth may be held accountable to the *Don't Rat* code of the streets. What makes this a particularly vulnerable area is that it is not necessary for us to maliciously violate a confidence in order to, in a youth's mind, betray them. There are two possible scenarios for betraying a trust to which we need to be sensitive.

The first is the "slip of the tongue." This is the small, unthinking breech of confidence; the act of leaving a file open where someone else may see it, or the off-hand comment in front of the wrong people. It may appear to us to be trivial or insignificant, but it is often interpreted by street-dependent youth as a major, calculated treachery.

The second is the promise that can't be kept. An example would be that of a teen mother coming to you, clearly upset. She wants to talk to you, but she doesn't know if she can. You reach out to her assuring her that it's OK; that whatever she tells you will be held in the strictest confidence. She decides that you are trustworthy and tells you that her boyfriend is sexually abusing her child. This is a confidence that you can't keep. You are obligated by law to report this information. In so doing, you have violated her trust, and possibly endangered her life.

This does not mean that you can't deal with issues like this. It only means that we need to be clear and honest about the level of confidentiality we can provide. To approach street-dependent youth with a "you can tell me anything" attitude is a dangerous lie. We need to present our boundaries on confidentiality and allow youth to make informed decisions about sharing information with us. If a youth comes to you and asks if they can tell you something in confidence, stop and think before you say *"yes."* An honest answer would be; you can tell me *some* things in confidence, other things I am legally obligated to report or to share with my supervisor. If need be, enter into a discussion concerning what those boundaries are, and then; and this is also important; *stick to those boundaries.* If the teen mother came to you, informed that you had a legal reporting obligation, and decided to tell you of the abuse anyway, you would already have her permission to act on it by her informed choice to share the information and the betrayal would come from *not* reporting it. Too often, however, we promise a level of confidentiality that we simply can't keep or we destroy trust by allowing no right to confidentiality at all.

It is not possible to overstate the importance of how we deal with confidentiality. This is an issue that young people themselves are aware of. At Youth Summit '94, the regional conference of the Northwest Network for Youth (representing services in Alaska, Idaho, Oregon, and Washington), a group of young people drafted a profile of their 'ideal' youth worker. There were 26 key traits described, with four of them highlighted for extra emphasis. One of the four highlighted qualities was *clear boundaries about what information can be shared.* This was further supported by one of the remaining traits, which was *sticks with agreements regarding confidentiality*

A common objection to this approach to questioning and confidentiality is; *but we need this information. How else are we going to document our services and create demographics on which to base our services? And how are we going to coordinate services with other agencies and share information?* This complaint seems valid when you look at early contacts with youth where these techniques are used. It is true that we don't get much information beyond the minimum required to meet an immediate need. What you will begin to notice, however, is that the youth will begin to develop trust in your services and return for more. This is the first therapeutic goal of any voluntary service for street-dependent youth; get them to come back. Do not confuse this with creating dependency. Rather, it is recognition of the fact that ==transition from street life is a long-term process.== If a youth does not develop trust you will not be able to deliver long-term services. Each time a youth returns for additional support or service, they build a little more trust and share a little more information. In time; and not too long of a time ==if you are consistent and trustworthy; you will overcome the fear street-dependent youth have of sharing information.== When that happens you will learn that street-dependent youth don't need the "3rd degree" to tell us what we need to know. The fact is that they want to share their lives and stories with adults; they just don't trust what we'll do with the information. Once they do trust us, you will be given more information than you need or want.

An additional benefit will be that the information will be accurate to the best of the youth's ability, which is not the case if you try to get your documentation before trust has been established. You'll find that if you ask for information too soon, you'll get it; youth will answer your questions and fill out your forms. The problem is, it will be mostly bullshit and you may not see that particular youth or anyone they associate with again. Word travels quickly on the street. If you are trustworthy, many youth will know that. The reverse is also true.

As for our ability to share information with other agencies in order to coordinate services, we need only keep in mind why we want to have that ability. The reason, of course, is that we feel that such information sharing and coordination will benefit the young person we are serving. If that's true, then all that's required is that we communicate how it's to their benefit and advantage and obtain their permission to share the information. If we are unable to obtain permission, all that means is that we haven't done an adequate job of clarifying the benefits and advantages or we haven't clearly thought through whether or not advantages actually exist. Sharing information for the sake of sharing information is not a benefit to anyone. In fact, it can often work to a youth's disadvantage. When we accept youth into our transitional living program they often come to us with a documented history of negative behaviors and observations from staff dealings with them in the past. It is our policy that our case managers do not read this information, but rather base their opinions and reactions on their personal experience. More often than not we find that the youth we deal with is far different from the youth who has been documented. By giving them a clean slate, they are often able to escape their past and create a new relationship and reputation; something that would have been very difficult to do if staff had developed preconceived opinions about them.

I've found in doing this presentation live that this section sometimes leaves people afraid to say anything to street-dependent youth. In some ways, that's good, I would much rather have people walking softly than carrying a big stick on this issue. But it's also not an accurate reflection of the types of relationships and conversations that you can establish with youth. You need not be fearful of talking with street-dependent youth, nor do you need to avoid asking questions. What you need to be is honest and trustworthy, and you need to not pry. Questions should be asked with open, stated purpose, not curiosity. This is especially true when asking for any type of identifying information, as this is the type of information that is most likely to conflict with the *Don't Rat* code of the streets. An example would be that of a youth telling you that they didn't get much sleep last night. Asking *what was the problem* is a much safer question than *where did you sleep*. Remember also that the key issue here is trust. Establish trust and street-dependent youth will be so open with you that you may not have to ask questions at all.

Code Three: Integrity

It may be difficult to understand how the concept of street integrity works as a code. In fact, when most people start learning about street-dependent youth and seeing the manner in which they deal with each other, it is often difficult to understand how the term "integrity" is applicable at all. Because of this, street-dependent youth tend to get labeled as "liars" or "manipulative" when the real problem is that we are misinterpreting issues of integrity. The reality is that integrity is one of the most highly valued concepts on the street, but, like so many of the concepts we have talked about, their concept of integrity is quite different from ours.

The Dynamic of Literalism

The primary difference between what you and I might call integrity and what you'll see on the street is that street integrity is, and this cannot be overstated, extremely literal. Communication to which we are accustomed tends to rely heavily on the implications contained in our statements. If I were to ask, for example, if the phone rang while I was out, I would not have to specify that what I was really interested in knowing was whether or not you answered the phone, and if any of the calls were for me. When you are communicating with street-dependent youth, however, expect to get only what you ask for.

The Factor of Arrested or Delayed Development

There is a significant contributing factor to why street communication is so literal. One of the strange dynamics of intervention with street-dependent youth is that, when working with a particular youth, you may be working with someone who is to all intents and purposes 3 different ages. Let's say that the youth you are working with is chronologically 16 years of age. In many ways their behaviors, their thoughts, and everything else about them is going to be like any other normal 16 year old. When you consider their life experience, however, particularly since they became involved in street life, it will seem that in some ways they are in their 40's. Then there is the trauma and abuse that they've been subjected to, resulting in significant levels of arrested or delayed emotional and psychological development. This factor creates behaviors and thought patterns that may more closely resemble a 6 or 7 year old child. This single human being in front of you is going to cycle through these 3 ages, sometimes in the course of a single sentence. They'll be expressing the desire of a 16 year old with the emotions of a 6 year old concerning a subject that would embarrass a 46 year old.

It is easy to see the "young child" part of street-dependent youth. When they play, they tend to play "young" and stuffed animals are in great demand on the streets. For example, we always to do a "real" Christmas at our transitional living program. What I mean by a "real" Christmas is the type of Christmas other young people experience, where they ask for something in particular, anticipate getting it, and then they open a package on Christmas morning to find what they wanted; and it's new, not a second hand donation. One year, one of our residents was a rather aggressive 17 year old male. He was a large youth who wore his anger on his sleeve. He dressed in black, with pointed studs and chains. His appearance was that of a hostile, scary guy who you would probably be nervous about meeting on the street. When we asked him what he wanted for Christmas we were scared of what he might ask for, and then very much surprised when he asked for a small, black teddy bear that he had seen in a window downtown. Watching him open that package on Christmas morning was like watching an innocent, bright eyed child, despite his appearance. Proudly walking around with that teddy bear was not a conflict for him, because parts of him are still the little kid we saw opening that package.

Those of you with personal experience with younger children will attest to the fact that they tend to be rather literal in both the way they communicate and the way they interpret what is said to them. I saw a great example of this one night while watching the first season of the new David Letterman show on CBS. One of Dave's guests was a 3 year old geography "wizard" who could do things such as name places on an unmarked map and chew American cheese slices into the shapes of US States. He had just finished telling Dave about a family vacation where they drove from his home in Colorado to Florida when Dave produced a state outline map of the United States. The conversation that followed went like this:

David asked: *"Can you show me Colorado, Florida, and all the states in between?"*

The Geography-Whiz replied: *"Sure."* Pointing to Colorado he said; *"Here's Colorado."* Pointing to Florida he said; *"Here's Florida."* And making a large circular motion with his hand over the states in between the two he said; *"And here's all the states in between."*

This, needless to say, resulted in laughter from the audience and a classic "dumb guy" look on Dave's face, but the 3 year old didn't seem to understand what he had done that was so funny. In his mind, and, in fact, in a literal interpretation of Dave's question, he had done exactly as Dave had asked. Obviously, Dave had meant for him to *name* the states between Colorado and Florida, but a literal response only required the whiz-kid to show him where those states were.

Communication on the Street

It is this type of literal interpretation and literal presentation of ideas that you're going to experience with street-dependent youth. The way street integrity operates as a "code" is that, when honesty is being judged on the street, it isn't what you mean that counts, it's what you say. This is one of the dynamics that makes working with street-dependent youth challenging, because "literalism" is not how we, as adults, are used to communicating. We tend to insinuate content and imply meaning by the way we speak. It is not generally necessary to specifically state every little nuance of meaning in order to get our message across. The only communication you can trust with street-dependent youth, however, is that communication which is specifically and literally stated. This requires you to, at all times, state your message in literal terms and interpret what is being said to you literally. If you are able to do that consistently, you will find that street-dependent youth tend to be reasonably honest and willing to keep agreements. If you are not able to be literal in your communication, and you slip into the realm of implied meanings, street-dependent youth will appear to be both dishonest and manipulative. The problem, however, will many times be a result of what your assumptions about the communications were, not what was actually communicated.

Here's an example of how communication assumptions can create misunderstandings. I had set an appointment for a young man to see an employment counselor. It was a morning appointment and that afternoon I was returning from lunch to my office when I saw him on the street. As we passed each other, we exchanged the following brief conversation:

I asked: *"Hi, how're you doing?"*
He answered: *"Fine."*
I then asked: *"Did you go to the employment office?"*
He answered: *"Yeah, I did."*
I ended the conversation with: *"Great, see ya' later."*

When I got to my office a few minutes later there was a phone message from the employment counselor. I returned the call and was a little bit irritated to find that, according to him, this young man did not show up for the appointment. Obviously, I concluded, I had just been lied to. Later that evening, I saw the youth at the drop-in center and talked to him about missing the appointment. I was at first confused by the fact that he was not trying to cover his lie, and was, in fact, quite open about not seeing the counselor. As the story unfolded I learned that he had made it to the bus, traveled to the employment office, but then stood outside for about 15 minutes trying to get up the nerve to go in. He finally was just too scared to do it, and left when the next bus came by. It began to occur to me that the reason why he wasn't trying to cover his lie was because he hadn't lied. That afternoon I had asked him if he had gone to the employment office. I didn't ask him if he had seen the employment counselor. I didn't ask him if he had kept the appointment. I didn't even ask him if he had set foot inside the building. When he answered *"yeah, I did,"* he was giving me an honest answer to a literal interpretation of the question I had asked.

This may seem as if they're just playing with words. It's very easy for us to take the position that they know what we mean and that this is just one of the ways that they're being manipulative. Your effectiveness with street-dependent youth will be much more productive however if you take the position that this truly is the way that they communicate. My experience has been that if you can train yourself to communicate clearly and literally and resist assuming content that has not been stated, street-dependent youth are as honest as any other population you may deal with. In some ways, due to the fact that they are literal, they may even be somewhat more honest.

We learned this lesson the hard way when we were in the development stages of our transitional living program. The model uses a *self-government* approach that includes both residents and staff in the management of the program. This is accomplished through an *agreement* process where staff and residents negotiate agreements by which everyone has to live. Obviously, for this to work, we need to trust that residents will be honest and keep the agreements that they make, especially when you consider that the vast majority of the agreements have no consequence attached to them. We've found that the youths' "honesty" is often directly proportional to how literal we are with the agreements that are made.

We experienced our first clear example of this over our *Bottom Line Rules*. While almost everything is negotiable at the program, we began with 3 things that we would never tolerate. These 3 non-negotiable Bottom Line Rules are; *No Sex in the House*, *No Violence in the House*, and *No Drugs in the House*. Very early in the program's life, working with our first group of residents, Portland experienced an uncharacteristically early spring day. The residents were out in the back yard enjoying the weather and the staff person on duty was inside with the windows open airing out the house. After a time, staff began to notice an aroma drifting in from the back yard that had the effect of, shall we say, peaking her professional curiosity. She went out to the back yard to see what was going on and, sure enough, there the residents sat rather openly smoking marijuana. The staff person was furious and couldn't believe how willing the residents were to flagrantly disregard the program's "bottom lines."

She confronted them with; *"What do you think you're doing? You know what the rules are here!"*

The residents responded with; *"Yeah, we know the rules. No drugs in the house. We're not in the house -- we're in the back yard!"*

The fact was that, as far as the residents were concerned, they weren't disregarding the rules. The problem was that we knew what the rule *meant* and the residents knew what the rule *said*. This incident resulted in a rather hastily called House Meeting, and now when you read our House Agreements you can see a little clause that states; *"In the House" includes the outside and surrounding property*. This experience is just one of hundreds of similar experiences we've had at the program. The amazing thing is how consistently the problem results from staff assuming an implied meaning for an agreement, when the residents have only committed to what is literally stated. We find that if we can be specific, clear, and literal in our communications, we deal with a fairly honest population who will keep agreements. It's when we begin to assume implied meanings that residents appear dishonest.

Another example of this had to do with the weekly house cleaning responsibilities that residents have. One week, a staff was not going to give a resident credit for cleaning the bathroom because the walls of the shower were filthy and the resident had left them untouched. When we looked at what was specifically stated had to be done when cleaning the bathroom, however, there was no mention of cleaning the walls. Once we negotiated that cleaning the shower walls be included in that responsibility, this problem never re-occurred.

When we are able to keep our communications clear and literal, both in what we say to young people and in our interpretation of what they say to us, establishing a level of honest communication with street-dependent youth is really not that difficult. When we assume content and imply meaning, however, our experience of street-dependent youth begins to feel dishonest and manipulative.

If we are trained to think literally we can often make sense out of situations that don't make sense. This technique was all that stood between me and total confusion once when a 16 year old female came to see me at my office in the drop-in center. During this time I was a case manager for a prostitution alternatives program and my office was located right in the heart of a high-vice district for adolescent prostitution. This particular girl, who was a client of mine, showed up fighting back tears and practically choking on restrained emotion. She didn't want to break down where the other youth might see her, so she asked me if I would meet her on the lawn outside of the downtown library. I agreed, and not too long after that we were sitting on the lawn and she began to tell me why she was so upset. It's important to point out that I was thinking of this as a counseling session so I was in full "counselor" mode while she was talking to me. After a time she paused at an appropriate place for me to offer her some feedback, and I, of course, had some appropriate things to offer. I began to speak and was able to get out maybe 4 or 5 words before she cut me off with:

"Fuck you, Jerry. You're not listening to what I'm saying!"

OK. I was an experienced youth worker. I could handle that. Obviously I had jumped in a little too quickly. Maybe she was leading up to something and I didn't quite have a handle on what she was talking about. I sat back and, in a moment, she began talking again. It wasn't too long before there was clearly no doubt in my mind what the issue was and what I, as her counselor, should be saying. There was another pause creating an appropriate place for me to offer some feedback and I (of course) had some appropriate things to offer. Once again, however, after maybe 4 or 5 of my appropriate words she cut me off with:

"Fuck you, Jerry. You're not listening to what I'm saying!"

To be perfectly honest, this was the point where I was starting to get a bit pissed. I thought to myself; *fine, I won't say a word.* Sitting back, I let her talk until she stopped talking altogether. From where I was sitting I could see a clock in a store window across the street and I allowed 2 full minutes to go by. I don't know if you have ever had the opportunity to sit with someone in total silence for 2 full minutes, but take my word, it's a significant period of time. After 2 minutes of silence I felt reasonably assured that it was now my turn to talk. Once more I began to offer the appropriate things that I had to say, and once more she abruptly cut me off after 4 or 5 words with:

"Fuck you, Jerry. You're not listening to what I'm saying!"

Finally I was sure of something. I was absolutely certain that I was definitely doing something wrong. I was still a bit uncertain as to exactly what it was that I was doing wrong, but I clearly wasn't getting the results I was hoping for. In a desperate attempt to figure out what to try next, I began to review the outline of this manual in my head, frantically searching for a concept that would make sense of all of this. This was in line with the Second Rule of Crisis Intervention, which is; *if what you're doing isn't working, quickly do something else.* When I reached the concept of street integrity and started thinking about how literal street-dependent youth tend to be, something suddenly dawned on me. She had said the exact same thing 3 times in a row. Every time I started to talk she had made a rather blunt, direct statement that, interpreted literally, was telling me that I wasn't listening. I had been assuming, of course, that what she meant was that I didn't *understand* what she was saying. It was possible, however, that she meant exactly what she had said; that when I was talking, I wasn't listening.

Looking at it from that perspective, it occurred to me that maybe this wasn't a counseling session in her mind. Maybe she wasn't looking for feedback or answers. Maybe she just wanted somebody to be there with her while she fell apart. I decided that, if that was true, my best intervention would be to sit back and shut up.

Without another word, I leaned back against the wall and shut my mouth. Once again, she began to talk and she continued to do so for the next 2 hours. She talked about prostitution, her life on the streets, her experience with sexual abuse, and problems she was having with drugs. Sometimes she seemed happy. Sometimes she seemed sad. Sometimes she was angry. Sometimes she wouldn't say anything; she'd just sit there in silence. She went through the entire spectrum of issues and emotions while I sat there without speaking a single syllable. I didn't even use *minimal encouragers*, those clever little statements that are used to keep people talking. Brilliant things like:

"Uh-huh."

"I see."

"And then what happened?"

Not a sound escaped my lips. Finally, she seemed to talk herself out and came over to hold on to me for a couple of minutes. She then got up and began to walk away, pausing only long enough to glance back at me and say:

"You know, that's what I like about you. You're not real quick, but you can usually figure out what's going on."

There are actually two very valuable lessons to be learned from this story. The first, of course, is to interpret things absolutely as literally as you can. It was when I was able to stop reading my assumptions into her statements that I was able to understand what it was that she needed in that moment and her behavior started to make sense. The second lesson has to do with the value of a passive intervention such as listening.

Passive Intervention

Sometimes when I tell that story people question whether sitting in silence for 2 hours while a youth spills their gut is really in a youth's best interest. Street-dependent youth, after all, are in a life-threatening environment. They may be on drugs and prostituting themselves to survive. Meanwhile, I just spent 2 hours not doing a damn thing except sitting there and letting her talk. The question of whether or not there is value in that is a legitimate one. My answer, however, is that, not only is there tremendous value in this type of intervention, but sometimes it is all that street-dependent youth really need from us.

Thinking out loud is one of the primary ways that we, as human beings, process information. We all need the opportunity to say things that we don't necessarily believe, just to try them on for size and to see how we feel about them. What's the first thing you do after you see a movie with a friend? The answer, of course, is that you talk about it. Why? You both saw the damn thing. The reason that you talk about it is because you are processing the information and talking out loud helps you to do that. The need to process information by talking out loud is so important that people who are isolated from other people begin to talk to themselves. This isn't because they're crazy, it's because they need to process information.

Helping professionals often use what I call the *filing cabinet* approach to counseling. That's where they are too quick to offer advice for every statement made to them. Conversations tend to sound like this:

"I'm having trouble sleeping at night."
"Have you tried warm milk?"
"Milk makes me sick."
"Do you want to see a doctor?"
"No, it's really just the taste."
"Have you tried putting chocolate in it?"

What we are doing when we use this approach is preventing people from processing. As a result they have difficulty figuring out what's really going on for them, making it impossible for us to be of any real help at all. In my example it's unlikely that the person's inability to sleep has anything to do with a physical condition, or is even the real problem. The only way either one of you will be able to determine the real problem and find an appropriate solution is to stop offering quick fixes and to let them talk it out.

Despite all of their obvious issues and challenges, street-dependent youth have incredible assets within themselves. You cannot survive as a drug-impaired, unemployed, homeless adolescent, living outside of traditional society and the law, by being stupid and incapable. You survive by being an incredibly capable and resourceful person who often only needs the opportunity to learn how capable you really are. Our challenge is to help them to recognize and tap into the strengths and abilities that they already possess. Many times, street-dependent youth don't need us to impart our wisdom to them. What they need is a sounding board that will enable them to figure out for themselves what's going on. Once they do that, you not only don't have to help them, you won't be able to stop them.

A young man I was working with had taken most of the tests for his GED, but kept putting off the final test; math. He kept coming up with every excuse in the world to not take that test and would miss any appointment that was scheduled for it. Finally, after it became obvious that he was deliberately avoiding the test, I asked him what was going on. What was it about this math test that he wasn't following through? In a burst of frustration and embarrassment, he said:

"I can't take the test because I'm just too stupid to understand math!"

That was the barrier. He wasn't taking the test because he truly believed that he was *too stupid to understand math*. I was in shock. He was going through life fully believing that he was *too stupid to understand math*, yet at the same time he was surviving on the streets by dealing drugs. He could do ounce-to-gram price conversions *in his head!* The problem was that he had never made the connection between his skill at drug dealing and math. All he needed to do was to realize that he already had the skills and translate them. When he was able to realize that, not only was he <u>not</u> *too stupid to understand math*, but that he had, in fact, been surviving *through* his math skills, the final GED test was no longer a barrier. Instead of thinking of street-dependent youth as empty vessels waiting to be filled with our training and education, think of them as a reservoir of potential and talent who only need our assistance to tap into their existing resources.

Whenever I forget this, all I have to do is remember a streetwork experience I had. It was shortly after a youth was murdered and a few of her friends approached one of our streetwork teams and said:

"Ya' know, when a kid in high school gets killed, they like, shut down the school and they bring in counselors and therapists and they let them deal with their grief and all this stuff. But out here when one of us dies it makes page five of the paper and that's it and nobody does nothing."

A bit embarrassed that we hadn't thought of this ourselves, we rather hastily organized a small gathering and a place where the youth could come to talk about their feelings. We spread the word on the street that at such-and-such a day and at such-and-such a time we were going to meet at a downtown park, and, after we gathered there, would be going someplace to talk. We really didn't know what kind of turnout to expect, but when the time came there were 45 - 50 youth gathering in the park. We had to wait about 30 minutes before the building would be available to us, and while we waited an amazing thing happened. The youth had all brought candles with them (I can't guarantee that they had all *bought* candles, but they had all brought them). Without direction from us, they lit the candles, formed a semi-circle, and gave each other the opportunity to stand before the group and say whatever they wanted to say. One youth, a girl of perhaps 14 or 15, stood in front of the group and made the following statement:

"As we're lighting these candles for all the kids who have died on the streets, let's not forget about the little kid who died in each one of us when we came to the streets."

I don't know about you, but that struck me as an incredibly insightful thing for a 15 year old youth who is surviving on the streets to say. It reminded me then, as it always does when I remember it, how much more there is to street-dependent youth than meets the eye. My role is not to go out there and impart wisdom to them. My role is to be a support and a resource that they can use to tap into the strength and knowledge that they already possess, and help them to use that strength in a more positive and effective manner.

Key Points - Codes of the Street

Code One: Survive
- Youth on the streets are in a life-threatening situation, and there is nothing unusual about youth dying on the streets. Behaviors are not judged by their moral or legal status, but by whether or not they help you to survive.
- Prostitution is viewed in the culture of the streets as degrading and disgusting, and something that you protect your loved ones from.
- Your status in the dominant culture will not protect you on the streets. Do not intervene directly in survival activities.

Code Two: Don't Rat
- It is a major violation of the code of the streets to share information outside of the culture. Getting known as a *snitch* is the worst thing that can happen to you, and youth can be and have been killed for that reputation.
- A serious inter-cultural conflict can develop from the clash between a youth's need for services and the "don't rat" code. Much of the "unmotivated" behavior we see is attributable to the ethical dilemma created by this conflict.
- Seeking information through questions, and issues of confidentiality are two ways we can either address or exasperate a youth's ethical dilemma, depending on how we approach and deal with these situations.

Code Three: Integrity
- Integrity is one of the most highly valued concepts on the streets, but a characteristic of street integrity is that it is extremely literal.
- The better you are at communicating and interpreting information literally, the more "honest" street-dependent youth will appear in their dealings with you, and the fewer misunderstandings and conflicts you will have.
- Street-dependent youth survive on the streets using skills and abilities that can be used to make a successful transition off of the streets. Our job is to tap into the strengths and resources that they already possess and to help them see how they can be used in a more productive manner.

2.0 Commentary:

Code One: Survive

As I write this I remember the 8.8 earthquake that occurred off of the coast of Chile on February 27, 2010. In the aftermath of that quake I was following developments by reading news accounts on the web, and started noticing a particular phenomenon, characterized by headlines such as:

- Hungry Chilean Looters Burn Stores (The Australian, March 1, 2010)
- Chile Battles Lawlessness, Desperation After Massive Earthquake (Chosun.com, March 1, 2010)
- Fires, Looting Plague Quake-Battered City (Wall Street Journal, March 1, 2010)
- Chile Troops, Police Attack Post-Quake Looting (Associated Press, March 1, 2010)
- Mayhem In Post-Quake Chile (Baltimore Sun, March 2, 2010)
- Chileans Protect, Feed Themselves After Quake (Newsday, March 3, 2010)

These are just a few of the headlines from news accounts of a wave of lawlessness, looting, and criminal behaviors that swept the quake-ravaged areas of Chile. In the aftermath of the earthquake, many Chilean people began stealing, robbing, vandalizing, and even murdering. But here's the important question to answer; why weren't they behaving this way *before* the quake?

Every population has a percentage of people who engage in criminal behaviors regardless of social structure or law enforcement; often estimated at around 10%. The remaining 90% do *not* engage in criminal behaviors, not *because* of law enforcement (the police and military are always far outnumbered by the general population), but because they are good people who want only to live in peace, take care of themselves and their families, and contribute to their community. This describes the Chilean people, as well, but something happened as a result of the earthquake. The social order was disrupted. Lines of communication were disrupted. Supply distribution was disrupted. Their sense of safety and security was jeopardized. The quake placed them in a circumstance where their very survival was in question, and these good people who never dreamed of being violent, looting, or vandalizing became nearly overnight, violent looters and vandals.

The Chilean people were not behaving as "Chilean" people behave, but as *people*; *any* people, *human beings*; behave when they find themselves in a life-threatening situation. They were behaving as *you* will behave in a similar situation. As we saw the headlines coming from Chile we needed to remember that the Chilean people were *not bad people*. They were *good people* desperately trying to survive a *bad situation*.

This is what I was talking about when I wrote "History is littered with sociological examples of this phenomenon." But we don't have to look to history to see this phenomenon played out; we only have to pay attention when events occur that threaten people's safety and security. This is how human beings react when in such situations and, until their sense of safety and security is restored, their behavior will not be governed or restrained by legal or moral codes; they will do what they need to do, *whatever* they need to do, to survive. We may pass judgment on *what they do*, but we should not pass judgment on *who they are;* because they are behaving as *we* would behave under similar circumstances.

But some of you may be thinking; what about Japan? On March 11, 2011, an earthquake even larger than the Chilean earthquake hit Japan and was subsequently followed by a devastating tsunami. As of this writing, Japan is still feeling the effects of and recovering from the disaster, but there was little in the way of the survival behaviors that we saw in Chile or that we see among adolescents on the streets. While there are some cultural explanations that are specific to the Japanese people, the real reason why we didn't see such behaviors has to do with the 72 hour rule.

In almost all resources discussing disaster planning it is encouraged that you create a "72 hour" kit; that is, store enough resources to sustain you through a 72 hour period. Have you ever wondered; why 72 hours? Why not 48, or 96? The reason is that 72 hours represents the approximate length of time that a human being will maintain old coping skills and adaptive behaviors before they begin to alter their behavior to adapt to new situations or environments. In other words, if your world suddenly changes you will continue to behave as you've always behaved for about 72 hours. After that, you will change your behavior to adapt to your new circumstances. You are told to keep a 72 hour kit because the authorities know that, unless they can restore the social structure and order within 72 hours, people will no longer maintain the social order that previously existed. The 72 hour kit is designed to keep you safe without outside assistance while order is restored. If it can't be restored within 72 hours, the authorities know that they are no longer *restoring* order; they are establishing a *new* order.

Look at the dates of the headlines from Chile that I cited above. The earliest is March 1st; exactly the 3rd day, 72 hours, following the February 27th quake. The Chilean people maintained the old social order for 72 hours but, when order was not restored within that time window, survival behaviors ensued. The difference in Japan was that, as devastating as the disaster may have been, help and resources were available to the victims of the disaster within the 72 hour window.

Incidentally, this speaks to the need for early intervention with runaway youth. If they can be reached and diverted from street influences within 72 hours of a runaway episode, there is a good chance of family reunification (assuming the family is intact enough to support reunification). After 72 hours on the streets they will begin to adapt to street cultural influences, and reunification will become much more difficult.

And consider what those street cultural influences are. There is nothing more threatening to a human being's sense of safety and security than to be living as an adolescent without any structures or supports in a violent world outside of social order and the law, with only your own cunning and "street smarts" protecting you from traffickers, drug dealers, and other exploitive adults. Many of these young people have *never* known protection from caretakers; in fact, have known only exploitation and abuse. They have learned to trust *no one* except themselves, and the world they inhabit is filled with one life-threatening danger after another. In that reality, how would *you* behave? How would *any* human being behave? Is it really that hard for us to understand how street-dependent youth behave?

I am not trying to gloss over or even justify the illegal or violent actions of youth on the streets. I'm simply trying to point out that you are not observing characteristics of *bad kids*. You are observing *predictable* human responses to life-threatening situations. In the book Mental Health and Emerging Adulthood among Homeless Young People by Les B. Whitbeck (based on a 3 year longitudinal study of homeless and runaway adolescents in the United States' Midwest region), the author states that "Aside from experiencing combat or living in a war zone, the vulnerability of homelessness may pose the greatest single situational risk for adolescent post-traumatic stress disorder[18]." I would only point out that when the level of desperation and violence that young people experience on the streets is considered, they *are* to all intents and purposes "living in a war zone." They do not behave as they do because of some made up cultural code; rather, the reality of life on the streets *requires* a code that condones illegal and immoral behaviors in order to enable young people to survive.

I will note that one of the survival behaviors mentioned in the original text is prostitution, and that prostitution as it relates to the culture of the streets is one of the areas where change can be seen since the original publication. Much as I described changes in street families, it's not so much that how I described issues related to prostitution in the original text are no longer accurate. Rather, formal prostitution and survival sex has evolved to additional or different manifestations. The attitude toward any form of commercial or bartered sex, however, regardless of the form that it takes, remains the same. It is a survival aid, nothing more, and it is regarded as the

---

[18] Page 77

lowest means to that end.

I ended my explanation of this code with a corollary; don't interfere with someone's survival; using a prostitution analogy as an example. I'd just like to clarify that you should pay attention to the *corollary*, not the *example*. Unrequested intervention into any form of street survival activity will not be met with appreciation, and, particularly for outreach workers (who are most likely to be presented with opportunities to do so), may place you in danger. However, this does not mean that you should ignore or condone such activities. Within programs, policy should be followed as street survival activities which involve drugs, sex, violence or illegalities should already be addressed by codified responses[19]. On the street (which refers to any location where you and the youth have equal status or right to be) your response should be limited (at least in terms of *intervening in the survival activity itself*) to acting to protect persons from injury (which means involving *appropriate* responders; e.g., police, paramedics) or *withdrawing* from the situation. Remember, this is to keep you safe and the youth safe, since your "status" does not protect you on the street, and you have no way of predicting the consequences to yourself or others as a result of your interference ("interference" being a much more appropriate term than "intervention" in these situations).

Code Two: Don't Rat

I stated that this code could be known by any number of names, but it was a bit of an oversight to not identify that the primary street language describing this code is "snitching." While I felt that the terminology "don't rat" was more easily understood by those not immersed in street culture, and while I *did* identify that the worst thing you can be known as on the street is a "snitch," I still should have been clearer about the cultural reference if for no other reason than to underscore just how deeply this code runs on the streets. So deeply, in fact, that over the years it has even entered into cultural parlance from, but beyond, the culture of the streets. "Snitch" is the name of a new 2013 movie release. The term "Snitches get Stitches" has appeared in numerous songs; in fact, it was adopted as the name for a Seattle punk rock band. A controversial *Stop Snitchin'* campaign aimed at getting criminal defendants to stop talking to police was established in 2004 (though its roots go back to the late '90's), and you can buy T-shirts, hats, mugs, and magnets with "Snitches get Stitches" or more expanded versions such as "Snitches get Stitches for being Punk Ass Bitches." Or even the more *accurate* variation, considering that snitching *can* and *has* resulted in death; "Snitches get Stitches and end up in Ditches."

---

[19] Note that these responses are not the same as "interfering with someone's survival" and are not likely to be reacted to as such, due to the fact that they are occurring on your "turf" and therefore are legitimately covered by your "codes."

But "snitching," as the mainstream understanding of it has evolved over the years has come to mean primarily cooperating with law enforcement[20]. While it does and always has carried that connotation, it is a serious mistake to interpret this street code as *only* meaning cooperating with law enforcement, for two reasons. First, when we interpret it as such we are limited by our *interpretation*. What we may not label as "snitching" due to a lack of direct law enforcement involvement may be interpreted on the streets quite differently. Whether this different interpretation is based on a different standard or a misunderstanding is irrelevant if you are the youth who gets labeled as a snitch. Either way your life may be in jeopardy.

Considering how serious the consequences of being labeled as a snitch are out on the streets, we don't want to rely on our interpretation of actions, particularly since *innocent until proven guilty* is not standard street practice. Youth have suffered consequences, serious, harmful consequences, for simply being *accused of* snitching or *labeled as* a snitch; sometimes with their punishers having no idea if the person is actually guilty of snitching, or even who or what they are accused of snitching about. It's not "Snitches get Questioned" or "Snitches get Investigated" or "Snitches get Trials." It's "Snitches get Stitches" ... period.

Second, the seriousness of this code begins to affect other behaviors and is the reason I caution against prying and over-questioning and offer guidance on how to act when in the realm of seeking information. As an analogy, think of someone with a fear of heights. Yes, you can be certain that they're not going to do any cliff jumping, but you can also be assured that they're going to stay *as far away from the edge* as possible. They may be in no greater danger 10 feet back than they are 20 feet back, but if their fear is great enough, they'll start hesitating to approach the edge *50 feet back* or more. Violation of the Don't Rat/Snitch code on the streets carries such severe consequences for youth that, unless and until they trust you and trust what will happen as a result of divulging information, they will be very hesitant to divulge information, dishonest in the information they divulge, slow to trust, and/or react by distancing themselves. In the worst case scenario you may put them in danger by how you seek information, what information you seek, or what you do with the information you get.

It is not my intention to put you in fear of asking questions of youth. We need information to assist them and they want to trust and talk to adults. I'm just asking you to know what you're doing, because there are huge potential downsides if you don't. The 5 step process I described in the original text is still the best way to be effective in this area, but I can give you some additional guidance on how to remember and apply the steps.

Just as a reminder, before asking anything you should answer the

---

[20] The new 2013 movie "Snitch" is about a guy working undercover for the DEA.

question; *why do you need to know?* Not only is that a necessary prerequisite to step 3 of the process, but it is also necessary to prevent prying and voyeuristic curiosity. If you can't *legitimately* answer that question with a reason that *benefits the young person*, then you have no need of the process at all because *you don't need to know the information*. Assuming, however, that you do have a legitimate need for the information, I'll remind you that I said that it is not necessary to present it as a rigid step-by-step process; rather, it is an *environment* in which you seek information. Because of that, you'll need to assess the environment in order to determine the appropriate application of the process.

Suppose I am a youth's case manager and have been working with them long enough to have developed a strong, trusting relationship. They already know my responsibilities and their rights around issues related to confidentiality, and I've been working with them at their request to get them back into school. In this situation I may only need to let them know what information I need and ask permission for it; not before each and every question, but certainly in the context of each session. Suppose instead that I am meeting a youth for the first time. I may need to go through each step *in order*, and even repeat some steps during the session. For example, I may only need to do step 1 (inform them that I need information) once, but I may need to do steps 2 & 3 several times giving them a heads up about what I'm asking next and clarifying why I'm going to ask[21]. Depending on their reaction, I may repeat steps 4 & 5 (clarifying the level of confidence they can expect and asking permission) to help them decide whether or not to share the information with me. It all comes down to maintaining an awareness that you're on thin ice, or more accurately judging just how thick the ice is, in order for you to cross safely.

And, speaking of ice, I use ICE as an acronym and analogy to help *me* remember exactly what steps I need to take to create a safe environment when seeking information. ICE stands for *Inform, Clarify,* and *Explain.* It's a slightly different way of describing the steps than I did in the original text, but it sure makes it easier for me to remember. Maybe it's just the way my mind works, but when I'm seeking information I remember the analogy that *I'm on thin ice,* so I first question if I even want to go there (why do I need this information). If I decide that I do, then I remember that I need to *inform* them that I need information, *clarify* what information I need, and *explain* why I need the information (sometimes it's easier as a two-word memory aid: *Inform That, Clarify What,* and *Explain Why*). After that, it's a simple matter to remember that the young person will have to *trust me to go out on the ice*; in other words, they need to have some idea of what will or could happen (so I'd better ensure that they know the limits of

---

[21] See the discussion of "7 +/- 2" in the next chapter.

confidentiality regarding information), and *I'll need to ask their permission to step out with me.* Yeah, I know it's corny, but it also works and helps me to remember how to apply the technique in the moment when I can't check my notes.

The Runaway and Homeless Youth Management Information System (RHYMIS) mentioned in the original text has changed over the years. It is now NEO-RHYMIS (NEO being National Extranet Optimized; the rest of the acronym remains the same) and it is far less onerous than it once was. What hasn't changed is service provider's need for documentation. Whether it be to satisfy reporting requirements for the patchwork quilt of funding sources that keeps their doors open, or for gathering information to properly assess a youth's situation and needs, young people can still expect to be asked to share an extraordinary amount of information when seeking assistance. This not only underscores the need to be aware of all the trust and cultural conflict issues I've already mentioned, it also highlights an aspect of information seeking that service providers often become desensitized to as a result of the volume of information they deal with when intervening in the lives of street-dependent youth; that much of the information we seek is highly personal, highly sensitive, highly embarrassing, and, in most relationships and social contexts, *none of anyone's damn business.*

Consider the information sought on many intake/assessment forms. A young person is expected to reveal information about their damaged family and relationships; their history of neglect, abandonment, or abuse; their sexual preferences, history, and activities; their drug use and history, as well as other illegal activities they may engage in; their mental health and history of treatment and diagnosis; their medical health and physical vulnerabilities; and a litany of other equally intimate details about their life. Imagine *you* are a young person being asked such things by someone you don't know or trust, who represents systems you *know* you *don't* trust, and who is expecting you to answer as though they were simply trying to determine whether you prefer your peanut butter chunky or smooth. In fact, here's an exercise you may wish to try. Take the intake/assessment forms that you use with young people and see if you would be comfortable sharing your *honest* answers to the same questions with *everyone* in your organization. If your answer is anywhere on a scale from hesitation to an outright "no" you will have some idea of the emotions that the young person sitting across from you is experiencing.

An additional problem is that most of our forms are not strength-based (meaning they only ask about a youth's deficits, needs, and problems, with little if any attention to a youth's abilities, interests, and aspirations) and are not in a youth's "language." By "language" I don't mean English, Spanish, etc., I'm referring to a youth's interpretation of the words we use. For example, what we call "abuse" is often seen by a young person as standard operating procedure. Sure, they were getting slapped around every day, and maybe the crap kicked out of them for various infractions as judged by their parents, but when a worker asks if there was physical abuse in their home they may very likely reply "no." This is not because they are trying to hide information, but because they didn't consider it *abuse*.

But what if we're not doing intakes or assessments? What if we're not "seeking information" but simply engaging in conversation or activity. This is actually the best way to get information as the relaxed context of a conversation will often reveal information that would otherwise be awkward to ask for directly. Unfortunately, it doesn't change the risks involved for the youth and may in fact "set them up" where they casually reveal something that they later regret saying. Equally unfortunately, a conversation doesn't really lend itself to application of the 5 step information-seeking process I've outlined. To keep yourself and the young person safe in conversational situations I have two recommendations:

1. Inform the youth early in the conversation, and remind as necessary (like when your questions get more personal), that you may ask some things that they may not be comfortable revealing. Give them permission in advance to tell you that they don't feel like answering or that it's *none of your business*. Let them know that such responses are more than OK and that you won't take offense; then be sure that your behavior demonstrates that it *is*, in fact, OK and that you *don't*, in fact, take offense.
2. If a youth, out of the comfort of a conversation, begins to move into areas where you have reporting requirements, *stop them* and remind them of your responsibilities. This requires that you really pay attention at all times in order to see where the conversation is going. If the conversation begins to move into a reportable area, interrupt if necessary and say something like; *I'm sorry to interrupt, but I want to remind you that if you tell me something like* [a reportable example], *I'm required to* [share your reporting obligations]. *I just want you to be aware of that before you continue.*

Of course, there is another perspective on this. Many might say that you don't want to interrupt their revelations; that in order to help them we need them to reveal reportable information and if they do so in an unguarded moment we should allow it to happen. I'm not arguing the end; that we need discovery concerning reportable issues; I'm arguing the means; that we should use entrapment, deceit, omission, or manipulation to make the discovery. By building a trusting and respectful relationship and empowering the young person to consciously control the information they reveal we will get a more honest and complete picture of the youth's experience and needs. Empowering young people to control their information actually encourages disclosure, whereas making a youth feel like they revealed things that they did not intend to reveal discourages further exploration and future information sharing.

While I hope that I have demonstrated the need for awareness and skill when dealing with street-dependent youth around issues of information, there is one last point I'd like to make. The Don't Rat/Snitch code of the streets is yet another area where we tend to separate ourselves from the young people with whom we work. It frustrates us when we are simply trying to help, and we wonder why "their culture" is governed by such rigid and unhelpful practices. Once again we get to see how *different* they are and how unusual their behavior is. But are they really so different than us? What about the long standing Police Code of Silence; the way unions sometimes protect incompetent employees; the way youth service providers sometimes send bad employees off with good recommendations (we all know it happens); or the way most organizations, families, or political groups tend to deal with issues "in-house." The fact is that *all* groups of people tend to distrust and hide information from *other* groups of people. It may be true that on the streets this behavior is exaggerated and extreme, but it really isn't accurate to approach it as a street-based pathology.

Code Three: Integrity

This is one section of the book where in retrospect I think I may have lost my way a bit. As I pointed out the literal aspects of street integrity I began to focus mostly on communication between workers and youth. I'm not saying that a focus on communication is a bad thing. In fact, the two areas of training and practice that I think are severely undervalued by trainers, supervisors, and youth workers alike are communications skills and negotiation techniques (both critical skills to develop if we are going to work *with* youth as partners). However, in going off on the communication tangent, I don't think I focused enough on the impact of the code of integrity itself.

Let's remember what a code is. It is often defined as a set of principles or laws. Street codes obviously are not laws, at least not in the legal sense, but they are principles; that is, *rules or standards of personal conduct*. Through principles, through behavior, we identify ourselves with larger systems and groups. Codes of the street, therefore, can be thought of as the manner in which one behaves in order to be accepted by and part of the culture of the streets.

It is easy to identify how the first two codes I described fit this measure. With the *survival* code the standard of personal conduct is that I am going to do whatever I need to do, and you as my larger cultural group are not going to hold me accountable to any moral or legal standards if my actions are in pursuit of survival. With the *don't rat/snitch* code the standard of personal conduct is that I am not going to take street business outside of the cultural group, and anyone who does so deserves retribution of the worst kind. But what is the standard of personal conduct around the "code" of integrity? All I described was that it was interpreted literally and is the root cause of a communication style that requires skills on our part to convey and receive meaning. That particular communication style is not a standard of personal conduct, though. Street-dependent youth haven't decided as a cultural group to communicate literally. They communicate literally primarily due to delayed or arrested development. So what is the standard of personal conduct that makes *integrity* a street code?

There are several parts of the original text where you see glimpses of this standard. In a later chapter I talk about self-alienation and quote a youth as saying:

"I may be nothin' more than a sleazy little street walking whore, but by God at least I'm honest about it!"

And then later, when describing a conversation a youth had with her pastor about Jesus dying for her sins, I quote:

"If he was trying to die for my sins, then he fucked up; because my sins are still here."

These and other statements are demonstrative of the things you'll hear and the behaviors you'll see that have their roots in the standard of personal conduct derived from the code of street integrity. That is, when you are on the streets you don't get to have a facade or a misrepresentation of who you are. The standard of conduct is to *be yourself*, and fuck anyone who can't handle it.

I strongly suspect that as you read this, those of you who work with street-dependent youth are already challenging me. You know about street names, adopted identities, and street stories (all addressed in later chapters). You know about the low self-esteem and incorrect self-image of many youth with whom you've worked. The youth I quoted above was in reality much more than a "sleazy little street walking whore" and I ended the section on integrity by pointing out the strengths and inner resources that street-dependent youth possess. In fact, we are often frustrated by a youth's self-sabotaging behaviors and how they tend to show us a young person who is very different from the young person we see and know them to be. And that's exactly the point; the literalness of the code of integrity applies not to who they actually *are*, but to who they *believe themselves to be*. Whether that belief system is tied to self-image and esteem or adopted identity doesn't matter; what they believe about themselves is the image they are going to project and the code of integrity, the standard of personal conduct that gives them a sense of belonging to the culture of the streets, is to *defend* and demand *respect* for that *image*.

I am not unaware of the irony involved in having a code that prohibits facades as part of a culture of young people who, from their street name to their identity to their history, misrepresent almost everything about themselves. The key to making sense of this is to understand that integrity involves a literal representation of two factors, one having to do with self-image and one having to do with survival, as this code is strongly influenced by the code of survival. In fact, nearly all street-codes have their roots in survival. The don't rat/snitch code, for example, draws its strength from the fact that if you get labeled as a snitch it will be very difficult for you to survive. The most benign consequence will be loss of group belonging and the most severe will be bodily injury or death. With the code of integrity you project a standard of behavior that represents what you *believe yourself to be* (for psycho-emotional survival) and what you need *others* to believe you to be (for group belonging and, at times, physical survival).

This sense of integrity plays out in its most observable form through behaviors and responses dealing with street *respect*. While this is widely believed to have its roots in African-American culture, street respect is the manifestation within street culture of the code of integrity. Street respect is simply the demand, backed up by force if necessary, that one be treated as one "should be treated" or as their stature, standing, or status deserves. Of course, how they "should be treated" and their stature, standing, or status is based on their perception of themselves and the image they feel they need to project for their survival, rather than on who they really are or what they really need. For this reason, the code of integrity often works against them as they may perceive disrespect in the most innocent of slights and be culturally required to "right" the situation, and that level of defensive justification works to keep them trapped in an internal and external image that works against transitioning out of street life. It is also the reason why they can't seem to let anything slide and will get caught up in street dramas and "avenging" things that we often perceive as insignificant.

One of my adolescent clients contacted me about 20 years after I worked with her. She had read the original version of *Street Culture* and was talking to me about the code of integrity. Her feedback was that she learned to be very careful about what she said on the streets, because once a statement was made, the code *required* her to follow through. You'll see this fact trap youth into future actions that they already may have reconsidered. For example, in the heat of the moment they may threaten to harm someone or take some other negative action. Even after talking it out with you and reconsidering the wisdom of the choice, they then go ahead and take the action. Why? Because they *said* they *would*. Their street credibility is now on the line if they fail to follow through. Unfortunately this doesn't translate into keeping commitments they make outside of the culture. Just because they agree to do something with a youth worker, that agreement *doesn't* require them to follow through. The code only requires follow-through where their *street credibility* is on the line. I should also point out, though, that we sometimes fail to interpret their communication literally and assume agreement or commitment where none has been made. Take, for example, a youth worker saying something like:

If I get you into the shelter tonight you can't bring in drugs and you'll have to turn in your weapons. Can you do that?

Here are some possible ways a youth might respond:

Yes.
I can do that.
Sure.
That sounds fair.
I understand.
That's the way it is at all shelters.
That makes sense.
Uh-huh.

Note that *not a single one of these responses*, when literally interpreted, indicates a commitment or agreement to not bringing in drugs or turning in weapons (just because they *can* do something doesn't mean that they *will* do something). There would be no street integrity conflict with a youth giving one of these answers, then failing to keep the shelter drug or weapon free.

In the introduction to this book I stated that helping youth transition off of the streets is about helping them make conceptual, not physical, changes. Nowhere is this more important than in how we respond to the behaviors stemming from the street code of integrity. On the one hand, we must not "disrespect" the identity they show us. To do so *requires* them to defend, and therefore strengthens, that identity. But on the other hand, if we are going to help them to transition out of street life, we have to change both their self-image as well as their beliefs around the image they need *others* to see. This is why one of the best interventions we can offer is to give them opportunities to be someone *other* than who they are on the streets. Opportunity-based interventions, where they have experiences of responsibility, contribution, and non-street-based community, place them in situations where they need others to believe something *different* about themselves -- what *we* believe about them -- in order to succeed. We need to remember that we are competing with street-based community, so the greater the involvement we can offer the greater the impact we can have. We also need to remember that we are promoting change, and change takes time. Giving them opportunities to be responsible and contribute doesn't mean that they will be responsible and contribute right away. Our goal in creating these opportunities is to *influence* rather than to immediately see or expect behavioral change. This underscores the Positive Youth Development strategy of Meaningful Participation. By creating other communities to participate in that expect them to project a different image in order to belong, their own code of integrity will eventually require them to adopt a different, more pro-social standard of personal conduct; and that change in conduct will begin to impact their self-image.

An excellent example of this strategy can be seen in the story of young men who were in a program for adjudicated youth. These young men ended up in that program due to their involvement in crimes and assaultive behaviors; in some cases some pretty serious things. The program was experimenting with Positive Youth Development and involved the youth in coming up with ideas for community service. One of them had seen a news report about an elderly woman who was experiencing legal difficulties because her yard was full of trash and had become a problem for the neighborhood. The boys decided on a project to clean up her yard, and the program made the arrangements to make it happen.

As they were out there cleaning the yard, the elderly woman, who was a bit senile and not really fully aware of who these kids were, but knowing that they were helping her, brought out milk and cookies for them. As she was giving them the cookies she was thanking them for their help and at one point said; *"Can you imagine how much better this world would be if it only had more fine young men like you."* For some of them, this was the first time in their lives that anyone had seen them through such a grateful and positive perspective, and that one statement from that single elderly woman probably had greater impact on these boys than much of the therapy they were receiving at the program.

Final Thoughts

I want to remind you of something I stated at the beginning of the original text; *an in-depth study of all of the codes and subtle variations of the rules and regulations on the street is beyond the scope of this book.* It's absolutely critical to remember that while I have focused on 3 specific codes of the street, they are by no means the only codes you will encounter. They were selected specifically because they tend to be universal, consequential, and govern the behaviors that are often problematic for youth workers. There are a myriad of other codes that exist on the streets, however, some of which may not be universal, but exist only within a defined sub-group of the culture or within a street family. While my hope is to clarify these primary problematic codes and offer you ways to navigate them, I equally hope to raise your awareness of the fact that street-dependent youth are not living in our world or by our rules. If we are going to work with them effectively we have to accept the fact that they are not going to behave as we expect and wish them to behave. When we see behaviors that don't make sense to us, it doesn't necessarily mean that there is something "wrong" with this young person; it very well may be that they are operating from a perspective that we don't share or know, but that in the context of their world, their behavior is entirely rational and makes perfect sense. Don't explain behavior you don't understand with assumptions, rather, use it to indicate an area of growth and learning for you. Until we understand the world through their eyes we will have no idea how to help them see the world differently.

A youth who is going to survive must transition out of street culture and this transition cannot be made unless concepts of time are addressed and changed

Concepts of Time

When doing this as a live presentation I share with the audience a piece of information I've learned from my study of public speaking. Periodically I make efforts to increase my skills by reading books or listening to tapes on the art of live presentation. I once even attended a workshop titled *How to Give a Winning Presentation* for no other reason than to see how the presenter would handle that much pressure! The confusing thing about studying public speaking is that there are so many different ideas on the subject, some of which actually contradict each other, that I often feel less knowledgeable than I was before I started studying. What makes it worthwhile, however, is that there are some common themes that tend to emerge from the different perspectives. The one that I'd like to call your attention to is this; *when attending or listening to an oral presentation, within three days you will only remember 10% of what was said.*

The reason why I point this out is to let you know that; if it's true that you may only remember 10% of this material; this is the 10% that you will want to remember.

Our concept of time affects everything we do. Our behaviors, thought processes, reactions, beliefs, choices, and decisions, will all in some manner be impacted by our concept of time. Street-dependent youth are no different in this respect, but their concept of time can be very different from how time is perceived in the dominant culture. For these reasons, a street-dependent youth's concept of time is perhaps the single most important concept for us to understand.

Time as a Concept

It's important to recognize the premise that time is a concept. It is not a table, or a chair, or any other such physical manifestation. Rather, time is something that we *made up* in order to regulate our lives. Throughout history there have been different ways of measuring time, and different cultures have developed various calendars for measuring the passage of years. Even in the modern world we take great liberties with time. Every autumn we arbitrarily decide to create an extra hour one day by turning back our clocks. We then give that hour back the following spring. Where time zones meet, next door neighbors can be an hour apart in their measurement of time. The International Date Line, which marks the point at which new days begin on our planet, is nothing more than an imaginary line that has been arbitrarily decided upon by the nations of Earth. You'll notice that it is not even a *straight* line, but rather it zigzags across the ocean. This was done in order to ensure that certain island groups remain within the same time zone, although several island nations are now attempting to extend their territories across the Date Line in order to be able to claim that they were first into the new millennium (which, by the way, begins in the year 2001, not the year 2000 as is commonly believed).

These are just some of the ways in which we are able to conceptualize time to meet our needs. This creates the possibility that we are not all going to conceptualize time in the same way and you will see some unique cultural perspectives toward time as you look at nations around the planet. Practically speaking, however, most of us have developed a similar concept of time, at least in general terms. That concept is what we call the past, the present, and the future.

Past, Present, and Future

The past is what has happened, but is not happening now. When most of us look at our past we think of it as a continuum. It's like a long line stretching behind us. We can't really see where it begins, because it becomes less defined as we remember our early years. Some of us can remember back to our first year. I can remember back to maybe my third year, and beyond that things are not quite so clear. Still, where it is defined, we have the ability to order events on it and to use those events as reference points in our life. We can remember that event A happened before event B. This concept of the past is so well defined that we can even write it down; most of us having done a "time-line" at some point in our lives.

The present is what is currently happening, but will not be happening soon and has not happened before. While we tend to think of the present as being a "point" in time; one that will very soon be a reference point in our memory of the past; the truth is that our concept of the present is generally much broader than we realize. This is probably attributable to two main factors; a seven day week cycle and a time oriented market system. Almost everything we do is by schedule or appointment. We work 9 - 5, Monday through Friday. We schedule appointments for medical care, haircuts, auto repair; even social engagements are scheduled activities. These two factors combine to give us a concept of the present that generally spans one week. When we think about what we need to be doing now, in the present, most of us are really thinking about what we need to be doing this week.

Finally, we have the future. The future is what's going to be happening, but is not happening now and has not happened before. The future tends to be conceptualized as a mirror image of your past. It is also a line, only this line stretches before us, losing definition depending on our capacity for long range planning. I've met people who can tell me what they'll be doing 10 years from now. Other people are able to plan months into the future, and still others can only manage to plan ahead a few weeks at a time. Like your past, you can order events on the line. The difference, however, is that these events haven't happened yet, allowing you to rearrange them at will. You may plan to do event A before event B but, if you wish, you may change that plan and do event B before event A. Your concept of the future gives you movable reference points for where you might go as opposed to your concept of the past which gives you fixed reference points for where you have been.

A Street-dependent Youth's Past

A street-dependent youth's concept of time will also include the past, present, and future. Once again, however, they don't have the same perception of these concepts that we do. To a street-dependent youth the past can also be considered what has happened, but is not happening now. It is not, however, a continuum on which you can identify a particular point in time. Instead, it more closely resembles a vast, disorganized warehouse, and everything that is not the present gets stored without organization.

Trauma and "Screened" Memories

The biggest contributing factor to this concept of the past is that, when you are dealing with youth on the streets, you are dealing with victims of trauma. Most street-dependent youth have experienced some form of trauma before they came to the streets, and they all experience trauma on a daily basis while they are on the streets. The inevitable result of trauma is that there are parts of your life experience that you will not be able to recall. The conscious mind has a built-in self-protection that helps you survive trauma by blocking, or screening out, certain aspects of your memory. If you experience a serious trauma, even if you remain conscious during the experience, there will be pieces of that event that you simply don't remember. I read about a plane crash in South America a few years back, and there was a story of a passenger who survived. The plane was in trouble for about fifteen minutes before it actually went down. The survivor related that he remembered coming out of the bathroom and had no further memories until he was in the field with rescuers surrounding him. The fifteen minutes of terror that he must have experienced as he knew the plane was going down had mercifully been erased from his memory by his own mind and his own need to escape that memory. Your conscious mind will not retain the most traumatic parts of your experiences simply because you cannot live every day with that much horror in your memory. Your mind, therefore, creates a block, or, what I refer to as a *screened* memory.

Street-dependent youth tend to have such an excessively screened memory that it becomes impossible to see their past as a line stretching behind them. Any attempt to do so will encounter so many blank spots or holes in the line that it ends up more closely resembling a jumbled pile of unconnected events with little or no reference to each other. These "blank spots" are often quite large. One of the techniques I've developed for working with street-dependent youth is called *life mapping*. This technique is basically a glorified time-line that includes reference points and graphics to create a history of the youth's life. While there are many goals in life mapping, one of the key purposes is to identify where these "blank spots" are as this helps to indicate when primary traumas such as sexual abuse may have occurred in the youth's life. It is not uncommon to see blank areas on a life map that span five or six years, where a youth literally does not recall where they were, what they were doing, or what happened to them. This is a result of their screened memory.

Being unable to develop a "continuum" concept of their past on which they can order events, they instead throw all memories into the "storage area." As a result, when recalling past events they do so in a random, disordered manner. This not only confuses the structure of past events, but it also alters the emotional and psychological attachment to those events. You'll hear a youth relate an event that happened many years ago, but their apparent connection to that event and the emotions that they are showing would lead you to believe that it happened today. By the same token, a youth may express a current event as though it were ancient history. You'll hear them talk about their past, and in the first telling events were ordered A, B, and C. The next time they tell the story you notice that the order has changed, with event C happening before events A and B. With each retelling of the story the order, psychological connection and emotional attachment seems to change.

This is another characteristic that results in street-dependent youth being labeled as manipulators and liars. We assume that they have access to the past in the same way that we do, and then we see psycho-emotional confusion, events that keep changing their order, and sometimes even the events themselves change. We therefore conclude that the youth is making these stories up, playing fast and loose with reality, and that they're lying to us. The truth is that they are not making it up, but rather they are literally unable to recall past events in the same way that we do.

This, then, becomes one of our biggest challenges. If we are going to help street-dependent youth piece their lives together, and help them figure out where they are at and where they are going, we may have to hear a story several times before we can get a clear idea of what has actually occurred.

Even at that, what we may end up with is a lap full of "puzzle pieces" with some of the pieces missing. It will then be up to us to try to fit the pieces together in order to create a coherent picture of the youth's past.

A Street-dependent Youth's Present

In looking at a street-dependent youth's concept of the present, it is similar in that the present is what is currently happening, but will not be happening soon, and has not happened before. Where this concept differs is in the span of the present, or how broad of a concept it is. Street-dependent youth do not think in terms of a week, but tend to be very focused on points in time. The present is what they can hear, see, and feel. We're talking about a concept of the present that at best spans a few hours. More often than not it only spans minutes, or sometimes even seconds. If an event is not currently happening right in front of them, then it is not considered to be a present event. Instead, it slips into the past, and into that vast storage area where it can quickly be misplaced. Psychological and emotional distance from the event can fully develop in a matter of moments.

Working with Time - Opportunities and Pitfalls

The difference between a street-dependent youth's concept of past and present and a more traditional view of these concepts creates both opportunities and potential pitfalls for youth workers. One of the greatest opportunities is the result of the interaction between a street-dependent youth's narrow concepts of the present compared to our broader view. This interaction means that when an event has slipped into a youth's past it is entirely feasible that it will still be in your present. This can provide you with an incredibly helpful tool; particularly if you're dealing with any kind of conflict situation where you are involved in some sort of head-to-head power struggle with a youth, or their anger is directed at you. If you confront the struggle or the anger, it is likely that you will either get nowhere or escalate the situation. If you realize, however, that in a very short period of time this will be a past event for the youth which will create psychological and emotional distance from the event, then you can simply back off for a few minutes. I want to be clear that I am not advising you to either back down or to not deal with the situation. What I'm suggesting is that a few minutes will allow the situation to become a past event for the youth while it remains a current event for you. This will allow you to come back and resolve your current issue with the youth while they are in a frame of mind to look at it objectively as a past event. Strategies such as calling a "time out" or suggesting that you pause to get a glass of water can work well to buy you time for the event to slip out of the present.

It is important when using this technique to make sure that you don't create a new "present" event for the youth. After allowing it to slip into a youth's past, keep it there with your language. For clarification, consider the following three examples. In all three the situation is that of a youth venting anger at you. In the first example you respond not using the suggested technique. In the second example you respond using the technique incorrectly. In the final example you respond with a correct use of the technique.

Example #1 -- While a youth is venting anger at you, you confront them with; "*why are you so angry with me?*"

Example #2 -- You do not respond to a youth's anger right away. Instead, you back off for a few minutes, then come back and say; "*can we talk now, or are you still angry with me?*"

Example # 3 -- You do not respond to a youth's anger right away. Instead, you back off for a few minutes, then come back and say; "*I don't understand what was going on. Why were you so angry with me?*"

In the first example there is no time allowed for the youth to develop distance from the emotions. The demand to explain their feelings has the effect of keeping the feelings present and escalating them by requiring the youth to defend them. The probable outcome of this intervention is an increase in the youth's anger.

In the second example the youth is allowed to gain distance from the angry emotions and receives no feedback to support or escalate them. When attempting to deal with the event, however, the worker first defines it as a new present event (can we talk *now*) and then asks the youth to examine anger in the present (are you *still* angry with me). The probable outcome of this intervention is to re-create the event that existed before backing off.

In the final example the youth is allowed to gain distance from the angry emotions and receives no feedback to support or escalate them. In this case, however, the event is not recreated in the present because language is used that supports its place in the past (I don't understand what *was* going on). The youth is then asked to examine *past* anger (Why *were* you so angry with me). The probable outcome of this intervention is consideration of a past event, leaving both youth and worker free to objectively resolve issues.

By allowing events to slip out of a youth's concept of the present and dealing with them as past events, youth often are able to let go of their emotional investment in positions, and deal objectively with what for you is still a current issue.

In the mid 1980's, I ran a component program for an organization known as *Project LUCK*, or *Link Up the Community for Kids*. This was a demonstration project created at a time when it was being recognized that traditional youth-service approaches were not meeting the needs of street-dependent youth. Rather than creating new services, the idea behind Project LUCK was to network existing services and specialize components of those services to meet the needs of the street-dependent youth population.

My piece of Project LUCK was housed at a youth service center with an existing Big Brother/Big Sister program. I directed what was called the Youth Advocate Component of Project LUCK. This was primarily a Big Brother/Big Sister program that had been adapted to serve as a mentoring service for street-dependent youth. My job was to recruit volunteers and train them to work with street-dependent youth in order to provide them with recreational outlets, assist them in accessing services, and act as adult mentors. One of our earliest lessons was that it didn't work very well to have a pool of volunteers and a pool of youth and create random matches. We quickly designed opportunities for youth and the volunteers to interact with each other in order to self-select.

One day we were on an outing with a female in the program. She had been in Project LUCK for less than one month, so we really didn't know her very well. This particular day, however, was her birthday. In recognition of that, I and the two volunteers that she seemed most comfortable with took her and her dog (which she had adopted as soon as she had moved into housing) on a picnic lunch. Each of the 3 of us had picked up a small gift for her birthday. The gifts were nothing dramatic, but we knew that she wasn't getting any other gifts so it was just our way to acknowledge that this was her birthday. What we didn't know at the time was that she had some major issues associated with the giving of gifts.

This was a youth who had been betrayed by everyone in her life who had ever said they cared about her. The result of those experiences was that *caring* was a very loaded concept for her. In her mind, if somebody said or showed that they cared, what that meant was that they were going to use or hurt her somehow. She also believed that anyone who offered gifts was, in effect, saying that they cared about you. When we offered her the birthday gifts, we inadvertently put her in a very difficult position. She needed the services of Project LUCK to accomplish the goals she had set for herself, but if she acknowledged the gifts she'd believe that we cared about her and would therefore have to leave the program in order to self-protect. Her need for the services was so strong that she exhibited one of the strangest responses I have ever experienced; she ignored the fact that we were offering gifts. There is no way to describe to you just how strange this response was. Imagine 3 people wishing this girl a happy birthday and offering gifts, but every behavior, word, and action on her part was as if it wasn't happening. It was *very* odd.

We responded by putting the gifts away and backing off. After about five minutes, I got up and asked if she wanted to take her dog for a walk. She said that she did and we got up and started walking through the park. After a short distance I began a conversation, as follows:

"*Do you remember when we offered you gifts for your birthday, and you ignored it?*"
Without hesitation, she responded: *Yeah."*

I then said: *"Can you help me understand what was going on, because that didn't make any sense to me."*

Again, without hesitation she began to explain to me what she was thinking at the time. We had a long, very detailed conversation about the event, which is how I learned about her associations with caring and gift giving. The important thing to bear in mind about this is that we were having an open, detailed discussion about an event that 5 minutes earlier she couldn't even acknowledge was happening. The reason we were able to do this is because, for her, it was a past event. I allowed her to examine it as a past event with my language, by using phrases such as; "do you <u>remember</u>," and "what <u>was</u> going on." If I had been able to tape record our conversation and played it back for you now, you probably would not be able to determine from anything said whether the event we were discussing had happened 5 minutes ago or 5 years ago. You would only know that we were discussing an event that had happened in the past. By dealing with it as a past event, I was not only able to learn about her association to caring and gift giving, but I was also able to help her see new associations. The result of this intervention was that she stayed in the program, and she accepted the gifts.

This is a very versatile technique that can be used in a number of situations. If you find yourself in a difficult spot with a youth where things just don't seem to be working, drop it for a few minutes. Then bring it up again as a past event. You will usually encounter far less resistance from the youth who is able to let their defenses down because, for them, it's not happening anymore. For them, they're talking about something that had happened in the past.

Unfortunately, the same dynamic that creates this opportunity for us also presents us with one of our biggest pitfalls in working with street-dependent youth. We need to be honest and acknowledge that, no matter how much we care about and respect the young people we are working with, they can be very skillfully obnoxious at times. We are human. We get our buttons pushed. We can leave an interaction with a youth with feelings of anger, or hurt, or frustration. The potential pitfall is that, long after the youth has let it go, they can still be present feelings for you. The risk is that you will recreate the experience in the youth's new present, because you have not yet let go of *your* feelings.

Let's say that you need to set a limit with a youth and they react with anger. You feel attacked, frustrated, and upset. You see the youth the next day and, for you, the event is still current. You feel the anger and the frustration and probably a sense of dread about having to deal with this youth again as soon as you see them coming. The result is that, no matter how professionally you conduct yourself, some of your reaction to that youth will be from anger, frustration, and dread; and you're kidding yourself if you think the youth will not pick up on those feelings. You will then have created a new present experience for the youth and the relationship between you and the youth will continue to be tense.

On the other hand, if you are able to let go of these feelings and put them behind you, you'll find that the youth naturally tends to do that as well. No matter how bad your last encounter with a youth was, the next one can be a fresh opportunity for a positive interaction. The key to being able to let go of these feelings is to develop the ability to deal with anger, even anger that appears to be personally directed at you, without taking it personally. We will be discussing this issue in more detail later in this manual, but, for now, realize that if you can let it go, more often than not, the youth will have already let it go.

Earlier I described an incident where we called Children's Protective Services to take a baby into custody. The reactions of the youth were such that most of our volunteers, and several of our staff, had been nervous about coming back the next night due to the fact that the youth had been very creative and graphic with the threats they had made in anger. People were concerned about putting themselves in front of these youth again because they didn't know what the youths' attitudes were going to be, or what was going to happen. As it turned out, their attitude was that it was over and done with. They expressed their feelings at the time, when it was a present event, and the next night it was simply something that had happened in the past. Again, if you can let it go, they will let it go. Where we get into trouble is when we hold on to the feelings and issues and re-create the event as a new present experience for young people.

A Street-dependent Youth's Future

For those of you who are paying close attention, you'll notice that I haven't touched upon the subject of the future. That's because, when it comes to street-dependent youth, there is very little to say about a future concept. Like our more traditional concept, street-dependent youth will also view the future as what is not happening now, and has not happened before. Unlike our traditional concept, however, street-dependent youth additionally view the future as what is *not going to happen*. For street-dependent youth, the future is not tangible. It doesn't exist and therefore it is not a medium that they can work with. There are 3 major contributing factors to this concept, or lack of concept, relating to the future.

The first factor is, simply, that street-dependent youth are adolescents. In many cases, due to the arrested development we've already discussed, there are parts of their conceptual ability that are even younger than their chronological age. Even adolescents who have had a healthy, non-traumatic life have difficulty with conceptualizing the future. Think back to your own teenage years and how difficult it was for you to think in terms of the future. Most of us were not very skilled in that area.

When you add to that a consideration of a street-dependent youth's development, many of them are working with the future conceptual ability of a pre-teen. This greatly increases the difficulty with a future concept for a very practical reason. For example, I remember when I was 10 years old I asked my mother if we could get something. I don't even recall what it was I wanted, but I remember distinctly her response, which was; *maybe we can get it next year.* That was what she said, but what I heard was; *you ain't getting it.* The reason why I interpreted her words that way is because a year was one tenth of my life; it was an *inconceivable* period of time. Now that I'm in my 40's, years go by every time I blink. If someone asked me today if we could get something and I responded *maybe we can get it next year,* I'd be panicking tonight about what I need to do in order to get it that *quickly.* The simple fact is that as you age your ability to conceptualize the future increases.

The second factor is related to a street-dependent youth's narrow concept of the present. This is complicated by the nature of street life which, as we discussed under the code of survival, is an inherently dangerous, life-threatening environment. An environment such as this, consisting of continuous crisis and trauma, not only keeps the present concept narrow, but it also focuses conscious attention on the immediacy of situations. Therefore, in addition to the rather limited scope of their present concept, street-dependent youth tend to be anchored in that narrow scope out of a perceived need to stay alert to immediate threats. This type of focused, anchoring in the present makes it very difficult to conceptualize the future.

Finally, the third factor is that a person's future concept tends to be a mirror image of whatever past concept they hold. For street-dependent youth, the past is a picture of confusion, disorientation, powerlessness, trauma, and pain. It is an unpleasant picture that, in any form of mirror image, remains unpleasant. The result is that efforts to conceptualize the future are usually experienced in a manner that repels them and discourages continued efforts.

The combination of these 3 factors makes development of a future concept challenging (due to their age and developmental level), unsupported (due to the nature of street life anchoring them in the present), and unpleasant (due to the beliefs that they have based on past experience). It should, therefore, come as little surprise that a future concept can be virtually non-existent among street-dependent youth.

The Challenge for Services

Unfortunately, this creates major challenges in developing services. No matter how they are designed, portions of our services are going to have to be provided on a scheduled or appointment basis. This is especially true when coordinating with community services, such as medical or education programs. Street-dependent youth have developed a notorious reputation for not keeping appointments and the underlying cause of this reputation is the near total lack of a future time concept. When we work from an appointment base with a population that has little future concept, missed appointments are inevitable. In addition, their future concept often creates a climate for conflict between workers and youth. Consider that the young person has reached a point where they are willing to deal with their issues enough to face them and take action, and they set aside the ethical bind of not "snitching" and going outside of their culture. They then come to you requesting a service and you respond with an appointment two weeks in the future. What the youth may hear in your offer is *service denied*, because two weeks is an inconceivable period of time for them. The next thing you know, the youth is angry with you and storms out with no intention of keeping the appointment. You, then, become angry with the youth because you have often done an incredible job of networking and advocacy in order to get an appointment that *quickly* since it usually takes a month to get the appointment, and your hard work is rewarded by verbal abuse from the youth and looking like a fool once again with your referral source as yet another of your clients fails to keep an appointment. This all too common occurrence is caused by our failure to provide services in a manner consistent with a street-dependent youth's concept of time.

I've found the following technique to be effective. When a youth comes to me requesting a service that I know will take weeks to provide, I'll respond by telling the youth that appointments are difficult to get and take a long time. I'll agree to work on getting the appointment, and then request that the youth come back and see me tomorrow for ... for whatever reason I can think of. I will then set the appointment up immediately, while, at the same time, I continue to set short-term appointments with the youth to keep them returning for services. When the appointment is a day or two away I'll say *remember when you asked me for such and such? I have an appointment for you tomorrow.* This approach is working within their concept of time and has proved to greatly increase a youth's ability to keep appointments.

It is important to point out that it is never appropriate or advisable to lie to the youth about the appointment. Dishonesty in any form never works well with street-dependent youth. If the youth asks about the appointment, I am not advising that you disguise the fact that you have already set one up. I am, however, advising that you keep the youth's focus on the short-term appointments. For example:

"Can you come see me tomorrow? I have some time to look into GED programs with you."

"Yeah, OK. Hey, what ever happened with that medical thing?"

"I've set up an appointment, but it's not for a while yet. If you come see me tomorrow we can start getting this GED stuff out of the way before you have to deal with that."

The better able you are to work in the short-term the greater will be the youth's ability to follow through.

In the Youth Advocacy program I described earlier, one of the approaches we used to keep youth involved who had not yet been matched with an advocate was a weekly recreation group. When we first began doing these groups, we would contact the youth in their placements and get their commitment to attend. Every week we would call them up and say; *we're doing a group next Thursday, do you want to come?* We worked hard to make the group activities exciting, fun, and culturally appropriate. Our efforts were rewarded with two major results. First, almost all of the youth eagerly agreed to attend and, second, almost none of them actually did. We couldn't figure out what we were doing wrong until one week when I called one of the girls in the program and discovered the problem through a conversation that went something like as follows:

I said: *"We're doing another Thursday night group next week. Do you think you'll be able to make it?"*

She replied: *"Yeah, sounds good. I'll ... oh, I don't know, Jerry, call me next week!"*

That was when it dawned on us that our mistake had to do with their concept of time. We changed our tactics and began calling youth on the day of the group and saying; *we're doing a group <u>tonight</u>, do you want to come?* Attendance skyrocketed. After a few weeks, we were able to start calling them the day before the group, and they kept coming. Pretty soon it became part of their routine, and we didn't have to call them at all.

It's important to remember that the burden is on you to keep these dynamics in mind. It is unlikely that, when presenting youth with a future appointment, they will respond with; *thanks anyway, but, you know, I have no concept of the future so that really doesn't work for me.* A more common response is for them to either get angry, or to agree to the appointment and then simply blow it off. If you do keep this concept in mind, however, and adjust your approach accordingly, you will find that you can greatly increase the follow-through of the young people you work with.

The Ratio of Time

A part of this concept that I haven't yet mentioned is that there is generally a 3-to-1 time ratio between a street-dependent youth's sense of time and the sense that we in the dominant culture seem to have. This is primarily caused by the 24 hour activity of the streets. We tend to live our lives with a daily routine consisting of 8 hours of activity, 8 hours of down time, and 8 hours of sleep. The streets, on the other hand, are 24 hours of activity, with down time and sleep being things that are grabbed when and where you can get them. The way a day feels to them can be the way 3 of our days feel to us. This is a factor that needs to be considered in long-term work with youth. If you have a technique or intervention that requires you to see a client once a week, applying that intervention to street-dependent youth will require you to see them 2-to-3 times a week in order to have similar results.

The Time Trap

Despite the problems that we as service providers encounter when dealing with a street-dependent youth's concept of time, the biggest problem is that this concept of time doesn't work for them. When I say it doesn't work for them, I'm referring to the fact that their concept of time doesn't work outside of their culture. Obviously, it works very well within the culture of the streets, but a youth who does not transition out of street life dies; maybe not today, but the streets mean death in the long run. Therefore, a youth who is going to survive must transition out of street culture and this transition cannot be made unless concepts of time are addressed and changed. This "time barrier" is often overlooked in terms of its impact on keeping youth locked into street activities. Prostitution is a prime example, where the traditional belief is that youth are reluctant to exit the life primarily for economic reasons. The question you hear all of the time is; *how can we attract them with minimum wage jobs when they can turn a few tricks and make hundreds of dollars?* My experience has convinced me that money is not the issue. Without getting into the economic concepts that we will discuss later, it is actually concepts of time that create the trap and you'll find that a youth can establish a better lifestyle economically working a minimum wage job. But they can't work a minimum wage job as long as they have a street-developed concept of time, which is what keeps them working the streets.

Consider that when a youth goes out and pulls a date, they are rewarded instantly. Both the means and the end of their act occur in the present. Then we discuss legal employment with them. What we are offering is that they get up in the morning, go to work for hours, and come home with nothing to show for it. We then ask them to do that again, and again, and again, and again. They have now completed one week. We then ask them to repeat that entire experience, and maybe by the end of the second week they will finally see reward for their labor. This simply doesn't make sense to them. By the end of the first or second day they're going to be thinking; *what am I knocking myself out for? I'm not getting anything for this effort!* They then get drawn back to a moment by moment lifestyle, one of which they are able to conceive.

During a counseling session with a youth who had recently returned to prostitution after a brief try at legal employment, I was exploring what it was about prostitution that she found attractive. I found her response significant for two reasons. First, it was immediate; there was absolutely no hesitation when I asked her about attracting factors. Second, it was the *only* attracting factor that she was able to identify. Her response was:

"*I like living hour to hour. I just don't get this week to week shit!*"

Obviously then, if we are to help youth transition out of street life, we are going to have to address concepts of time. We can't do that, however, by forcing them into a world where their concepts don't work, and hoping that they'll somehow be appropriately molded. Rather, we have to start by meeting them where they're at and then working slowly to expand those concepts. There are 3 essential factors in accomplishing this goal; *immediacy, repetition, and consistency.*

Immediacy

Being immediate is the necessary first step in transitioning a youth's concept of time. This is the step that allows you to meet the youth where they are already at. Skipping this step means that you are requiring the youth to make a conceptual leap into the time-sense that we desire them to have, which is a leap that few youth are successful at making without assistance. The danger with immediate response, however, is that, if not properly executed it can often serve to reinforce a youth's existing concept rather than provide a basis for expanding that concept. The key is to provide immediate responses that are connected to long-term results. This meets the youth's need for instant gratification while exposing them to a broader concept of time.

An example of this technique can be seen in the design of our transitional living program. Residents in the program live by an *evaluation* system and their ability to stay in the program is dependent on their evaluations. Evaluations are heavily influenced by *productive time*, which is credit for hours spent in activities that the program considers a productive use of the resident's time. The result is that a youth who is employed may have to wait two or three weeks to get a paycheck, but they receive productive time at the program on a daily basis. This system allows them to get daily gratification by earning productive time, weekly gratification through the evaluations, and long-term gratification through the benefits of employment. While the system works within their current concept of time, it also serves to gradually expand on that concept.

Repetition

Repetition is the key to mastery in any area. Great sports figures do not spend their practice hours on complicated and fancy moves in the hopes that they will have the opportunity to perform them. Instead, they practice the basics over and over again. Repetition of the simple tasks, as mundane as it seems, is the foundation for success in any activity. This foundation remains true when working to expand a person's concept of time. The technique is to identify the basic factors in an expanded view of time and create activities that allow repeated exposure to those factors.

One of the methods we utilize at our transitional living program is weekly schedules created by the residents. Each Sunday night the residents fill out a schedule predicting what they will be doing with the rest of their week. They are asked to list appointments, work, school, recreation, and anything else they can think of. A key part of the schedule is that the dates are blank and need to be filled in. Residents need to write in the start and end date of the week, as well as the day and date for each of the individual days in that week. We do not hold them to the activities that they list; we just ask them to go through the exercise of writing it all down. We do, however, hold them to correct dates and will not accept a schedule that is incorrectly dated.

When a resident first moves in from the streets and we explain the process of the Sunday schedules to them, their reaction is often to look at us as though we've just landed from Mars. Their attitude can be; *let me get this straight. You want me to tell you on Sunday, what I'm going to be doing on Friday?* Our attitude in response is to ask them to make the effort, to take their best educated guess and to try to write something down. If you look at the schedules from residents who are fairly new to the program it can appear to be a pointless exercise, with half-hearted efforts that don't even come close to what their week really ends up looking like. Every week, however, they are repeating the exercise of having to think in terms of a seven day period, including specifying the days and dates of that period. By repetition of this exercise, after several months their schedules actually start looking like what their week ends up being and the youth begins to develop the ability to think and act in concepts of weeks instead of days. It is repetition of the basics that creates this change.

Consistency

Consistency is the final key, and perhaps the most important one. It is not only their concept of time that keeps youth trapped in street life, it is also a belief system that the world is random, and most of them have not developed the concept of cause and effect. It is not possible for them to gain control in their lives because they believe that control does not exist. This is one of the reasons that we often see such an attraction to and fascination with the occult, witchcraft, and Satanism. It isn't that these youth are evil; rather what you're witnessing is a desperate attempt to find some way to gain control and power in their lives. At the same time that we are working to expand their concept of time, it is critical that we challenge the belief that everything is random and that there is no way to gain control. The way we do this is through consistency.

When describing the Advocacy program groups, I mentioned that they occurred on Thursday nights. While we changed our approach to getting youth to attend, we never changed the time or day of the group. It was that consistency in time that made it possible for us to count on attendance even after we stopped calling youth. It simply became part of their routine and something they counted on. This not only began to challenge their belief in a random world, but it actually encouraged attendance because it was something that wasn't random. It's important to point out that youth don't desire randomness; it's simply what they believe. Create opportunities for them to experience security and consistency and you will be creating something that is very attractive to them.

By creating consistency you will not only be countering the belief in randomness, you will also be providing an attractive framework for long-term involvement and therefore expanded concepts of time. Look for any opportunity you have to create consistency with time related issues. The House Meetings of our transitional living program have been at 7:00 PM on Wednesdays since we opened our doors in 1987. Our emergency shelter program requires youth to arrive before 9:30 PM unless otherwise provided for by their case manager. This then provides another consistent time reference in their daily schedule and provides clear examples of cause and effect. If a youth does not make it by 9:30, their reserved bed space is given to another youth needing shelter. We have designed our programs to pay such close attention to consistency around time that we have purchased clocks for both our transitional living and emergency shelter programs that receive radio signals from the atomic clock in Boulder, Colorado.

One of the worst things that services can do is reinforce the concept that the world is random by being inconsistent. If a program states that A will happen if a youth does B, and then does not follow-through with that, we have then in effect verified that the world is random and reinforced concepts that will keep a youth involved in street life. No matter how difficult it may appear in the moment, do not rescue youth from the consequences of their actions. As seductive as the short-term results of doing so may be (you feel good and the youth likes and appreciates you), you have just reinforced beliefs and concepts that will work against a youth's transition out of a life-threatening environment.

There is one note of caution. There are many times when we are, to all intents and purposes, doing triage work with a youth's issues. That is, there may be a need to respond in a way that is not ideal in terms of one of their issues, in order to address a more immediate need. An example of this may be a youth who arrives very late for a medical appointment. Depending on the nature of the medical need, it may be more urgent to treat the youth while they are present than to expand their concept of time by rescheduling. This section of the manual is focusing on the issue of time with street-dependent youth, but you will always need to make decisions as to what is the most important response to give in any individual situation.

The long-term effect of holding youth accountable with consistency is that you tap into their tremendous reservoirs of resources and strength. When youth are able to finally embrace the concept that their actions control the effects in their lives there is no limit to what they can accomplish. Up until that point their progress is generally slow and undirected. We have accepted residents from juvenile institutions or other highly structured environments where their experience had been to do what they are told to do, without question. They then arrive at our programs where they are given full responsibility for their decisions and the response we often get is that they do everything they can to get somebody to make their decisions for them. It's when they realize that nobody is going to bail them out; that nobody is going to make this decision for them or take responsibility from them, that they really begin to really bloom. It's when youth finally believe that their decisions and actions create their futures that we see them make their greatest progress.

Key Points - Concepts of Time

- Time is a concept, and street-dependent youth experience time differently than we do in the dominant culture.
- Due to past and continuing trauma, street-dependent youth have gaps in their memories that prevent them from seeing the past as a continuum. Rather, the past is viewed as a big storage area from which it is difficult to retrieve memories in an ordered, consistent manner.
- A street-dependent youth's concept of the present is immediate; what they can hear, see, and feel.
- Street youth have very little ability to conceive of the future. For them, it is not a medium that exists or can be worked with.
- One of the greatest challenges for service providers is learning to work within a street-dependent youth's concept of time, while also working to expand upon that concept. It is their concept of time that is responsible for many youth's failure to transition out of street life.
- The 3 most important factors in impacting a youth's concept of time are immediacy, repetition, and consistency.

2.0 Commentary:

And the winner is (drum roll) -- The Republic of Kiribati (pronounced KIR-ee-bas); beating out the Catham Islands, Tonga, Fiji, and Hawaii. I'm referring, of course, to who won the competition to be able to claim that they were first into the new millennium. Kiribati won the title by having the

International Date Line arbitrarily shifted more than *2,000 miles* east to put it on the other side of their Caroline Island, which was then renamed *Millennium* Island.

I think I can honestly report that the biggest change over the past years affecting the content of this section is that I am no longer in my 40's [sigh]. Beyond wishing that time were a flexible enough concept that I could make myself younger, there really is nothing I would change in this section, and the concepts of time that I describe remain one of the most important aspects of working with street-dependent youth -- in fact, *all* youth -- that we need to understand, develop skills around, and upon which we need to influence conceptual change. Unfortunately, not only has there been little change in the street-developed concept of time, I have also observed very little change in how services work with these concepts. Our failure to consider the impact of time concepts in the design and implementation of services continues to be one of the greatest barriers to effective work with street-dependent youth (IMHO).

Case management services are a good example. The case management structure remains the primary way youth services work with street-dependent youth in the long-term to assist them in leaving street life. This structure involves 1-on-1 meetings between an assigned case manager and a young person, focusing on the facilitation and coordination of services, the provision of specific resources, and the development of long and short term goals. It is a medical model with its roots in the nursing profession and a history dating back to the 1800's. The standard is for clients to meet with their case manager once per week, and my observations[22] of case management programs for street-dependent youth around the nation generally utilize this once per week standard. But I'll remind you of the 3-to-1 ratio that I proposed in the original text. If we are going to apply a technique or intervention to street-dependent youth and expect it to be effective, we need to adjust it to consider their time concept. A technique such as case management, designed for a once per week application, would need to see a street-dependent youth 2-to-3 times per week; but I haven't seen any case management programs for this population that are designed for that level of support.

There is a very practical reason for this. A case manager can expect to dedicate up to 3 hours of time or more to each youth, even if they only meet with them once per week; 1 hour for actually working with the youth, and 1-to-2 hours for paperwork, advocacy/networking, and case planning/supervision. That same case manager can expect that up to 25%

---

[22] While Street Culture was originally released when I was the director of Janus Youth Program's Willamette Bridge in Portland, Oregon (a continuum of services for street-dependent youth ranging from streetwork/outreach to independent living) I have, since 1999, been an independent consultant/trainer working with youth programs nation-wide.

of their time (or more) may be consumed by an assortment of meetings that seem to permeate the social service culture[23], leaving only 30 hours at best to dedicate to actual case management for a full time worker. At 3 hours per youth, that means a manageable case load of 10 young people. Making the adjustment for a youth's concept of time would drop that case load to 3-to-5 youth. But I challenge you to find a case management service for street-dependent youth where 3-to-5, or even 10, is the actual case load size. The industry standard is probably 20-to-25 youth, and I have seen case load sizes as high as *65 young people*.

But let's assume that within a case management program every youth is getting their full hour weekly. What does this look like from their perspective? Each week consists of 7 days with 24 hours in each day, for a total of 168 hours. That means that for every hour a case manager spends with a young person, that young person is immersed in and influenced by the culture of the streets for *167 hours*. For all the hard work and dedication on the part of the case manager, they exert influence over the youth's perspectives, actions, and decisions for less than *0.6% of a youth's week*.

Granted, most youth receiving services are involved in structures beyond case management, but these structures are often fragmented, uncoordinated, and in the case of street-based services such as streetwork/outreach programs and/or drop-in centers, may actually be viewed by youth as *part of* the street culture. The reality is that our primary intervention approach with street-dependent youth is generally incapable of adjusting to accommodate a street time concept due to the small case load size it would require, and the structure itself may not be the best approach to this population even if adjustments were feasible.

But that is not the only issue. Immediacy, repetition, and consistency, identified as the 3 most important factors impacting a youth's concept of time, are all areas that I've observed agencies and workers continue to struggle with at best, and ignore at worst. The pitfalls of immediacy that I identified; that being that if immediacy is not properly executed it may serve to *reinforce* a youth's existing concept rather than provide a basis for *expanding* that concept; make it all the more important that workers discuss and consider the nature of their immediate responses. While immediacy should be a consideration in programming, such as the "productive time" structure that I described in the original text, it also needs to be considered in how you respond to the random, crisis orientation of a youth's lifestyle. Positive immediate responses are those that make a youth feel *heard* and provide them with the *necessary information* to get their needs met without negating time requirements, but that does not mean always *immediately*

---

[23] Which always reminds me of Dave Barry's quote: "If you had to identify, in one word, the reason why the human race has not achieved, and never will achieve, its full potential, that word would be 'meetings'."

meeting their wants and needs. For example, when working with youth on a scheduled appointment basis (the manner in which case management is structured) I generally present a "15 minute" rule. This rule is stated each and every time I set an appointment with a youth (repetition). While I adjust how the information is conveyed depending on the young person I am speaking to, the information that is conveyed includes the following.

- Our appointment begins at (x) and ends at (xx).
- If you are up to 15 minutes late we will still meet, but our time will still end at (xx), so we'll have 15 minutes less time for the appointment.
- If you contact me during that 15 minute window (or earlier) we can set a new start time, but unless we reschedule the appointment the meeting will still end at (xx), so being late means less time together (This allows them to show up after the 15 minute window and still meet, however).
- If you are more than 15 minutes late without contacting me, we will reschedule rather than meet.

Note that there is absolutely no emotion, judgment, or disappointment involved. They can consistently be more than 15 minutes late without contacting me and it will not impact our *relationship* at all. It will, however, impact what they are able to get from our relationship, at least in the short term, but they'll know in advance what they'll get and how to get more. I will be available to them as agreed between (x) and (xx), and if they show up after the 15 minute window without contacting me, I will immediately give full attention to rescheduling the appointment and giving whatever information they need to deal with the missed appointment without anger or criticism; but I will not alter time structures to protect them from cause and effect or support a belief in the randomness or inconsequence of time. I will always immediately *respond* to them, but I will not always immediately *provide* for them. It is the living example of the saying *lack of planning on your part does not constitute an emergency on my part*. Failure to be true to that saying means that you will always be working in crisis mode, putting out one fire after another, and in so doing you will be supporting and reinforcing the random, crisis orientation of street life rather than exposing youth to an alternative that will ultimately work better for them.

Workers often view such procedures as described above as being too "harsh" and I will remind you of the triage exception that you don't want to place addressing time concepts over more important critical needs. But my observation is that workers often tend to view *every* need as critical[24] to the point where they aren't managing time concepts at all, but simply responding to every request a youth presents no matter when or how it comes in. This not only turns immediacy from an intervention technique

---

[24] This is sometimes more the result of a worker either not having the skills or the desire to deal with a youth's displeasure than it is with viewing the situation as a true "crisis."

that moves youth forward into a response pattern that holds youth back, but it also makes it hard to implement the other 2 important factors; *repetition* and *consistency*.

If I set appointments, but then adjust myself to whenever the young person decides to show up, I can guarantee that I will always be adjusting myself to the youth's random schedule. This, in the long run, won't work out well for either one of us. But if a young person understands the game plan, and then through a series of repeated experiences has that game plan reinforced, what begins to happen is that you find yourself working with youth who *keep appointments*, and you no longer need to "govern" their behavior with such structures. In the recreation night example I gave in the original text, after a period of time youth no longer needed reminder or encouragement, it simply became a predictable structure in their life and they found the predictability of the structure gave them a sought after sense of safety and security. Obviously, this bleeds over into consistency, which is the primary source of a sense of safety and security, but repetition in and of itself is important for another reason, one that actually has little to do with street-dependent youth.

One of the constant complaints that I hear from workers who deal with youth is captured in statements such as:
- *They just don't listen*
- *I told (him/her) and they ignored me*
- *They should know, they've been told*
- *There's a sign clearly posted, they just don't care about the rules*

Or, the ultimate in frustration:
- *Geez! Do I have to keep telling them over and over?*

Well, since you asked ... yes, you do.

I'd be willing to bet that while there may be some "kill your TV" folks out there, a good percentage of you spend some at least time in front of the screen. Have you ever noticed how you keep seeing the same commercial over and over again, sometimes even more than once during the same commercial break? Why? Is this just poor planning on the part of advertisers? Or is it possible that they are keenly aware of something of which we should all have greater awareness? formula, perhaps? Maybe something like *seven plus or minus two (7 +/- 2)*?

Seven plus or minus two (or, another way to think of it is five to nine) was first referred to in a 1955 paper by George A. Miller titled <u>The Magical Number Seven, Plus or Minus Two -- Some Limits on Our Capacity for Processing Information</u>. Miller proposed that the human capacity to process information was limited to 7 +/- 2 "chunks" and that "chunks" beyond that limit were not retained in short term memory. Since that time, 7 +/- 2 has also been proposed as the number of times the human brain needs to be exposed to information before it begins ... *begins* ... to "stick."

Why do you see the same commercial repeated over and over, or why do they repeat a phone number several times in a row? Because advertisers know that it takes *repetition* to get information across to people.

This is why repetition is so critical. Not only is repetition the basis of skill development, it also addresses the human capacity; not the "youth" capacity, but the *human capacity; to process and retain information*. To help young people "get it" and begin to alter their concepts, you absolutely have to use repetition that fits the 7 +/- 2 structure. First, when offering information, make sure it is packaged in 7 +/- 2 "chunks." Case managers who ask youth to learn, understand, or accomplish 20 different things in the coming week are just setting the youth up for failure, as they are unlikely to even *comprehend* what they need to do, especially when the 20 different things were presented to them only *once*. Which brings us to the second requirement of repetition; make sure that the information you offer is given once, then again, then again, then again, then again, and realize that you are now at the *minimum* number of times that information needs to be repeated. A good standard is that when giving young people tasks to do or things to learn, stick to the low end of the scale (no more than 5). When trying to get a message across, go for the high end of the scale (at least 9), and in both cases go for a diversity of deliveries as well, to ensure that you address different learning styles and to speak to all the different ways an individual youth may process information. The better you are at proper chunking and repetition, the less you'll wonder why young people aren't listening to you.

I visited a youth drop-in center that had this concept down. There was a particular rule regarding access to the refrigerator. I've seen the same rule in other drop-in centers (the rule itself is unimportant) and almost every time I see it there is a sign on the refrigerator presenting the rule. At this center, however, there were *4 of the same sign* on the front of the refrigerator, *2 more on each side*, and a few *scattered along the walls* in the kitchen area. You could not walk through the kitchen area without getting exposed to that *one, single message* over and over and over again. When I asked, they reported that they had a high level of cooperation with the rule; in my estimation due to the fact that they had a high level of *repetition* in presenting the expectation.

Another nice thing about repetition is that it breeds consistency, which I've already identified as the underlying cause of a sense of safety and security. I talked about the importance of consistency in earning and building trust, but this is such a critical skill to effective youth work that it deserves additional focus here. It is also, in my observation and opinion, one of areas in which many youth services are the most ... well ... *inconsistent*. These inconsistencies take many forms; from different responses to similar situations among staff members (one will let you do something that another will not, or one will enforce rules and hold youth accountable where another will be flexible in enforcement); to programs that rely too greatly on staff discretion as opposed to program guidelines and structure, often resulting in different youth getting vastly different treatment and results from the same program. In either case, it makes it difficult for young people to predict what other people will do and what situations will occur (which directly impacts their ability to develop trust) and inhibits their ability to feel safe and secure within the environment of the program or relationship. Think about that for a moment. We are working with youth experiencing homelessness and suffering from various levels of past and present trauma and abuse. To be of any help to them at all, they absolutely have to be able to develop a trusting relationship with us where they feel safe and secure in our presence. Every time we are inconsistent in our treatment of them or responses to them, we make it harder for them to do that, and inhibit their ability to shed their negative, self-protective behaviors and accept help from us. Yet developing consistency within our programs is not only something that we often pay little attention to, it is actually sometimes *not even valued as an intervention approach.* There are two primary reasons why this may be the case.

The first has to do with a phobia. The American Psychiatric Association defines a "phobia" as an irrational and excessive fear of an object or situation, usually involving a feeling of endangerment or a fear of harm. For something to be a phobia, there must be fear involved, and that fear must be *irrational* (fear of cracks in a sidewalk is irrational because they are unlikely to hurt you; fear of stepping in front of a speeding truck is rational) and *excessive* (cowering under your desk when you see a mouse may be excessive; doing the same thing when you see a gunman is not). When you understand this, you then understand that a phobia is not about the feelings or behaviors, it is about their relationship to the stimulus. It only becomes a phobia when your response is out of proportion to the stimulus.

Ephebiphobia, a recognized psychological phobia for which support groups and treatment options exist, is *the fear of youth and teenagers.* It describes the irrational and excessive response to teenagers and their behaviors demonstrated by both individual adults as well as groups of adults, such as mass media and politicians. Those of us who work with young people can easily point to examples of Ephebiphobia in action when we confront negative stereotypes or deal with what we perceive as irrational fears when we advocate for young people. What is harder for us, and often more harmful to young people, is our ability to recognize Ephebiphobia within our *own* field of youth work. Whenever we make decisions or put rules in place that are more about our own comfort level than they are about the needs of a youth, we are letting our Ephebiphobia show. Whenever we fail to share power or decisions with young people because we fear what they may do with it, our Ephebiphobia wins out. I'll remind you, I am not talking about *rational* and *proportional* cautions and responses;

I'm talking about things where we don't give young people a chance because we fear the worst in them instead of expecting the best of them.

But it is not this level of Ephebiphobia that inhibits a young person's ability to develop trust and feel safe and secure, as oddly enough we can *consistently* be ephebiphobic in our approach. The challenge to our consistency that has its roots in Ephebiphobia is when our behavior is affected by our fear of a youth's *responses and reactions*; that is, when we are reluctant or unwilling to implement consistency, expectations, and accountability out of a fear that youth will respond negatively, demonstrate displeasure, act aggressively toward or not "like" staff or their actions, and, where voluntary programs are concerned, potentially withdraw their participation.

But consistency, expectations, and accountability are exactly what young people need to become healthy and accomplished adults, and to develop trust and a sense of safety and security. While it is important to ensure that we are providing consistency, expectations, and accountability in ways that are supportive, respectful and honoring of each individual's dignity, it is a serious disservice to youth for us to fail to provide these things out of a fear that young people will react negatively or withdraw. While it may often be *uncomfortable* for us, we have to remember that the measure of our support is not in whether or not a youth *likes* us or what we're doing; it is whether or not our actions are helpful to them in the long run, and if young people are getting what they *need* from us. If young people are not experiencing consistency; if they are not receiving expectations to live up to; if they are not seeing their accountable for their lives and their behaviors ... then the answer to that is, unfortunately, "no."

But even if we do not fear a young person's response, we sometimes fudge on consistency in order to avoid conflict due to a lack of skill. It is so easy, and so unpleasant and unproductive, to get into "power struggles" with young people that we may sometimes be inconsistent due to a cost/benefit analysis. Is it really worth it to get into a big power struggle over this relatively minor issue in the name of consistency? That's the wrong question, because it is always important to be consistent[25]. The trick is in knowing how to stay out of *power struggles*. When you develop that skill, which I will address in a later chapter, you find that you no longer have to choose between being consistent or avoiding power struggles and we no longer end up reacting *irrationally* or *excessively*.

Consistency can also be challenging when we rely too heavily on an individual staff person's skills and authority. Do not misunderstand; I am not criticizing individualized treatment, staff decision-making, or "meeting youth where they're at." My concern is when a program becomes little more

---

[25] Again, within the guidelines of the "triage exception."

than an extension of each individual staff person's discretion, disconnected from unifying guidelines, goals, and objectives. While it is obvious that such reliance on staff discretion may create inconsistency in the treatment of different youth[26], it can also create inconsistencies in an individual youth's treatment due to responses becoming *situational* as opposed to *programmatic*. But of even greater concern is the impact of a human condition called *preferential bias*.

Preferential bias is the name for the natural human instinct to impose patterns on and predict our world. In every domain of our lives (and we have hundreds of domains) we each have natural preferences. What we believe about the world and the people in our lives, and how we interact with both, is determined largely by the sum total of all of our personal preferential biases. Some of our preferential biases are very subtle, but others can be easily seen. Whether subtle or apparent, preferential biases are a major contributor to how each of us responds to others

Let me give you an example from politics, since the political left/right spectrum is an obvious example of preferential bias. Michele Bachmann is the Republican (right-leaning) U.S. Representative for Minnesota's 6th congressional district. As she was positioning herself for a bid for the Republican presidential nomination, she stated in New Hampshire that this was the State known for the "Shot heard 'round the World" during the American Revolution. As the "Shot heard 'round the World" was fired in *Massachusetts*, people with politically left-leaning preferential biases jumped all over her, labeling her everything from ignorant to an outright idiot. People with politically *right*-leaning preferential biases excused her statement as an innocent mistake; who hasn't misspoken, particularly when they're tired? Compare this to a similar situation during the 2008 presidential campaign. Democrat (left-leaning) Barak Obama stated that "I've now been in 57 States; I think one left to go." As there are only 50 States, people with politically right-leaning preferential biases were all over him, labeling him everything from ignorant to an outright idiot. People with politically *left*-leaning preferential biases excused his statement as an innocent mistake; who hasn't misspoken, particularly when they're tired? These are examples of how preferential biases color our thoughts and actions.

Because they affect how we interpret our world, our preferential biases have direct impact on our relationships. When we meet someone who has preferential biases that are compatible with ours, we develop a friendship. If our preferential biases are extremely compatible, we have a very close friend, perhaps even a lover. When, however, our preferential biases are *not* compatible, we tend to find the other person not very likable. If our

---

[26] And I'll remind you here that you are never working with individual youth, so such inconsistencies often have repercussions beyond the primary relationship.

preferential biases are in *conflict*, we may really dislike them, and may even consider them an enemy or target of our disdain (see the Bachmann/Obama example above).

Unfortunately, as much as we would like them to be (and as beneficial as it would be if they were), professional relationships are not immune to preferential bias. How it affects the relationship is directly related to the "match" between the helper's and the helpee's preferential biases. Broadly speaking, there are 5 potential matches, and each is listed on the following chart describing how the match affects the nature of the relationship and the helper/helpee's view of each other:

Helper	Helpee	Biases are:	The relationship feels:
▲	⇧	**Compatible** Not necessarily a perfect PB match, but dominant PB's are compatible.	**Positive and Productive** Helper's view of Helpee: Motivated and Cooperative Helpee's view of Helper: Caring and Supportive
▶	⇨	**Helper Compatible** Compatible from the *Helper's* perspective, but not from the Helpee's.	**Neutral with limited Productivity** Helper's view of Helpee: Motivated and Cooperative Helpee's view of Helper: Caring but Unsupportive
◀	⇦	**Helpee Compatible** Compatible from the *Helpee's* perspective, but not from the Helper's.	**Neutral with limited Productivity** Helper's view of Helpee: Resistant but Cooperative Helpee's view of Helper: Supportive but Uncaring

Helper	Helpee	Biases are:	The relationship feels:
←	⇒	**Incompatible** Not compatible from either perspective.	**Negative and Unproductive** Helper's view of Helpee: Resistant and Uncooperative Helpee's view of Helper: Uncaring and Unsupportive
→	⇐	**Conflicting** PB's are in conflict from one or both perspectives.	**Hostile and Counter-productive** Helper's view of Helpee: Manipulative and Threatening Helpee's view of Helper: Abusive and Threatening

Note that only when preferential biases are compatible is the relationship *caring and supportive*, a key qualifier of the one of the three Protective Factors that fosters innate resilience and is required for Positive Youth Development.

Considering the impact of preferential biases on helper/helpee relationships creates a rather sobering perspective on our ability to assist young people who are coming to us for help. In our position as a helper, all other things being equal, we have *only a 40% chance* of being in a professional relationship where we truly feel we are helping (the helpee appears motivated and cooperative), and *50% of the time* that we feel that way, *we'll be wrong* (the helpee really won't be getting the help they need from us). Sucks to be a helper, huh? But, if you think that's bad, look at it from the *helpee's* perspective. As a helpee, all other things being equal, you have *only a 60% chance* of being in a professional relationship where you feel you are being helped (the helper at least appears either caring or supportive), and *2 out of 3 times* that you feel that way, *you'll be wrong* (you really won't be getting the help you need from them). But it's even worse than that, because of the *80% of the time* that you're really not getting your needs met, *3 out of 4 times you'll be seen as the problem* (you are either resistant, uncooperative, manipulative or threatening from the helper's perspective; the "power" side of the relationship).

What this means is that whether or not a program is helpful or unhelpful to a young person, and whether or not any individual young person is viewed in a positive or negative light, is to a large degree determined by *pure, dumb luck*, and whether or not they are working with a staff who has compatible, incompatible, or conflicting preferential biases. If a young person gets matched with a case manager/teacher/parole office with *compatible* preferential biases, then that young person receives the help they need in the context of a positive relationship, and they are viewed as motivated and cooperative. *That same young person*, however, may be matched with a case manager/teacher/parole office with *conflicting* preferential biases, and suddenly that young person receives counter-productive treatment in the context of a hostile relationship and they are viewed as manipulative and threatening. The interplay of helper/helpee preferential biases also explains why one staff can get along great with and assist a young person, while others who are equally skilled are not able to connect with or be helpful to them. In the original text when I describe the volunteer Youth Advocate program I stated that; "*One of our earliest lessons was that it didn't work very well to have a pool of volunteers and a pool of youth and create random matches.*" It is because of the inability to measure and match preferential biases that such random matches were unsuccessful.

Obviously, in order to be of the greatest assistance to the greatest number of young people, we will want to compensate for the impact of preferential bias in professional relationships. Can that be done? The good news is, yes. All we have to do is be completely aware of all of our personal preferential biases and consciously act to keep them out of our professional relationships. Now for the bad news; unless we become highly evolved, spiritually enlightened beings, it will not be possible for us to be *completely* aware of *all* of our many preferential biases in all the different domains, nor to keep them from influencing our professional relationships. Additionally, we and every young person we meet are in a state of *constantly changing personal preferential biases*. Every experience we have or new knowledge we obtain influences our preferential biases in many domains. The simple act of reading this information about preferential biases is going to affect your preferential biases. This is particularly the case with young people who are in a very volatile developmental state; their preferential biases can change in a *moment*. This is one reason why an unproductive relationship may sometimes suddenly become productive seemingly at random, or a productive relationship suddenly becomes difficult and challenging.

How does a program or school compensate for the impact of preferential bias? The short and unfortunate answer is, too few of them actually do so intentionally, relying instead on the skill level and awareness of individual personnel. The result is high levels of staff burn-out and turnover; programs that eventually evolve to serving only a specific type of young person; on-going challenges and conflict with difficult-to-serve populations (who are generally difficult-to-serve because their preferential biases deviate from cultural norms, such as members of subcultures, like street-dependent youth); and high levels of negative descriptors when discussing client behaviors (e.g.; manipulative, unmotivated, untrustworthy, aggressive). But just because few programs intentionally address this concern doesn't mean that it can't be addressed. It is possible to compensate for the impact of preferential bias, and that is accomplished through *program structure.*

When there is a program structure; that is, specific guidelines and procedures for the provision of services that are *consistently* adhered to; it serves as a kind of preferential bias "compensator" or "matcher" by inserting a structure within which the helper and the helpee interact. Instead of the relationship being determined by the match between the preferential biases of the helper/helpee, the helper works through the structure, thus taking their personal preferential biases out of the equation. It's true that the structure will have its own preferential biases, but these are determined by goals and outcomes (in other words, the structure will be preferentially biased towards what he program is trying to accomplish for young people), and they are *static*; they don't change based on mood or emotion and are not affected by the preferential biases of the young person.

The effect of guidelines and procedures is that any staff person with a basic level of skill and a thorough understanding of and consistent application of the program structure can work effectively with *any* young person. From the young person's perspective, the determination of their success or failure in the program is the match between their preferential biases and the preferential biases of the *program structure*, not any *individual staff*. The structure in effect becomes a mirror to the young person's choices; if they want what the program has to offer (determined by the goals and outcomes the program is designed to achieve), then they succeed. If they *don't* want what the program has to offer, then they "fail," but failure in this case is not a deficit or a problem, it is simply a *choice*. Regardless of whether they choose to succeed or fail in the *program*, they have a compatible preferential bias relationship with all *staff*, because both parties are matching their preferential biases to the program structure, not to each other. And, if a young person chooses to not work the program due to incompatible or conflicting preferential biases with the structure, they don't get "blamed" for their "failure" because *there's no blame or failure involved ...* they simply made a choice. In either case, they are able to maintain a caring and supportive relationship with staff, allowing them to benefit from Positive Youth Development Protective Factors whether or not they actually "succeed" in the program.

The case for consistency is not only that it builds trust and develops a sense of safety and security, it is also to ensure that young people have the best opportunity to benefit from our involvement and do not take the blame when they don't. Providing situational responses and being inconsistent in our treatment of young people, intentionally or unintentionally, often *appears* justifiable because it can *feel* better as we are working *intuitively* in line with our personal preferential biases. However, our good feeling does not change the negative impacts on the young person. Being consistent and working within a program structure often does not *feel* as good as we may sometimes be working counter-intuitively in *conflict* with our personal preferential biases. However, our bad feeling does not change the positive impacts on the young person. It's important to remember that our measurement of success is not in how our work impacts *us*, but rather in how it benefits the young people who trust us with their lives. We need to *consistently* keep that in mind.

Working with street-dependent youth is the equivalent of walking through an emotional minefield.

Time-related Behaviors

Several of the more challenging behaviors that street-dependent youth exhibit directly result from their concept of time. It should be clearly understood that all behaviors, including yours, are influenced by an individual's concept of time, but there are 3 specific areas where a time-influenced behavior presents a unique or difficult challenge for adults. These three behaviors are cockiness, prejudice, and violence.

Cockiness

There is an aggressive, "cocky" behavior often exhibited by street-dependent youth that anyone who has worked with the population for longer than, say, 2 or 3 seconds knows all too intimately. They can be "in your face," loud, unreasonable, and more than a little obnoxious. Far from a redeeming quality, this behavior is one of the primary reasons street-dependent youth have gained a reputation as "bad" kids who are difficult to work with. We tend to react to this behavior based on the interpretation that the youth is being disrespectful or trying to "put us down," and we often fall into a knee-jerk response loosely associated with *kids need to learn to respect their elders*. The problem with this reaction and the reason why any response that is associated with it either fails to change the behavior, or escalates the behavior, is that it is a misinterpretation of what the youth is communicating.

We are dealing with young people who are surviving on the streets, outside of society and the law, and living through situations in which most of us would fall apart. They're doing that to a large degree because of childhood experiences where they felt they had little or no power to influence or control their lives. Now in adolescence, they would rather survive on the streets, despite how horrible that may be, simply because it gives them some measure of control. They may continue to be exploited and abused on the streets, but, unlike the abuse that they may have experienced at home, they now at least have some choice in how, when, and by whom they are going to be abused. Power and control are core issues with street-dependent youth. But even with the small measure of control that they are able to exercise on the streets, they are confronted daily with an awareness that they are never truly in an equal power relationship with any member of the dominant culture. As difficult as it may be to grasp, even when youth create an event that gives them *situational power*, such as confronting you with a weapon, you still possess more power and authority than they do. This will become evident when the police show up and lend far more credibility to your account of the events than to the youth's. In every encounter, positive or negative, between you and a youth on the streets, you represent greater power than they possess and that represents a tremendous threat to them.

In addition to the threat that they perceive by our greater power, we also tend to be a mirror on their shame and self-loathing. They view us as representing everything they wish they could be but don't believe that they are. We're the good people, the people who fit in and have a place in the world. We're the clean, untainted souls that somehow have been spared the torment that they've experienced and their only explanation for that is that we are good and they are bad. Our very presence can fill them with self-disgust and we can make them feel so tainted that they can literally feel "dirty" around us. So they react with a cocky, aggressive, smart-alecky behavior that we interpret as offensive and an attempt to damage us in some way. But the behavior they are exhibiting is not designed to bring us down to their level. Rather, it is intended to equalize the power and to help them feel that on some level they are as good as we are. They are not trying to diminish us; they are attempting to elevate themselves.

The problem, of course, is that it's a terribly ineffective way to achieve that result and, more often than not, it doesn't work. Instead of equalizing the power, it more often results in a show of power by the more authoritative adult which only reinforces feelings of worthlessness and can escalate into a truly ugly situation, up to and including violence. But they are young, and hurt, and doing the best they can. The fact that their coping skills are poor in no way changes the intent of and need for the skills themselves. If we are able to respond to the intent of the poor skill, instead of reacting to its effect, we can then begin to transform negative experiences into positive outcomes.

Relationship to Time

Another factor to be considered is the relationship of the behavior to time. What is helpful to understand is that if a young person is being cocky and aggressive towards you, you can assume that something you are doing is being perceived by the youth as threatening or demeaning. This is generally the point where many listeners who truly care about young people decide to take a coffee break, based on the assumption that, if threatening or demeaning behavior on our part causes this response, then they'll never have to deal with it because they have nothing but respect for young people and value them as human beings. Unfortunately, even the most caring, respectful person is unable to avoid these situations, because the threatening or demeaning behavior does not have to be either conscious or malicious on your part.

The reality is that working with street-dependent youth is the equivalent of walking through an emotional minefield. You don't know what hurts. You don't know what "mines" you're going to encounter or how they may be set off. When you do trigger an emotion, the young person is unlikely to make a rational connection to what's going on around them. Instead, they are more likely to react to the old emotion out of context and perceive events around them in connection with how they experienced that emotion in the past. The way you're standing in the doorway might be the way her father stood there before he came in and raped her at night. This doesn't mean that she'll perceive you as her father and fear that you are about to rape her, but it does mean that she will react to you as a threat. The tone in your voice or a particular word you use may be the tone or word that was used by a date that beat the crap out of him the night before. Again, he won't perceive that he's in the same situation, but he'll experience the emotion and respond and react to the threat.

Responding with Respect

Without malicious intent and without doing anything wrong, you can find yourself confronted by an angry, aggressive youth who is treating you like you are the enemy. What you need to do is step out of your own defensiveness long enough to realize that at that moment and for whatever reason, you *are* the enemy. Something you have done or are doing, regardless of your actions or intent, is being perceived by that youth as threatening or demeaning. And if you can accept that, then you can also accept that the best way to de-escalate the situation is to do what you would suggest to someone who *was* being threatening or demeaning. In other words, use the youth's behavior as your signal to show respect. The most effective intervention in these situations is to stop all other behaviors and focus on respect.

Earlier I described a drop-in center with a second floor entrance. Youth would check in at a desk there, and then go downstairs to the main room on the first floor. One night a young girl came in after just losing her place to live. Everything she owned in the world was in a single brown paper bag. It included two pairs of dirty blue jeans, a package of new underwear that she had received for her birthday; and, since it was the only birthday gift she had received, she hadn't opened them yet; and finally her most cherished possession in the world: an AC/DC rock group shirt. The drop-in center had lockers available for youth to store their possessions and she handed the bag to the staff on duty asking that he lock it up for her. He said he would, but as there was a line of youth behind her waiting to get in, he set it down by the desk while he proceeded to check in the other youth. It turned out to be a very busy evening and as a result the staff ended up forgetting to lock up her bag before he went home, leaving it sitting by the desk.

That was the beginning of a series of unfortunate events. The next morning a shipment of donated clothing arrived and all the clothes were in brown paper bags. The people who brought the clothing simply placed it inside the entrance, which meant that it was all stacked around the check-in desk. Later that morning a volunteer crew came in and were given the task of sorting all the donated clothing and putting it out for youth to access. Naturally, any clothes that were in brown paper bags by the desk they sorted and put out. That afternoon youth came to the center as usual and accessed clothing. The end result of all of this was that when the girl showed up at the drop-in center the next evening she went downstairs and the first thing she saw was another youth wearing her AC/DC shirt.

She went ballistic. She immediately stormed upstairs to the staff at the desk and verbally ripped him a new asshole. She then came downstairs again and stood there seething with anger, punching and kicking at the wall. When street-dependent youth are this angry, it is almost visible; their anger takes up space around them and you can virtually see it, like heat rising off of a radiator. When I saw this I quickly moved over to the general area that she was in, not because I was going to do anything immediately, but because there were many other youth there and I wanted to be nearby in case the situation began to spread. However, as soon as she saw me move over I became the target for all her anger. I found myself being bitched up one side and down the other and, I have to admit, one thing street-dependent youth excel at is anger. I was being bitched out by a pro. It borders on being a skill, and if you can somehow remove yourself their abilities in this area become almost admirable. It's a very difficult thing to experience personally, however, and it's hard to stay neutral when you are the target. But I managed to maintain, and simply stood there and patiently listened while she graphically described what a bunch of incompetent shits we all were.

At this particular program staff has the authority to issue a "vacation" to youth who are out of control or not following the rules. A "vacation" is simply requiring the youth to immediately leave and not return for "x" number of days. This girl was fully expecting me to issue a vacation in response to her behavior and, I'm convinced, was hoping for it, because that would have been her way of finding validation for her anger. My issuing of the vacation would have allowed her to leave in righteous indignation with our "asshole" status confirmed in her mind. My choice to ride out her anger was confusing her to the point where she needed to push the issue and remind me of the response I was supposed to give, so she plopped herself down defiantly in a chair, glared at me and said:

"*So now I suppose you're going to kick me out of here, uh?*"

To which I replied, as calmly and respectfully as I could:

"No, I'm not. We made a mistake and you have a right to be angry. So you can bitch me out all you want to as long as you don't forget that I'm on your side."

That response was the one thing that she hadn't been prepared for. The fact that I would show her respect in the face of her anger, acknowledge our mistake, and validate that she had a right to be angry about it was an outcome that she hadn't even considered. She stared at me blankly for a few seconds, and then the anger dissipated into a flood of tears.

We went upstairs to one of the counseling rooms and began to talk. During that conversation she admitted for the first time in her life that she had been sexually abused by her father. Not that this admission came as a newsflash to us; her behavior had *sexual abuse* written all over it. But it was a tremendous breakthrough for her in that she had never before discussed it with anyone. And the truth is that this was what was going on for her in this outburst of anger. It never really was about the dirty blue jeans, the underwear, or the AC/DC shirt. Rather, the incident of the staff not taking care of things that were important to her and betraying that trust unleashed the stored up feelings of violation and betrayal that she had never dealt with from being sexually abused. That's why she could get so outrageously angry over a shopping bag with a few dirty items of clothing, because the anger was really about her experience in childhood.

By responding to anger with respect I was able to end a volatile situation at the center in a way that resulted in therapeutic progress for the youth. I understand that every program is going to have its bottom lines and its rules and regulations that you must ensure the participants are adhering to. But at the same time, try not to forget to look past the behavior to the emotions and the feelings that the behavior is masking. By responding to the emotions and feelings, rather than the surface behavior, you can generally meet the needs of your program in a way that creates a success for the youth, though this often means setting your own emotions and ego aside. What I'm asking you to do; to respond to anger with respect; is not at all easy. We are human beings who need respect ourselves and our normal reaction will be to want to lash out or to stop the attack with a show of power and authority. But if you can remember in the moment why you've chosen to work with street-dependent youth, then it is easier to remember that what is needed is a therapeutic response, not a gut level reaction. If you have a youth who is escalating into anger and you can remember to use respect to respond to their feelings, it often won't get to the point where they're threatening the program or violating your bottom lines.

Prejudice

Prejudice is a time-related behavior with which most of us have an extremely difficult time. On the surface, street-dependent youth are a population that can appear to be racist, sexist, and exhibit a wide range of prejudice and bigotry. Particularly in social services we are very conscious of this. Issues of diversity and working against "ism's" have their foundation in social services. Funding sources demand attention to these issues and we develop and attend diversity and cultural competency trainings. One of our goals as a field is to break down barriers against such things as race and sexual orientation and eliminate all forms of "ism" and prejudice. These issues are at the forefront of our consciousness. Then we find ourselves working with a population that uses words like "nigger" and "spic" and exhibits overt gestures of racism and bigotry. Our immediate reaction is to address the issue by challenging them and letting them know that it's not OK what they believe, that we're all one planet, we're all one people. But if you try that sometime you'll find that their response to us is the same response we would receive if we had just done something to *shame* them, which is a very dangerous thing to do to a person with low self-esteem. It's not the response we would expect from a bigot, and it often leaves workers confused and unsure how to proceed.

The fact is that when you respond to their displays of bigotry from a perspective on their beliefs you are communicating to them that you see them as a bigot. The reason why you get a shamed response is because being seen as a bigot shames them. And the reason why it shames them is that in most cases you are *not* dealing with a bigot. In fact, you are dealing with an extremely open, caring, non-judgmental person who also has little tolerance for bigots. I am not going to try to convince you that there is no prejudice or bigotry among street-dependent youth. The culture of the streets tends to be a microcosm of our dominant culture. Bigotry and prejudice are issues that taint all of our social interactions, and there is no reason why the streets would be immune. I will state with conviction, however, that as a population street-dependent youth are probably the most non-judgmental population you will ever meet, simply because, from their perspective, nothing and no one is lower than they are.

Street-dependent youth see themselves as the bottom of the food chain, like slugs crawling in the sewer. Because of their experience, the way they view themselves, and the oppression and unfair treatment they feel they've experienced, they have tremendous regard for other groups and a highly developed sense of justice. Of course, if that's true, then it's a legitimate question to ask why they display overt gestures of racism and bigotry. And the answer is that when you are witnessing these overt expressions of hatred what you are really seeing is another coping skill. Much like their cocky attitudes, this skill is a poor and ineffective one, but it none-the-less has a purpose other than the expression of true feelings.

As already stated, this population feels worthless, as though there is no place for them on the planet and that their existence is somehow an affront to all that is good and clean. Nobody can go on day-to-day with feelings of worthlessness that extreme. Many people with self-esteem that low would simply kill themselves rather than face another day. But these youth are in a culture of survival and the conflict generated from a clash between a constant struggle to survive and feelings that you, and the world, would be better off if you were dead, creates a need for some way to cope; some way to feel like you are worth your next breath. The way they do this; the admittedly poor and ineffective way that they do this; is to attempt to elevate themselves by putting others down. It is an attempt to create, at least for the moment, the belief that something or someone is less valuable than they are. Most overt expressions of hatred are not about hatred of others, they are about hatred of the self. What you are dealing with is not an issue of belief and that is why responding to the perceived belief system is inappropriate. You are dealing with a crisis of self-esteem. It is time related because, at the moment of the expression of hatred toward others, the youth is feeling hatred toward themselves.

There was a girl at the drop-in center who was so vehemently prejudiced against blacks that when we hired an African-American staff member we felt we needed to hold a special staff meeting to deal specifically with the issue of what her reaction was going to be to an African-American staff. As it turned out, her reaction was that within three days he was her favorite staff member and she suddenly didn't like Mexicans. It never was about her feelings toward African-Americans, and it did not become about her feelings towards Mexicans. Her expressions of hatred had always been about her feelings toward herself.

If you can avoid your own gut-level repulsion toward the behavior, you'll see things that seem in conflict with the youth's expressions. The same person who is ranting on about "niggers" and "spics" will hang with and be very close to black and Hispanic friends. When they are exhibiting bigotry what they are actually feeling is degraded, not hateful, and an attack on their hatefulness will result in heaping shame on top of degradation. What really is needing to be addressed is their feelings about themselves, because that's the issue that they're struggling with at the moment.

Responding to Prejudice

One of our most difficult challenges is how to interact with them 1-on-1 when they're making hateful attacks on others. Do you simply ignore the language and keep on interacting with them despite the words that they are using to put down others? The proper response is somewhat dependent upon the situation. If you're a street outreach worker dealing with youth through voluntary association on their terms you could pick between two alternatives. The first is to ignore it completely, simply not respond positively or negatively to the language and look for opportunities to respond to the feelings behind the language. If you are not able to do that for whatever reason, your other alternative is to simply withdraw; excuse yourself and take your leave. But it can be extremely dangerous, both to the youth and to you, to get into an attack on their bigotry while on the streets.

If you are in a more controlled environment, such as a program, it is recommended that there be a norm established around language. In programs I operate we have a "Bottom Line" rule that prohibits what we call "verbal abuse" which is defined as any attack against a person's personality or character, or language used to harass or intimidate. With an established norm you can intervene on expressions of bigotry in a safe way, because your intervention will be about the norm, not about the youth's beliefs[27]. Your intervention then lacks any judgmental overtones. You are not attempting to force an artificial concept of how people should be or condemn the youth for their feelings. You are not expecting all of them to be friends, or even to like each other. You are simply expecting that they will abide by the norms while in the program. And by dealing with it as a norm, as opposed to a judgment, you will often find that you can achieve your goal of addressing bigoted beliefs.

At our transitional living program we once accepted a white supremacist skinhead and an African-American gang member at the same time. By not forcing them to like each other, but rather simply expecting that they both accept a norm around how they would deal with each other while in the program, both of them felt safe enough to drop their aggressive stances. The result was that they ended up as friends and the hatred they had for each other when they moved in was forgotten without any work on the part of the staff.

There will be situations where these responses are inadequate and you will feel a need to address directly the language a youth is using. The technique to use in these situations is to make it about you, not about them or their beliefs. In other words, avoid statements like:

You shouldn't talk about other people that way.

A better response would be:

I'm sorry, I have reactions to certain words. It's difficult for me to talk when I hear words like "nigger."

Be certain that your response keeps the focus on you and doesn't communicate judgment. The previous statement could also have been phrased:

I don't like language like this.

That statement, however, would generally be *heard* as:

I don't like you when you speak that way.

Remembering that you are dealing with a person who is having a crisis

---

[27] See the discussion of preferential bias in the chapter on "Time."

of self-esteem, you'll want to be sure that your response avoids adding to their negative feelings about themselves.

Violence

The final time-related behavior that deserves special attention is violence. If for no other reason than personal safety, you should always be aware of the fact that this is a population with a high potential for violent behavior. I hope that it comes across in this manual that my personal opinion about street-dependent youth is that they are intelligent, wonderful human beings who are full of potential and deserve our respect and the opportunity to make something of their lives. If you didn't agree with this perspective prior to reading this, I hope that I've opened your mind to considering it. But there's an old saying that goes; *you don't want to keep your mind so open that your brains fall out*. No matter how highly one regards street-dependent youth, you must always remember that at this point in their lives they belong to an angry, drug affected, heavily armed, criminalized population with poor impulse control. It is shear foolishness not to consider the potential for violence for both your safety and the safety of the young people with whom you work.

There is good news here. Almost all violence, at least in terms of violence that's directed towards you and other staff, is both predictable and avoidable. The key to doing this requires 2 commitments. First, you must make violence avoidance a priority outcome. That is, you must be willing to temporarily suspend other lesser priority outcomes in certain circumstances in order to avoid violence. Second, you must make the commitment to develop the skills necessary to recognize the causes of violence and respond to them appropriately.

I would like to clarify that this book does not adequately address all of those skills. De-escalation skills and dealing with angry people is an entire presentation unto itself, and you are strongly encouraged to seek additional training in this area. The purpose and goal of this book is to provide you with an understanding of the causes of violence when working with street-dependent youth and to give you ways in which you can assess the potential for violence before it occurs. While I will be giving you a general approach to use in these situations, I will once again state that additional training is required to be effective in dealing with violent people.

The Causes of Violence

There are 3 separate and distinct factors that make up every violent outburst. The first and basic underlying cause of all violence among this population is simply the inherent nature of street life. This is where I may sound a bit like Ronald Reagan's approach to the former Soviet Union, but he was correct in his basic premise; the way to avoid violence and survive in a violent culture is to be prepared for and willing to use a level of violence that is greater than the threat. This does not necessarily mean that you are by nature a violent person. It only indicates that you are a *rational* person, because in a violent culture your alternative is annihilation.

The culture of the streets is by nature violent. Anyone on the streets who chooses to be passive and non-confrontational is choosing to be a victim ripe for exploitation. You'll see youth who make this choice. They are the ones with the bruises who are constantly being raped, beaten, and ripped off. A more common choice is to be the biggest bad-ass you can be, to be armed and ready to take somebody's head off if they look at you cross-eyed. These youth tend to be untouched. More times than not, their willingness to engage in violence keeps them safe from the engagement and, when it doesn't, it has prepared them to win. The thing to realize is that while this behavior appears to us that they are violent by nature, perhaps even seeking violence, the truth is that violence is not the intent of their behavior. The intent is personal safety.

In any situation where the youth perceives a threat, rightly or wrongly, their primary coping skill will be a rapid escalation to violence. What this means is that any perceived threat immediately escalates to what we would consider a crisis situation, since the potential for violence exists within every threat. How we all are affected by a crisis situation is the second factor that comes into play. The fact is that a crisis situation affects your concept of time. Notice that I am not applying this only to street-dependent youth. When you yourself are in a crisis situation, your concept of time will be affected in exactly the same manner.

Take a moment to think back to the last major crisis in your own life. What were you thinking about? My guess is that it was not what appointments you had the following week, or even what you were going to be doing the next day. You would have been incapable of doing that, because a crisis situation will trigger a *fight or flight* response in all human beings. Once that response is triggered, your concept of time will narrow. You will be incapable of focusing on anything beyond the immediate present, the here and now. You will also begin to think very quickly, which is responsible for the way time seems to move very slowly and short periods of time appear to last abnormally long. Now consider that your concept of time in a crisis situation has been narrowed to what I've described as a street-dependent youth's normal concept of time. If that's the case, what does a crisis situation do to their concept of time? It narrows it, only now you end up with a human being who is thinking in split seconds. They may be thinking so quickly that, to all intents and purposes, they're really not thinking at all. This is why in many cases when you discuss an incident after a youth has engaged in violence they are often as surprised and in the dark about it as everybody else. While we sometimes interpret this response as the youth avoiding dealing with or taking responsibility for their behavior, the truth is that often it was not a thoughtful response and a conscious choice. They simply reached the inevitable conclusion of an escalation of survival behavior.

The final factor that precedes violence relates to the youth's concept of integrity. If the nature of street life is the charge, and the effect of crisis on your concept of time is the fuse, then the youth's concept of integrity is the spark. Remember that street-developed integrity, though it is very different from what your concept of integrity may be, is one of the youth's most highly valued concepts. In reaction to a perceived threat, due to the nature of the culture that the youth is acclimated to, the youth will begin an escalation to violence as their primary coping skill. The crisis nature of the situation will result in a compression of time, rendering the youth virtually incapable of processing thought. The escalation will include threats, aggressive posturing, verbal attacks and other bravado. If something does not occur to de-escalate this situation, a point will be reached where it comes down to the integrity of the youth's word. At that point, there will be violence.

It is often thought that violence erupts out of nowhere, and the type of violence I'm describing could be viewed that way to an untrained observer. When the actual event of violence takes place, it generally does not begin with poking, then shoving, then hitting, and so on. Rather, it can often seem as though it were "a bolt out of the blue;" an instant switch from a non-violent position to an extremely violent one. However, if you can train yourself to be sensitive to the nature of what precipitates violence in street-dependent youth, then you can remove the element of surprise. The build-up to violence will include pacing, increasing tension and anxiety, the tendency to be "larger" and to take up more room, anger and rapid eye movement, and increasing hostility and verbal aggression.

Responding to Potential Violence

Our tendency is to respond in reaction to behavior such as this by countering the escalation with authority. This very rarely works, and a good rule of thumb is to never, ever, put a street-dependent youth in a position to *put up or shut up*, because they will be far more likely to *put up* than to *shut up*. A better response is to recognize the behavior early on and realize that the youth is looking for a way out. For your safety and theirs, give them one. Your best response to avoid violence is to simply back off. I want to be clear, I am not saying that you need to allow them to threaten and intimidate you in order to get their way. When I recommend that you back off, I am not suggesting that you back down or fail to deal with whatever situation is occurring. What I am suggesting is that you alter the situation in order to de-escalate it. Neither you, nor your ability to address whatever issue is going on, are harmed in any way by taking a time out. Simply say something like:

"Wait a minute. I don't know how we got here, but it's not where I want to be and it doesn't seem to be very pleasant for either one of us. I'm sorry if I've done anything to offend you. That wasn't my intention. Why don't we both take a short break and we can talk about it in a few minutes."

Then take your break, possibly even with the youth. Go get a glass of water and talk about something else for a minute. Then, when you bring it back to the issue, deal with it as a past event.

So, a <u>while back</u> we <u>were</u> talking about issue X. What <u>was</u> your side of the story?

Here are two examples of situations that ended in violence, and in both cases it's probable that the violence would not have occurred had the staff involved acted differently. The first case involves a situation in a private lock-up facility where two girls were on clean-up detail after the evening meal. As they were washing the dishes and utensils they began to have an energetic discussion. I describe it as an "energetic discussion" because everything is escalated to a different level of intensity with street-dependent youth. You will often see an interaction that, interpreted through our standards and norms, may be viewed as an argument or hostility. When you intervene, however, both youth think you're nuts and wonder why you've got a problem with their "conversation." This was the case in this situation. It was later related by both youth that neither was threatened or concerned; in their mind they were simply debating an issue. To the worker in the other room, however, it was loud and sounded hostile. She went through the swinging kitchen door and saw the two youth at the sink, speaking loudly, one with a knife in her hand. Again, in later reports from both youth, the knife was not a factor. That simply was the utensil being washed at the moment and was being used like a finger to punctuate a point.

Without any hesitation or question the staff ordered one youth out of the kitchen and began to confront the youth who held the knife as though she were making an armed threat. The youth was placed in the position of going from a debate with another youth to being accused of assault with a deadly weapon by staff, with no time for explanation or response. The result was that the youth dug in her heels, refusing to put the knife down while she tried to figure out how to get out of the situation. The staff continued to confront her, finally saying something that I would strongly urge you never to say to a street-dependent youth with a knife, which was:

"Give me the knife or I'm going to take it from you."

To which the youth responded:

"If you try to take it away from me, I'm gonna' cut ya'."

The staff person interpreted this as a threat to her authority that she could not let go, and immediately moved in to take the knife from the youth. You can guess what happened next. The end result was that the staff was hospitalized with a knife wound and the youth was jailed in a state lock-up facility with an assault with a deadly weapon charge. Yet the likelihood exists that if the staff had come through the door and simply said *what's going on* or *can I help here?* and then discussed the situation with the two youth, the outcome would have been free of violence.

In this second example, all 3 factors that precipitate violence are present, but it demonstrates another form they may take. In this case, the threatening bravado is implied by a stance. While you can be sure that the threatening language is occurring in the youth's thoughts, it is never verbalized. The youth's stance, however, delivers the message to anyone who is trained to receive it. This situation occurred in a group home where a female resident had just finished baking some cookies from scratch. This was the first time in her life that she had ever baked cookies, which meant two things. One, she had a tremendous amount of pride and satisfaction baked into those cookies, and, two -- they weren't very good cookies.

One of the staff made a disparaging comment about them to another staff which the girl overheard. It made her very angry and she reacted by storming across the room and turning her back on the staff. She stood facing the wall with her arms folded tightly across her chest and was radiating anger; the almost visible radiation of anger that street-dependent youth are capable of. The staff that had made the comment saw this and decided that the youth's reaction was "socially inappropriate." She walked up behind the youth and placed both hands on her shoulders with the intention of turning the youth to face her. It was like grabbing a small thermo-nuclear device. The staff was on the ground before she knew what happened. More important, however, is that the staff was on the ground before the *youth* knew what happened. In telling the story later the youth stated that she hadn't known that she had decked the staff, and when she realized that she had decked her, the first impulse that she had was to give the staff a hug. She figured, however, that she had already blown it, so she went ahead and decked the staff again. But that's not the point of the story. The point is that it's likely that the episode of violence would have been avoided if the staff had reacted differently. She could have given the girl some space and let her cool off. She could have apologized for the comment, or better yet, not made the comment in the first place.

It is not my intention to make excuses for youth's violent behavior. We are all responsible for our actions, and I will state for the record that youth are responsible for their acts of violence. But we are professionals working with youth who have big issues, and we are responsible for our behavior as well. If you stick your hand in a crocodile's mouth you don't blame the crocodile when he bites it off. If you are working with street-dependent youth, escalation to violence is predictable and there are actions that you can take to avoid it.

Sometimes it's as simple as letting a matter go. A staff in our emergency shelter was hit by a gang-involved youth in response to an intervention he made. The youth was being verbally abusive, which is not permitted in the program. The staff member intervened, explained to the youth that he could not use that language if he was going to remain in the shelter, and asked for the youth's cooperation. The youth stopped the behavior and walked away from the staff. This is the point where the intervention should have ended, but the staff wanted to make certain that the youth understood exactly why verbally abusive language was not allowed. He followed the youth explaining to him why the behavior was wrong. That's when he got hit.

The majority of times that I have heard of a staff in a program being assaulted or hurt by a youth I have been able to trace it back to a point where the staff made a mistake. Street-dependent youth are volatile; you are working with emotional bombs. If a member of a Police Bomb Squad tries to diffuse a bomb by hitting it with a hammer, we're not surprised when the bomb explodes. Well, we know that street-dependent youth are filled with rage, drug affected, and quick to resort to violence. If you make the choice to work with them, then it's your responsibility to learn how to do it in a way that's safe.

Key Points - Time-Related Behaviors

Cockiness
- A street-dependent youth's "cocky" attitude is a poor attempt to cope with feeling dis-empowered or threatened. If they are being cocky and directing the behavior at you, you can assume that something you are doing is being perceived as threatening or demeaning.
- The best way to address cocky behavior that is directed at you is to respond with respect.

Prejudice
- Overt expressions of prejudice are generally not an expression of a youth's attitudes towards others, but rather an expression of their attitude toward themselves. Most prejudiced behavior is a poor coping skill indicating a crisis of self-esteem, not hatred of others.
- A proper response to prejudiced behaviors depends on the situation and environment. However, in all cases, responses should avoid shame or attacking a person's beliefs.

Violence

- Violence and aggression are a defense that helps to keep youth safe on the streets. With an understanding of how violence is precipitated, most violent behavior, at least in terms of violence directed at staff, is both predictable and avoidable.
- Avoiding violence is a matter of treating youth respectfully and allowing space when needed.

2.0 Commentary:

There are two points I made when discussing time-related behaviors that I would like to expand upon, and I'll begin with where I talked about a youth's need for power and control. I first mentioned this need earlier in the book when I spoke of the importance of consistency and proposed that seeking power and control was the underlying attraction to things such as the occult, witchcraft, and Satanism. When discussing time-related behaviors I identify that need as one of the reasons why young people might rather survive on the streets; a somewhat controversial statement that implies a measure of choice. We advocate for street-dependent youth by presenting them as victims of abuse, neglect, and abandonment, and propose that they are on the streets not by choice, but by circumstance; all of which is true, but it may not be entirely accurate. To be part of the solution we absolutely must accurately understand what we're dealing with. If we do not, we are far more likely to be part of the problem.

In my opinion, efforts to help with this population have always been plagued by a level of inaccuracy in our descriptions, perhaps with the most obvious example being our choice of labeling the population as "homeless" youth. While it is true that many young people are without a stable place to live and experience long periods of housing instability, the moniker is inaccurate and has been problematic within the field on 4 different levels. First, as I identified in the introduction, being on the streets is a conceptual, not a socio-economic, condition. My statement that "*it generally doesn't take much more than a few minutes at [a transitional living program] for an observer to conclude that the residents are far from 'off the street' in terms of attitude and behaviors*" points out the problem with labeling them as homeless. If we define them as homeless then we can't help but think of the solution as giving them a home; the result being a strong focus on "roof-based" services such as shelters, host and group homes, apartments, and even a steady trend toward the "housing first[28]" model of services designed for the chronically

---

[28] The Housing First model places emphasis on rapid access to permanent or at least stable housing as a prerequisite to addressing other issues. It assumes that a lack of housing is the foundation of other problems/issues and that solving the housing problem facilitates solving other problems.

homeless. But homelessness and particularly chronic homelessness is not the problem with youth on our streets. "Homeless" may be a situational description of a point in time circumstance, but evidence that it is not "the problem" can be seen in the high number of young people who won't seek shelter and/or are unsuccessful in housing programs.

Chronic homelessness is a problem among adults, not young people, and the second consequence of our inaccurately labeling them as "homeless youth" is that they are often viewed simply as younger homeless adults. But "homeless" youth and homeless adults are completely different populations; on the streets for different reasons and with unique and different needs. By calling them "homeless youth" we have lumped them in as a subcategory of the "homelessness" issue, with the result being that youth-specific needs often get lost in planning efforts addressing homelessness and the real issues rarely get adequately addressed. In fact, our efforts may sometimes be counter-productive as young people must identify with homeless services and cultures in order to get any of their needs met, which may have the effect of preparing them to accept a "homeless" identity during a critical developmental period of their lives.

A third consequence of defining the problem as youth "homelessness" is that a significant percentage of the young people we see on the streets really aren't *homeless*; at least not in the traditional understanding of the term. If we consider a "home" to be a place where one is accepted, nurtured and loved, and feels connected to family and to caring, supportive relationships, then we may indeed consider them "homeless." But that does not mean that they are actually *houseless* in the sense that they don't have a place that they could and sporadically do go to for shelter. It's true that many youth on the streets have been out-and-out abandoned, rejected, or are otherwise denied access to an option for housing, but it's equally true that many "homeless" youth maintain contact with family members and other relations, and often stay at home for brief or extended periods of time. This is not a question of whether or not these particular youth should be counted among the population; it is an indicator that we may have misidentified the problem.

Finally, there may actually be a hint of racism in our clinging to the "homeless" label; if not in our intent, at least in an unintended consequence of our reliance on the term. In many areas, non-European populations are under-represented, and many communities have had a difficult time building bridges between primarily white youth services and those serving youth of color. Certainly one contributor to this is a difference between European and non-European cultures, where there is a much greater reliance on extended families in the latter. However another contributor, perhaps the more significant contributor, is that many non-European cultures simply do not identify with the label "homeless." They may be in similar circumstances with similar needs and requiring similar support, but they don't self-identify as homeless and therefore do not see "homeless youth services" as viable options.

"Homeless" may be an accurate situational description in some cases, but it really fails us in accurately describing the problem. This is one reason why there are so many labels used that attempt to describe the same population[29]. My personal choice, as you have seen throughout this book, is *street-dependent* youth; where *street* represents any temporary, unstable, or out-of-home circumstance. This label, while it has its own inaccuracies, at least helps us to understand that the problem is not one of *homelessness*; it is one of *dependency*. The question then becomes; on what exactly are they dependent upon the "streets" for?

This brings us back to what I've identified as one of the strongest motivators for street survival behaviors, and, in fact, one of the reasons why some young people choose the streets over abuse and neglect and others do not; the desire to exercise power and control in their lives. But having power and control is simply a *means*. The *end*, that is, the outcome of exercising power and control is meeting a *developmental* need for a sense of safety and structure; to feel that they are safe in the world and that daily events are somewhat predictable. In a child's ideal developmental process this sense of safety and structure will be derived from *external* sources; caring and supportive adults who guide and protect a young person and provide a "blueprint" for how the youth can eventually create and maintain their *internal* sense of safety and structure. When young people grow up in environments where, for whatever reason; be it incompetency, neglect, abuse, or traumatic events; they are unable to derive a sense of safety and structure *externally* from the adults in their lives, they will then seek their safety and structure *internally*, years before they are developmentally prepared to do so.

In addition to being developmentally unprepared, they are seeking an internal sense of safety and structure within a society that is equally unprepared for young people to survive independent of adult caretakers and systems. As a result, they gravitate to options outside of adult support and supervision; options that take many forms but would generally be referred to as *the streets*[30]. On the streets they find an environment where exercise of internal power and control is not only accepted, it is how one survives. It feels as though they have finally found a "fit" and they begin to build their community and their support system among others in similar circumstances. Perhaps most regrettable, they even find adults who are

---

[29] Homeless youth, street youth, alienated youth, unaccompanied youth, throw-away youth; to name a few.
[30] The *streets* being a "catch-all" term describing any type of temporary, unstable, or out-of-home circumstance, as well as any lifestyle predominantly influenced by socially unacceptable structures for safety and survival such as street families, gangs or self-organized homeless camps.

willing to offer them the external sense of safety and structure that they longed for, but never received. From our perspective, these adults do so through the exploitation of vulnerable youth, but from the youth's perspective it feels as though the adult is taking an interest in them and is willing to be there for them no matter who they are or what they do; the very definition of the resiliency Protective Factor we call a *caring, supportive relationship*.

This then becomes the attraction to, and the trap of, the streets. Young people who are not getting their developmental needs met by pro-social structures and healthy adults find that, by taking power and control into their own hands, they can get these needs met on the streets. Adolescent development is a natural process of growth that requires young people to seek ways to meet their basic physical and social needs and to build competencies. When they are unable to do so within a healthy, externally-provided environment of safety and structure they become dependent on the streets for their developmental needs. We also know from Positive Youth Development that young people thrive in a Protective Factor environment where they are exposed to caring, supportive relationships, high expectations, and meaningful participation. When young people lack these Protective Factors they seek them out on their own; again, finding each of these on the streets *from their perspective*. We can argue whether what they find on the streets really *are* Protective Factors, but for the young person who has not experienced the safety and structure provided by *true* caring, supportive relationships; the sense of competence and capability derived from *true* high expectations; and the sense of being valued and belonging that results from *true* meaningful participation; what they experience on the streets feels to them like the "real thing."

It is not life events or the issues resulting from life events that create street-dependency. Many young people on the streets have been sexually or physically abused; but many young people who have been sexually or physically abused are not on the streets. The difference is in whether or not a young person has, from their perspective, been able to secure an external sense of safety and structure. If they have not, at least to a limited degree, they will exercise internal power and control and eventually create a sense of safety in a circumstance and environment that we would describe as "street-life." Two young people could experience the same type and level of family dysfunction, abuse, and neglect, but the one that is able to maintain some sense of external safety and structure; whether it be other adult relationships such as extended family, teachers, or coaches; or from structures, such as school, sports, or organized activities (e.g.; scouting, 4-H); may very well not end up on the streets. What this means is that the young person who does end up on the streets has *given up on* and *no longer believes in* the ability to derive a sense of safety and structure from adults, and they have accepted self-reliance as the only means to safety on which they can depend.

This is why so many efforts to assist street-dependent youth find the population challenging and are limited in their success. We begin with a flawed assumption; that the problem is their "homelessness" created by their history of abuse, neglect, or a litany of other surface issues; when the *real* problem is that they have become street-dependent for their developmental needs due to a failure to secure a sense of safety and structure from the adults and communities in their lives. Understanding this helps to explain the high percentage of LGBTQ[31] and former foster care youth that we find among street populations, with *each* group representing between 20% and 40% of the population, depending on the area. Each of these groups represents individuals who have often had a very difficult time establishing bonded relationships and developing trust in adults to provide safety and structure. LGBTQ youth are at high risk of experiencing a lack of acceptance within their families and communities due to their sexuality, while foster care youth have experienced loss and trauma precipitating their entry into the foster care system and then may continue to experience trauma, separation, and even abuse as they grow up in that system. That these two populations are prone to giving up on placing their trust in adults for safety and structure and comprise such a large percentage of the street-dependent population should come as no surprise.

Having expanded on my first point; that we have misidentified the problem; the second point which could benefit from greater discussion is specific to the time-related behaviors discussed in this chapter; or, even more specifically, to how we approach these and other behaviors. In discussing the 3 behaviors of cockiness, prejudice, and violence, I made the point that all behaviors are time-related in that they are a response to present situations and feelings, and that these 3 were only highlighted as examples of behaviors that youth workers often find problematic or challenging. The question really becomes how best to professionally respond when addressing *any* challenging or problematic behaviors; since I believe that the mark of a professional is to be able to professionally *respond* regardless of how you are personally *reacting*. There will be many behaviors where your personal reaction will be negative and human; but in order to de-escalate the behavior and address it in a way that is *helpful to the young*

---

[31] Lesbian, Gay, Bisexual, Transgendered, and Questioning. There is a lack of consensus on the proper acronym for these populations, ranging from the order of the letters (GLBTQ is often seen as opposed to LGBTQ); to the inclusion of some letters (the Q is often omitted, simply listing LGBT or GLBT); and even to the addition of some letters, such as LGBTQQ (or LGBTQ$_2$), with the second Q representing Queer; or the addition of an I (Intersex[ed]); or the addition of *another* I (Interested); or the addition of an A (Asexual); or the addition of 2S (Two Spirited, describing mixed gender Native Americans). This book uses LGBTQ as representative of all self-identified sexual minority populations.

person you will need to subjugate your reaction to a professional response. While the second step in your ability to do that is to have enough experience to override your personal reactions, the first step is in knowing what to do.

Before I discuss specific skills it's helpful to remember what you're dealing with; which is why I spent so much time discussing the real problem. If you are approaching the problem as "homeless" youth, then challenging and problematic behaviors can only be explained by negative characterizations of the young person. You are only trying to help, so they must be ungrateful little snots; aggressive, manipulative, "bad" kids who don't want to be helped. If, however, you understand that you are dealing with a fearful child who is feeling unsafe in the world, does not trust adults to provide them with safety and structure (often for very good reasons), and feels (rightly or wrongly) that giving up any measure of personal power and control is *extremely* threatening if not *life* threatening, then behaviors that we find challenging and problematic not only become less inconsistent with what we perceive as the problem, they actually begin to make sense and become both rational and predictable. It also helps us to understand that any approach that threatens their sense of power and control is going to escalate rather than de-escalate the behavior. Traditional adult-child responses tend to be punitive, authoritarian, and controlling; and have the dual detriment of being consistent with our human reactions but counter-productive and ineffective. What is productive and effective; that is, the professional response that often seems counter-intuitive to how we are personally reacting, are interventions that are based in *respect*.

In the study I previously referred to under "Codes" the author observes that "*Most homeless youth cannot or do not want to return to childhood, but they are not prepared for adulthood*[32]." The latter part of that statement highlights the need for street-dependent youth to have the guidance and assistance of caring, supportive adults. But the former part of the statement clarifies that when young people have lost faith in adults and begin to rely on an internal sense of power and control for safety and structure in their lives, it is difficult if not impossible to "turn back the clock" and return to a state of childhood where you trust in and defer to the power and control of others. We are, in effect, dealing with human beings who not only won't submit to external authority, but will in fact find external displays of authority *existentially* threatening, and they will rebel against them *even when it is in their best interest to submit*. The old constructs of adult-child relationships no longer apply, and any approach that relies on adult authority and privilege will evoke responses that work against your efforts and their interests. Instead, we

---

[32] Mental Health and Emerging Adulthood among Homeless Young People, The Midwest Longitudinal Study of Homeless and Runaway Adolescents; Les B. Whitbeck, page 3.

must engage street-dependent youth using a partnership approach that allows them to maintain their sense of power and control.

Early in my career I had the privilege of knowing a personal mentor of mine named Linda Zingaro, the founder of a continuum of programs for street-dependent youth in Vancouver, British Columbia back in the late 1970's, early 1980's. While the concept of child-rights is still a controversial one today, back then it was almost unheard of. Advocating an approach that treats young people as partners with rights to self-determination was dismissed by most traditional youth-service professionals as near insanity; unworthy of discussion, particularly when discussing at-risk young people who are surviving in a criminal subculture on our streets. My perspective on this was shaped by Linda's, who taught me that whether or not you recognize a child's *right* to exercise self-determination and survive by their own authority is a completely moot point as long as they have the *power* to do so. That leaves us with only two effective choices in response to the crisis of young people surviving on our streets. One choice would be a universal, systemic response that secures and provides for adolescents against their will until they reach the age of majority; which is neither practical nor affordable, and not even clearly in the best interest of society or the child. Our second choice is to recognize young people's *power* even if we don't acknowledge their *rights*, and engage them as self-determining partners using voluntary rather than authoritarian approaches.

This is the philosophical justification for respect-based intervention. If you are seeking the cooperation of a human being who has the power to self-determine and finds external control existentially threatening, you absolutely have to work from a place of respect. The minute you are perceived as disrespectful, the self-determining individual will withdraw their cooperation or challenge your authority. Note that I didn't say that the *street-dependent youth* will do so; *any* self-determining individual will react this way. That being the case, what does respect-based intervention look like?

Many of the techniques I suggested for responding to the identified time-related behaviors in the original text were examples of respect-based intervention. For example, when discussing violence I advised against backing young people into corners, even if that means de-escalating situations by backing off yourself (which I will re-clarify is not the same as backing *down* or not dealing with a situation). The reason why this is a respect-based approach is because it acknowledges that people; particularly young people acculturated to street life; often need a "face saving" time lag to cooperate with requests. Since our goal is to engage cooperation as opposed to compel compliance, our interventions should avoid presentation as a "do what I say" mandate within an authoritarian or confrontational approach. We should escalate our intervention only after allowing a reasonable time for a young person to offer cooperation rather than accept capitulation.

Another characteristic of respect-based interventions is that they are always professional and never personal. Whether we are making a simple request or applying a consequence such as denying service or asking a young person to leave our program, it should be presented in a neutral, respectful, and consistent manner. If a young person elects to behave in a way which results in our having to enforce a boundary or apply a consequence, then that is what we will do. It is never about who they are as a person; it is always about the choices they are making. We will always appreciate and respect them, but we will also always do our job. Our ultimate goal is to create a relationship where we do not have to intervene, enforce boundaries, or apply consequences at all. This is something we do if necessary, but it is not our desired outcome or the way we wish to spend our time. While it may be unrealistic to assume that we will ever completely achieve that level of relationship with all young people, it should always be the goal that we are *attempting* to achieve, and the best path to that goal is to use 4 qualifiers in all of our communications; be *clear*, be *direct*, be *matter of fact*, and be *honest*.

To be *clear* means to prioritize our message over our eloquence. Don't use two paragraphs when two sentences (or two words) will do. Excess verbiage tends to confuse issues. In fact, a good standard is that if we can't say it in 2 or 3 sentences, we shouldn't bother saying it at all; because a young person won't be listening to us after 2 or 3 sentences anyway. We'll know this to be true when we see their eyes glaze over, at which point all they're hearing is "blah, blah, blah." Within those sentences, don't use $16.00 words when there are simpler words that mean the same thing. It's not that young people don't have knowledge, but they often lack vocabulary. For example, a young woman was talking to a doctor who asked her about the type of contraception she was using. The young woman replied *"what's that?"* The doctor was visibly taken aback and stated in a surprised voice; *"You mean you've never heard of birth control?"* The young woman looked at the doctor like she was the stupidest human being on the planet and said; *"Well, of course I've heard of birth control. I've just never heard of that 'ception shit!"* The problem here was not with the young woman's knowledge; she simply lacked vocabulary. But even when vocabulary isn't the problem, clarity sometimes suffers when we speak *generally* about *specifics*. For example, don't say *you're pushing the limits* if the problem is that they're showing up late for appointments. A young person can deal with specific, identified behaviors, but they often don't get euphemisms or behavioral generalities[33]. The clearer and more specific we can be, the more respectful the conversation will feel to the young person.

---

[33] Remember the literal communication style described under the street code of integrity.

To be *direct* means to not be hesitant or reluctant. Don't beat around the bush. Get to the point and say it. This not only helps with *clarity*, but it also helps with *honesty* (see below), or, at least, reduces the appearance of dishonesty. When we are hesitant, reluctant, or indirect it is often interpreted by the young person as us withholding information or being dishonest or manipulative. This is one of the areas where our natural communication style doesn't translate well to the streets. We often feel that people being blunt and direct is disrespectful, whereas on the streets it is a sign of respect and the exact opposite behavior is what feels disrespectful. This is another reason to avoid euphemism. While our intent is to "soften the blow" or make a conversation "easier," the effect is that street-dependent youth will feel that we are being dishonest or disrespectful, and we will antagonize rather than sooth. An outreach client who had been raped was talking with a rape advocate who kept referring to the rape as "the incident" (Were you injured during the incident? Did anyone witness the incident?). After about the fifth reference to "the incident" the young woman angrily confronted the advocate with; "*Fuck you! I didn't have an 'incident.' I was raped!*" It goes against our personal communication comfort; and I am not saying to use the most graphic language you can think of; but to be perceived as respectful when dealing with street-dependent youth, don't *allude* to what you're talking about; just *say* it.

To be *matter of fact* is not just a communication style, it actually has to be the emotional place from which we are communicating. Whatever we're dealing with isn't personal. It doesn't make us happy, or sad, or angry, or contemptuous; it just *is*. We are simply stating facts and giving information. The more we can just present the information with the same level of assuredness as we would present any other factual information, the easier it will be for the young person to hear us and the more respectful the communication will feel.

And finally; and this is often the hardest one for us; to be *honest* means to be absolutely, scrupulously honest. The more dishonesty that creeps into our conversation, the more a young person will feel disrespected; and, in fact, the more they will actually *be* disrespected. If nothing else we owe them honesty, and not being honest is a sure fire way to perpetuate their distrust in adults. This is particularly true when we are exercising external power and control over their choices or behaviors. Does the young person *need* to be quieter, or are *we* bothered by their volume? Is there a program reason why they need to look at their behavior with their partner, or do *we* resent the way they are treating him or her? Note that either of the options in these examples can be legitimate topics for intervention, as long as we're honest about what the issue *really* is. Don't say things like *you can't do that here* if there are no program rules or guidelines that prohibit the behavior. This doesn't mean that we can't intervene, it just means that our intervention shouldn't be justified based on a rule that we just made up. Young people are extremely skilled at detecting dishonesty (and hypocrisy, by the way) and, after detection, they will tend to tune out *everything* we are saying.

I've sometimes been asked, well, what about when you can't be honest? Situations such as maintaining personal boundaries or protecting confidentiality may mean that we can't give them the information they are seeking. Situations such as this come up all of the time and are absolutely legitimate, but they do not require dishonesty. If you can't share information either for boundary or confidentiality reasons, you can *honesty* tell them why you can't share the information. Being honest doesn't require you to tell them everything; it simply requires that you are honest about why you're not telling them.

Respect-based intervention requires that we are transparent in our actions and that young people are clear about expectations and boundaries. This means that we always talk openly about our expectations and that we never change our behavior without discussing it. Let young people know what we are doing and why we are doing it; and this begins at the very start of our relationship; defining the nature of the relationship and allowing for the various directions it may take.

I believe that one of the mistakes often made when youth workers are establishing relationships with young people is that we are predisposed to present the benefits we have to offer and disinclined to inform the young person of the less attractive features of being involved with us. The result is that when the time comes for us to set boundaries or assess skills and abilities or reflect upon behaviors or apply consequences, it comes as a huge surprise to the young person and feels disrespectful; as though we are arbitrarily "changing the game." All they knew was that things were going to be great and they'd have access to all kinds of goodies and benefits; we never said we that were going to be on their case about stuff.

Respect-based intervention requires that we respect their ability to make informed choices and handle both the positive and the negative aspects of interventions. This means that when we are first establishing our relationship with young people they need to be shown the complete picture of what the relationship involves and what it may look like. Later, if we need to have a "difficult" conversation, set a limit or boundary, or apply a consequence, it won't be quite as challenging or feel quite as disrespectful from the youth's perspective because they will have had advance knowledge that these interventions were going to be a part of their experience.

For example, let's say you're enrolling someone in a job readiness program. It's fine to tell them the benefits; that involvement in the program will give them marketable job skills and help them to gain employment. But what happens if, after enrollment, your assessment determines that they really aren't employable right now? Perhaps you discover mental health issues that need to be addressed first. To the young person it would feel disrespectful; as though you were pulling the rug out from under them; if they hadn't been told that such assessments were going to be taking place and that the "benefits" were dependent upon the outcome of such assessments. If, however, the orientation to the program included this information then the result would not feel disrespectful because it was understood in advance.

Creating advance understanding is not only respectful, it can also be beneficial to us in terms of discovering the best way to convey information or engage an individual young person. For example, when I directed a transitional living group home for street-dependent youth I was often involved in providing the initial orientation for new residents. As it was a voluntary program that young people made a decision to enter, the orientation was always very amicable; they were excited that they had been accepted and would be moving in with a completely clean slate. The orientations always felt very pleasant and comfortable for us both, and they were non-confrontational and conflict-free. Yet I knew that there would come a time in the future when things may not be so amicable, so out of respect for the young person it was my job to make sure that they had the same knowledge and information that I had. To ensure that they did, my orientations always included a canned speech that went something like this:

"Part of my job is to uphold limits and give you feedback on your choices and actions. Sometimes we're going to disagree and I'm going to be giving you feedback that you might not like, or we're going to be on different sides of a conflict. When this happens, how do you want me to deal with you?"

Giving this speech had two benefits. First, it shared information with the young person helping them to understand my role and what our relationship might look like as it developed. This not only showed respect for their capacity to understand and participate in the relationship, but it also ensured that they were making an informed choice about entering into the relationship in the first place. Second, it provided *me* with useful information on how to approach the young person when the inevitable conflict takes place. I remember one young woman told me; *never say 'you need to ...' If you do, I'll probably go ballistic.* Trust that I made a mental note of that and never used that phase when setting limits with her (it also allowed me to open up a conversation about the life experience she had that created her reaction to that phrase). Another advantage of this approach is that, when in conflict with the young person, a part of them registers that you are dealing with them as they *requested* to be dealt with. This recognition serves as a sign of respect that goes a long way toward de-escalating the conflict.

It should be noted that this is a negotiation. If you ask how they would like to be dealt with and you get a response like; *shut up, back off, and leave me the fuck alone*; just think to yourself, *that's an interesting opening position.* You then come back with something like; *my job requires that I don't do that, so what's another option we can consider?* You then continue the negotiation until *you* agree on an approach that works for *both* of you.

When using respect-based intervention, there are two communication tools that all youth workers should have at their disposal and use liberally when working with street-dependent youth. They are often counter-intuitive, but they are extremely effective. These tools are the power of *apology* and *gratitude*. They are counter-intuitive because neither depends on having something to apologize or be grateful for; they are simply useful approaches in respect-based intervention. To demonstrate, here are two examples from my own experience where I used apology and gratitude.

In the first example, I was preparing for a youth forum within a shelter program and had set an easel out on the floor. As I went to get other supplies, I saw one young man start to remove the easel I had just set up. I explained that I had placed the easel there for use in the youth forum and asked if he would please leave it where it is. I then went about my other business, but returned just in time to see that he had taken it again and was trying to hide it between the washers. I went up to him, retrieved the easel and said; *Please leave the easel where it is. If you take it again I'll have to ask you to leave the forum.*

He responded loudly with; "*Geez, why do you have to be such an asshole about it?!?*" There were many ways I could have responded to his outburst, but the way I responded was with an *apology*; "*I'm sorry if I'm coming across as an asshole, that's not my intent. I just need the easel to be left where it is.*"

That was the end of our interaction, and the youth did not take the easel again, nor did we have any further dealings that night. However, as I was leaving, a friend of his gave me a note that he had asked her to pass on to me. The note said:

What up yo. I'm sorry 4 calling you an asshole. I was out of line. I reacted badly. I will try to refrain from reacting so harsh next time. Sorry again.

The second example involves a youth who came storming into a drop-in center I supervised during an evening when I was working the floor. He appeared extremely angry and agitated. He knew that I was in charge of the center and when he saw me across the room he pointed and loudly shouted; "*YOU! We need to talk!*"

He rapidly approached me shouting; "*Your goon* [staff's name] *told me I wasn't who I am! Some other youth used my name to get in here, and* [staff's name] *told me that I was using a fake name, but I have ID* (the ID is now being held defiantly in my face) *so he's wrong!*"

I knew nothing of this situation, but I could assume that the youth was denied entry earlier based on some confusion over identity. It might have been his fault; it might have been staff's fault. At this point, knowing who was at fault didn't matter. The identity issue had obviously been resolved as the youth was accessing the center. The only thing left to resolve was the issue of a pissed-off youth in my face.

I first responded with a clarification; *"We don't have any 'goon's' working here. Are you referring to one of our floor staff?"*

"Yeah."

"*Thank you*," I said, using the *gratitude* technique. It never hurts to thank people, even for the smallest concession. He had at least acknowledged that he was referring to a staff person, not a "goon," and so I thanked him for that. I then apologized.

"It sounds like we may have made a mistake earlier. If we made a mistake, please accept our apology."

He looked at me for a moment, and then said *"OK."*

That was the end of it. Done. Over. *Never* underestimate the power of apology and gratitude.

As an aside, please note that in the above example I did not admit to a mistake. I had no way of knowing whether *we* had made a mistake or *he* had. I simply clarified that *if* the mistake was ours, we're sorry. Note also that I did not place the blame on the individual staff person in question. I intentionally said that *we* may have made a mistake. Staff should always operate as a consistent team. Everything you do, *we* do.

The more you are able to let respect govern your interventions, the more effective, and brief, your interventions are likely to be. But one of the areas where interventions go off the rails is when we get sucked into *power struggles*.

A "power struggle" takes place whenever an adult and a young person are unwilling to relinquish power or control to the other. It may be about choices or decisions, but, particularly with street-dependent youth, power struggles are often created around *situations*. There is a very simple reason for this. We've established that street-dependent youth rely on an internal sense of power and control, yet they are rarely in a situation, particularly when dealing with adults, where they actually *have* real power and control. When people to whom power is an issue find themselves powerless, they create *situational* power. gain, we're talking about *people*, not just street-dependent youth. Have you ever been at a store, obviously in a hurry, and the clerk is taking their own sweet time in serving you? That's an example of situational power. Now, you can get into a power struggle with that clerk, but do you think that doing so is likely to make them serve you faster or slower? In this situation, and in almost every situation where we get into a power struggle with a young person, just getting into the power struggle means *that we have already lost*. Our goal is to develop a caring, supportive relationship, build trust, and show respect. Power struggles create distance, build resentment, and show disrespect. If we "win" the power struggle, the young person will find us existentially threatening. If we "lose" the power struggle, we will lose the young person's respect.

If you find yourself in a power struggle, since you've already lost, the worst thing you can do is to try to win. Your only alternative really is to *alter or withdraw from the situation.* Let's take the example of the clerk intentionally moving too slowly. What if you said; *you know what ... I'll just get this stuff later*, and you walked out of the store? In that case you will have completely altered the situation to where the clerk no longer has situational power over you. Certainly you may be slightly inconvenienced by not getting your purchase right then, but it may be a small price to pay to avoid a power struggle with the clerk or to allow them to continue to screw with you. Whenever you find yourself in a power struggle with a young person, *stop trying to win* and look for ways to alter or withdraw from the situation.

Of course, we are our own greatest barrier to being able to alter or withdraw from a power struggle. I once read an article about disciplining youth without power struggles that said; *I have never seen a power drunk child without a power drunk adult real close by*[34]. It is often our own egos, our own unwillingness to let something go, our own unwillingness to let a young person "win," that prevents us from withdrawing from power struggles. But remember that professional response needs to trump personal reaction. Nowhere is this truer than when you find yourself in a power struggle.

Realizing that if you get into a power struggle you have already lost, then the best professional response is to avoid power struggles in the first place. Granted this is easier said than done; particularly when dealing with young people for whom power and control are core issues; who are powerless people prone to creating situational power; and when your job as staff is often to set limits or enforce boundaries. However, even though it may not always be possible to avoid situations of power *imbalance*, it is possible to avoid power *struggles* if you follow two simple rules; first, *choose your battles*; and, second, *don't fight.*

When we *choose our battles*, it means that we don't exercise power or control just because we're the adults. We only do so when it is necessary to set limits or enforce boundaries. Outside of that, we don't care if young people create situational power; in fact, we may even encourage it. We want them to exercise power and control in their lives; our only concern is that they do so in healthy ways. We don't have any problem letting a young person "win" as long as nobody really "loses."

When we do choose a battle, however, we ensure that it does not become a power struggle because we *don't fight.* We should be on solid ground by having chosen our battle carefully, so at that point it is simply a communication issue. All of the previously stated communication

---

[34] Eighteen Ways To Avoid Power Struggles, by Jane Nelsen

techniques apply (be *clear*, be *direct*, be *matter of fact*, and be *honest*) and, additionally, we are not going to *debate* or *argue*. We will state our position, and then *restate* it as long as necessary.

An extremely helpful tool in avoiding debate or argument is the "Never-the-less/Regardless" technique. After stating your position, you then rely on "never-the-less" or "regardless" as a response to anything that the young person says in an attempt to challenge, argue, or debate the point. For example, a program was having a problem with some residents intimidating and bullying other residents by "staring them down." Staff was having a hard time intervening because residents would argue with them about their involvement in this somewhat nebulous behavior. They were able to begin to address this issue when they implemented the *never-the-less/regardless* technique, which would go something like as follows:

Staff would see a youth staring down another youth. They intervene by saying; "*Johnny, staring people down is not acceptable here.*"

The young person might come back with something like: "*What are you talking about? I wasn't doing nothin'!*"

Staff's response: "*Never-the-less (or regardless), staring people down is not acceptable here.*"

"*But I didn't do anything. You're trippin', man!*"

"*Never-the-less (or regardless), staring people down is not acceptable here.*"

"*You're just picking on me! Everybody does it and you don't get in their face!*"

"*Never-the-less (or regardless), staring people down is not acceptable here.*"

No matter how or how often the youth challenges you, tries to argue with you, or tries to draw you into a debate about the behavior or their participation in it, the response is a simple formula: "Never-the-less (or regardless)" and then you restate the expectation.

A variation of this technique is helpful when you have to impose changes or restrictions within a program. I call this variation *scripting*, because it relies on actually creating a "script" that all staff follow. This not only helps with consistency, but it enables all staff to avoid power struggles as the changes are implemented. As an example, what follows is an actual script developed for a drop-in center program that was experiencing numbers too large for the available staff, and problems with young people bringing in weapons and drugs concealed in their gear. The week prior to implementing changes necessary to keep the program safe, all staff rehearsed and followed this script to inform young people of the upcoming changes:

How to Explain

Identify that you have two things they need to know about next week:
One (first):
- Beginning next Monday we're changing drop-in hours.

- Drop-in will be from (AM) to (   ).
- Snacks will be available, but there won't be any services during drop-in.
- If you need services (be able to define services), come during service hours in the afternoon between (PM) and (   ). Access will be limited to staff available, so you may want to make an appointment or call first.

Two (second):
- We have to do something about the drugs, weapons and restricted items (stolen goods, pornography, paraphernalia, etc.) that are being brought into the [program]. Until these problems stop, you may not bring backpacks, bags, sleeping bags (etc.) into the [program] UNLESS you are willing to show us the contents. If you are wearing particularly bulky clothing we may ask you to empty your pockets as well.

    NOTE: Do not use "search" language. They are being given a voluntary choice to show us the contents of what they are bringing in, or else not bring it in.

How to Respond

Why? (drop-in/services)

We don't have enough staff to supervise drop-in and provide services, so we are separating the two. That way if all you want to do is hang out there is time for that, but if you need services or want to work on something there will be time for staff to assist you.

Why? (showing contents)

It is our responsibility to keep the [program] safe and free of weapons, drugs and other restricted items (stolen goods, pornography, paraphernalia, etc.). We are aware that we have not been able to do that, because these items are coming in concealed in people's belongings. Until we can be sure that people are not bringing these items into the [program], we are asking people to not bring backpacks, bags, sleeping bags (etc.), or to show us the contents before entering.

What can I do in drop-in?

Drop-in is an opportunity for you to hang out, grab a snack, and relax a bit. Due to the small number of available staff, all services (be able to define services) are being moved to the afternoon service hours.

What are "snacks?"

During drop-in the kitchen will be closed*. The program will provide snacks ranging from pastries to fruit and similar things, depending on what's available.

  * "Why" questions related to this issue should be answered

similarly to the drop-in/services answer -- we do not have enough staff to support kitchen use.
How do I get services?
Make an appointment, call first, or stop by during service hours. Services will be limited by the number of available staff, so your best bet is to make an appointment or call first. If you stop by and staff is already busy, you may not be able to get services right away. (Youth may ask what a service is, so be able to define services)
(agitated) That's fucked; That's not fair; This is like a prison; Fuck this fuckin' fucked-up place (etc.)
(calm) I understand how you feel, and we're sorry we have to do things this way. // If and when we have more staff and people stop bringing in stuff that shouldn't be here, we can talk about making some adjustments. But, for now, // this is the only way we can keep everyone safe and meet everyone's needs.
(continued arguing) Utilize the *never-the-less/regardless* technique.

Note the use of the apology technique in response to youth who may be upset about the changes. By following this script, these rather dramatic changes were able to be implemented relatively smoothly, without confusion, and, most importantly, without power struggles.

As a final word on this subject I'll refer back to a statement I made earlier; that our goal is to engage cooperation as opposed to compel compliance. Whether we get cooperation or compliance is usually a result of whether we are *encouraging* cooperation instead of compliance, and which one of those we are encouraging depends largely on how we communicate. There are specific communication techniques that will either encourage or discourage cooperation, and if you discourage cooperation you will be left with no other alternative than to mandate compliance. The following is not an exhaustive list of all communications, but it will give you a solid basis for communicating in ways that encourage cooperation. I begin, however, by identifying some communications that *discourage* cooperation. Cooperation-discouraging communications fall into two categories; aggressive and passive. For demonstration I'll use an example of a youth leaving dirty dishes on the counter instead of putting them in the dishwasher.

Aggressive communications that *discourage* cooperation:
- Criticizing: You're too lazy to put your dishes in the dishwasher.
- Name-calling: Geez, you good-for-nothing, you're supposed to put your dishes in the dishwasher!
- Orders: Put your dishes in the dishwasher now!

- <u>Threats</u>: If you don't start putting your dishes in the dishwasher there are going to be serious consequences.
- <u>Blame and Accusation</u>: You left dirty dishes on the counter again? What's the matter with you, anyway? Can't you even clean up after yourself?
- <u>Warnings</u>: If you don't put your dishes in the dishwasher you're going to get in trouble.
- <u>Sarcasm</u>: Left your dirty dishes on the counter again, I see. Oh, don't worry yourself about it. You're obviously the only one who matters around here.
- <u>Moralizing</u>: Do you think that's considerate, leaving your dishes on the counter? Other people live here too, you know.

Passive **communications that *discourage* cooperation:**
- <u>Diagnosing</u>: You never do your dishes because you grew up in a sloppy household.
- <u>Evaluative Praise</u>: It's being a good resident to do your dishes. That would be really wonderful of you.
- <u>Questioning</u>: Why don't you ever put your dishes in the dishwasher? Don't you stop to think? Does it just not matter to you? What?
- <u>Advising</u>: If I were you, I'd be concerned with how leaving my dishes on the counter affected the other people in the house.
- <u>Diverting</u>: You think putting your dishes in the dishwasher is hard? In other programs you have to scrub them by hand!
- <u>Logical Argument</u>: If you leave your dishes all over the counter it's obviously going to cause tension and resentment.
- <u>Reassuring</u>: It'll be fine. Just put your dishes in the dishwasher and everything will work out great.
- "<u>Cutesipation</u>": Look at you cleaning up and putting your dishes in the dishwasher. It's so cute, like you're a little bird cleaning up your nest!
- <u>Martyrdom Statements</u>: You left your dishes on the counter again? I can't believe it! You're going to be the death of me. I wish you were in my position; then you'd understand the meaning of frustration!
- <u>Comparisons</u>: Why can't you be more like the other residents? They don't leave their dishes on the counter. And do you see the staff doing that? I don't think so!
- <u>Prophesy</u>: If you don't learn how to clean up after yourself you're going to have major problems with anyone you live with in the future.

Communication techniques that *encourage* cooperation:
- <u>Description</u> (what you see, or the problem):
    (*What you see*) I see dirty dishes that need to be in the dishwasher.
    (*The problem*) The problem with dirty dishes on the counter is that

they create cross-contamination and other sanitation issues.
- Give Information: Leaving dirty dishes on the counter violates our sanitation guidelines. (Note that this is different from *Logical Argument*, which is "if you do this, this will result." Giving Information is simply stating facts.)
- Identify *your* feelings: I feel frustrated when I see dirty dishes on the counter that should be in the dishwasher. (Do not confuse this with *Martyrdom Statements*. This is about what *you* are feeling, not what *they* are *making you feel* or *doing to you*.)
- Say it with a word: Tom, the dishes. (It is amazing how effective this technique is if utilized properly. Say it and move on. If you say it and stand over them impatiently waiting for them to comply, it becomes more like an *Order*.)
- Write a note: (*Written*) Please remember to put your dishes in the dishwasher when you're finished eating. Thank you. (This is a particularly useful technique to avoid calling people out in front of their peers, eliminating the need for them to challenge you to maintain peer status. If you know that dishes are a problem with a particular youth, slip them a note just before clean up begins. Note the use of the *gratitude* technique at the end of the note.)

Remember that it takes time for people to voluntarily change their actions and learn to cooperate, which is one of the many reasons that staff repetition and consistency are so critical. Also, not only do people need time to acquire new habits, but remember that most people need a "face-saving" time lag between a request being made and a response on their part. That's OK, since the goal is cooperation, not immediate compliance. Describe, give information, identify your feelings, say it with a word, or write a note, then go about your business assuming that they *will* cooperate. If you stand over them waiting for cooperation, you are setting up a power dynamic that they will feel obligated to resist.

Despite all of the valiant efforts that these youth make to survive, a street-dependent youth's decision to live is a fragile one.

Concepts Related to Identity

One of the more challenging concepts we encounter is a street-dependent youth's concept of identity. It's important to understand that our concept of identity is generally not who we are, but rather, who we perceive ourselves to be. As such a person's self-identity is often very different from your perception of that person. Regardless of what you may see or think of an individual, their life will be determined by how they see themselves.

When most young people first become involved in a street lifestyle, their identity is that of a powerless victim; due mainly to the life experience that predisposed them to the streets in the first place. They quickly learn, however, that a victim identity is not conducive to survival on the streets and, in a very short period of time, they will begin to develop and adopt a new identity.

The most apparent manifestation of identity adoption is the use of aliases, or "street names." The majority of youth that you will meet on or from the streets will initially present themselves under an assumed or "street" name. Sometimes the fact that they are not using a birth name is obvious; names such as "Thumper," or "Lost," or "Shadow." In other cases you will meet a "Crystal," or an "Angel;" names that may or may not be birth names. Still other times you will meet "Patty's" or "Ted's," assume them to be birth names, only to find out later that they are not. To add further confusion, if you are working with older street-dependent youth who become involved in the adult entertainment industry, they are likely to adopt a stage name as well.

Street Names

There are some important things to remember about adopted names. The first is that names are not chosen haphazardly or at random. Street names are adopted either by the youth because it helps define the survival identity they've created for themselves, or the name has been given to them by their street family. In either case, it represents far more than a simple nickname. It is who they are, and their entire identity may be at stake with that name. Because of this you have to be careful with how you respond to street names. An attack on the name, a joke about the name, abuse of the name, dismissing the name, will be perceived by the youth as an attack on them, a joke about them, abuse of them, or dismissal of them.

Sometimes a program will try to accelerate a youth's transition out of street life by forcibly removing the external trappings. They dictate a new way of dressing, speaking, and they disallow the use of a street name. While the goal is admirable, it is a mistake to believe that you can change what is going on inside of a person simply by changing their external world. Programs often make this mistake because it is true that a person can create change on the inside by making changes on the outside. For example, if you wish to be a positive, happy person, you can act as though you already are a positive, happy person and, in a very short period of time, you will begin to feel like and truly become positive and happy. While this is true of almost any characteristic or behavior that you may wish for yourself, the key that is usually missed in programs is that before you can externally create internal change, you must first internally *desire* the change. Programming that focuses on external changes that a youth does not believe in, desire, or accept, are far more likely to create manipulation, violence, and runaway behavior than they are to create change.

It is true that at some point in a youth's transition out of street life they will give up their street name, and one clear sign of progress is when we see this happen. But there are risks involved if you try to force that change. Like many other behaviors, street names are best viewed as a Band-Aid that is covering a healing wound. Do not attempt to rip it off unless you are willing to re-open that wound and deal with the bleeding. Trust that when the identity protection is no longer needed, when the name is no longer required to help the youth survive, they will stop using it without an external mandate.

I admit that this is sometimes not easy. I worked with one youth who insisted that I use her real name when we were alone, but if anyone else was around in possible earshot she wanted me to use her street name. Since most of the time I was working with her we were out on the streets it meant that I had to be constantly aware of the environment around us. If I used her real name and there was somebody ten feet behind me she'd get angry. She'd also get angry if I used her street name and there was nobody there.

We had an outreach worker who had first met a boy under his street name and then, at some point in their relationship, the boy had confessed his real name. The following day the worker saw him on the street and in an effort to establish a bond of familiarity she went up to him and said "hi" using the boy's real name. He didn't talk to her for almost a month. In that situation out on the streets the worker should have known to address the boy by his street name.

Because these names represent their identity, street-dependent youth take them very seriously. Our challenge is to acknowledge that fact and train ourselves to treat the names seriously even when it's difficult for us.

For example, one youth I worked with was a girl who had been hideously sexually abused and exploited her entire life. Her street name was "Cuddles." It was extremely difficult for me to be comfortable with that name, as it felt somewhat abusive as well. But it was important to her to be accepted by that name; it was, after all, one of the few things in her life over which she had some measure of control. I mitigated my discomfort by using the name as sparingly as possible, but I respected her wish to be addressed by that name.

In another example a youth came to a drop-in center as I was leaving and met me on the steps with some clothes she needed to lock up. She was about 16, and dressed like she had just stepped out of a video that MTV would find too sleazy to air. You did not need to be an expert in the field to figure out that this girl was involved in adolescent prostitution. As I had never met her before, I asked what name she wanted me to mark on the locker. She gave me a beaming little smile and identified herself as "Chastity." Cognitive dissonance or not, if Chastity was the name that she needed, it was the name that I would use.

Vicarious Traumatization

A small digression is appropriate here as this points out one of the primary occupational hazards of working with street-dependent youth, and the reason why we lose so many staff and volunteers to "burn-out." People who work with street-dependent youth are consistently exposed to psychological and emotional pain. Day in and day out we work with wounded children, and often we don't see the results of our work. Additionally, in many interventions, such as the examples around street names that I've used, it's necessary that your response is different, sometimes dramatically different, from your reaction. It's not uncommon for youth workers to develop a form of vicarious traumatization from this work. And one of the releases, sort of a safety valve that works well to counter the effects of this traumatization, is inappropriate humor.

I use the term "inappropriate" only to indicate that there is a specific time and place to express this form of humor. In terms of the need for its expression, it is very appropriate and can help to keep you sane. The humor I'm referring to is often labeled "foxhole" humor, derived from the humor soldiers express in combat. If you were to attend some of our after-shift debriefings without the context of our experience, there are times when you would think that we were very sick people. But it's a coping skill, and it allows us to go out again the next night. The important thing to remember about foxhole humor is that it should only be expressed in private, away from your work with youth, and among co-workers who understand and accept the intent of the humor. Certainly, when the young girl introduced herself as "Chastity," about 50 crude jokes and comments went through my head. My reaction to her, however, was respectful. It wasn't until later at a staff meeting that several of us voiced some inappropriate remarks. And I want to be clear that these remarks were not voiced in order to have a good laugh at her expense. They were voiced in order for us to be able to keep working in a world where 16 year old girls are named "Chastity" and have to prostitute themselves to survive.

Street Stories

Another behavior related to identity that gives many adults difficulty is the concept of lying. For many staff, lying is their bottom line, and they will accept almost any behavior except lying. I'm suggesting here that if you are going to work successfully with street-dependent youth, you are going to have to accept some forms of dishonesty. Remember also that there may be behavior that is experienced by you as dishonest, that wasn't, in fact, a dishonest action on the part of the youth. Rather, it was a misunderstanding caused by how literally street-dependent youth tend to communicate. Admittedly, however, there will be situations when a youth will simply be dishonest and tell you out-and-out lies. These lies often take the form of what we call "street stories," or, as someone once labeled them; "creative reality." These are the stories and experiences that youth simply make up, but it's important to realize that they do it for a reason other than just to see how big of a lie they can get away with. The fact is that they have enormous gaps in their memories. They also have an adopted self-image and identity that helps them rise above victim status and survive in the violent culture of the streets. The combination of identity adoption and missing memory is fertile ground to grow experiences and histories that have never occurred, but once developed fill in gaps in memory and help to support a survival identity.

Sometimes the stories are close enough to reality that it's difficult to tell fact from fiction. They may be intertwined with the truth, and they may sound entirely plausible. In other cases the stories will be so outrageous as to leave you in awe of the concept that the youth believes you are buying any part of it. One example that leaps to mind is a 14 year old male I was talking to on the street. Now, admittedly, I had only just met this youth, so I really didn't know very much about him or his history. Still, I was willing to bet a year's pay that he had never been a paratroop mercenary fighting Cubans in Angola. Call me jaded, but I just don't think that it happened.

Our reaction is often similar to the reaction we have to prejudice. We feel that it is not in this youth's best interest to be lying, so we want to challenge the fantasy, confront their deceit, and make an honest person out of them. We do this in the belief that it's harmful to allow them to believe this stuff and spread lies, so we tell them that we know that the story isn't true, that they didn't do this, that, or the other thing. It's a risky course of action, however, because these stories are another form of Band-Aid that street-dependent youth use to cover their psycho-emotional wounds. If you're going to rip that Band-Aid off you'd better be sure that you're qualified to deal with the wound, and that the youth is healed enough to survive it. The fact is that it's usually unnecessary to challenge them. Just as with street names, when they don't need these stories for self-protection they will voluntarily stop using them. But it can be risky to challenge them on the issue of lying, because on some level they know that these stories aren't true. When they are forced to confront the truth before they are ready, their entire defense mechanism, their entire survival identity, starts to unravel, leaving them with nothing but more shame. And a shamed street-dependent youth can easily end up being a dead one.

It's important to remember that, despite all of the valiant efforts that these youth make to survive, a street-dependent youth's decision to live is a fragile one. It doesn't take much for them to see themselves as being unworthy of existence, and you may not see it coming. I remember a class on sexual abuse that a staff member conducted once with a group of young girls. During the class the staff was very impressed with the participation of one youth in particular. She was very articulate and mature, and was so participatory and active in the group that the staff almost viewed her as a co-leader of the class. As soon as the class ended, however, this smiling, calm, well-adjusted youth went to the bathroom and slit both of her wrists. What you see on the outside is often in no way comparable to what they are experiencing on the inside.

So you have to be very careful in how you choose to respond to these stories. This is one of the massive gray areas that can make working with street-dependent youth so challenging. On the one hand, you don't want to feed into the lie or act like you believe, because then you run the risk of making the youth feel bad about deceiving you. On the other hand, you don't want to directly challenge the lie, either. So what do you do? You simply accept. That is to say, you don't acknowledge the stories, but neither do you challenge them. Instead, you simply accept that the story is true for *them*, and at the same time, you look for the truth in the story. Street stories may fill gaps in memory, but they do not occur in a vacuum. In every tale there will be some truth. Your job is to accept the filler, and respond to the truth. For example, it was obvious that the young man I was speaking to had never been a paratrooper in Angola, but it was equally obvious that there have been times in his life when he was in danger, when he felt threatened, and when he struggled to survive. I can respond to those feelings, which are true, without doing more than simply accepting that the story is the vehicle he is using to describe those feelings.

By using this method of intervention with street stories the youth will, over time, benefit from interactions with you. They will be getting their needs met, and slowly learn that they get the attention they need in response to the truth. With patience you will see the made up stories melt away in favor of honesty, and it will happen without the need for confrontation. Working with this population can be a slow, long-term process. They did not get to where they are overnight, and positive change will not occur overnight, either.

There is one thing I would like to caution you about. In discussing street stories I can leave you with the impression that you are going to know when the youth is lying. My example of the 14 year old who was a paratrooper in Angola is one where the lie was so apparent that it was almost comical. And there will be stories that are similarly ridiculous that you will encounter. But a bigger trap for us are the stories that are, on the surface, believable. An audience member in one of my presentations related that he had worked with a young woman who had told him about a childhood experience where she and her brother were at the beach, and the brother drowned. He believed the story, and he responded to her, and dealt with her from that point forward, as if the story were true, only later finding out that it wasn't. The result of his belief was that a barrier had been erected between him and the youth, because their entire relationship was based on a lie. His belief in that lie required her to remain invested in it. I am not telling you to not believe anything a street-dependent youth says, but I do advise that, regardless of how believable the story is, you only respond to what you can confirm and verify as the truth. Whether or not her brother actually died can be irrelevant to how you respond. What is true in that story is that she has experienced loss in her life. You are far safer to discuss the feelings, rather than the supposed events that caused them.

Suicide

Before we leave this topic, a few words need to be said about the issue of suicide in relation to street-dependent youth. Let me first clarify that this is not a suicide assessment or intervention training. You are strongly encouraged to seek additional and specific training on this topic. However, suicide in relation to street-dependent youth has some interesting particulars.

As a population, the suicide risk among street-dependent youth is probably less than with other populations of youth, due to the fact that their entire culture is based on a daily struggle to survive. The act of suicide is not conducive to that goal. However, ending that struggle through suicide can lie in a dangerously shallow place just beneath the surface, and, in many ways, their daily life can add up to one lengthy, covert suicide attempt. If the protective surface of the youth's identity, self-esteem, and will to survive is damaged too severely, it can be very easy for them to slip into overt suicidal behavior, and they can be fatally successful if they get to that point.

That's why I've discussed the dangers of stripping away their identity too quickly. You'll see more suicidal behavior when youth are in programs to help, then you will when they're out on the streets.

But there is another factor that can come into play, and that is how we respond to talk of suicide. I'll admit that there have been some days when I've personally made statements that could be interpreted as suicidal. For example, after a presentation that did not go well I may say something like; "*I wish I was dead.*" You probably make statements like this as well. When we make those statements, it really is only a figure of speech; the idea of actually killing ourselves is not even a part of our consciousness. Sometimes street-dependent youth describe feelings this way, as well. The difference is that when they make such statements we can immediately get hooked. Suddenly they're on a 24 hour watch and staff is paying all kinds of attention to them. The message they can get is that the way to get attention and support is to be suicidal. The result is that we play a role in creating a situation where suicidal behavior becomes a way to get their needs met, and a youth who may not be seriously suicidal becomes suicidal in their behavior; sometimes resulting in actual attempts.

It is not my intention to give you permission to discount talk of suicide, and I strongly encourage you to take all suicidal indicators extremely seriously. I do caution you, however, to avoid over-reaction and to learn to separate expressions of frustration and despair from actual suicidal intentions.

Key Points - Concepts Related to Identity

- In order to survive, youth on the streets adopt an identity that helps them overcome their "victim" histories and cope with the trauma of street life.
- The most obvious manifestation of identity adoption is the use of "street names". These names may encompass a youth's entire self-image, and care needs to be exercised when dealing with street names.
- "Street stories," or events described by youth that have never occurred, are not lies in the traditional sense. Rather they are a survival aid that helps youth fill in gaps in memory with a "history" that supports their adopted identity.

2.0 Commentary:

The original material states: *When most young people first become involved in a street lifestyle, their identity is that of a powerless victim.* I should clarify that the "powerless victim" identity predates their street involvement or, more accurately, predates their conclusion that they cannot trust in adults for safety and structure and must instead be self-determining. Having made that decision, they no longer see themselves as a powerless victim, but rather as someone who is unwilling to surrender their power and control to others and are therefore responsible for everything that happens to them. This is a difficult concept to understand from outside of the culture, so I want to be clear about what I'm trying to say. It's not that they are taking responsibility for their actions in the positive sense that such responsibility is commonly viewed. It is also not that they are totally in control of their decisions, choices, and actions. Rather it is that they are unwilling to submit to authority *that they do not trust*, and that they believe that whatever happens to them is *deserved* because of their belief in their own failures, flaws, or even their inherent *evil* nature. This is why they will submit to control and abuse by pimps, traffickers, drug dealers, and other exploitive adults, while rebelling against and resisting adults and systems with the intention of helping and protecting; because they *trust the intention* of the former in that it's clear, predictable, and they have a measure of control in the relationship, and they *do not trust* the intention of the latter in that it's not predictable and they have little or no control. Despite our view that they are being abused, exploited, and victimized, their view is that they are maintaining power and control because they *understand the rules* and are treated as they believe they *deserve* to be treated.

It is this conceptual point that is the basis for my disagreement with systems that operate from a "victim" perspective. I actually agree with that perspective to some degree for purposes of public advocacy, but I think it is mistake, or at least a technique with unintended consequences, to approach the young people as victims on a therapeutic and intervention level. In my opinion it is better to capitalize on their sense of responsibility and help them to realize that they have the power to be in control of their lives. They are not responsible for the actions of others, but they do not deserve to be treated that way and they already possess the skills and abilities to expect and demand different treatment. If, instead, we communicate to them that they are victims we run similar risks to those derived from labeling them "homeless" -- that they may accept the victim identity and in some ways lose their ability to be anything but a victim. They may regress to their pre-street "powerless victim" self-image and become functionally helpless. Or they may become "positive" victims; that is, subject themselves to the power and control of "helping" systems having simply transferred their dependency. The danger there is that when the systems are no longer available to them they may simply transfer their dependency to someone or something else, perhaps someone that does not have the same "best interest" in mind as did the system. But if they are to truly lead safe, stable, self-realized lives, they need to learn to be dependent upon themselves and change their perspective on what they are capable of and deserve. That is something that they will be extremely challenged in doing if the messages that they receive from us is that they are victims.

But I fear I'm in the minority on this issue. Over the years our non-punitive responses have moved decidedly toward the "victim" perspective. Take, for example, our attitudes toward youth involved in commercialized sex; something we have been struggling with since I entered the field over 40 years ago. We began by calling it prostitution, then, to distinguish it from the broader prostitution debate, referred to it as *juvenile* prostitution[35]. At some point we became uncomfortable with using the term "prostitution" at all due in part to the "voluntary exchange" argument and other issues raised by advocates of decriminalized or legalized prostitution, so to highlight a focus on lack of choice, we accepted the term "survival sex." Today we have evolved to "commercialized sex," and to make sure that we de-emphasize any act of volition on the part of the youth, CSEC, or the Commercial Sexual *Exploitation* of Children is the banner around which we rally. An unspoken goal in all of these terminologies is to de-emphasize the young person's responsibility for their actions and to see them as victims needing and deserving of our help. At the time of this writing, the webpage of the Office of Juvenile Justice and Delinquency Prevention that is dedicated to the Commercial Sexual Exploitation of Children[36] uses a variation of the term "victim" *27 times* (along with an additional 27 uses of variations of the word "exploit"). As stated earlier, the problem in this is not in how we represent the young people to the public, it is the unintended consequences of creating a victim identity when we allow that perspective to govern our approach to the youth.

Undoubtedly the best way to provide insight into the self-image and identity of street-dependent youth is to allow them to present it themselves; unfiltered and without interpretation. I have a limited ability to do so thanks to a writing project provided to me and presented with permission and without any identifying information. It was written by a young woman with whom I worked who had left the area, but remained in telephone contact with me nearly every day. She was going through a period where she was having a difficult time sorting out her thoughts and feelings, and I was unable to help her over the phone as she was mostly just breaking down and crying when she called. I suggested that she write her thoughts out, without thinking about or trying to make sense of them, and then we could sort them out together when she returned (this was also a way of keeping the thought of returning in her head). What follows is what she wrote and brought back. It is a difficult piece to read and absorb, particularly when

---

[35] Which was seriously flawed, as it left out anyone 18 years of age or older.
[36] http://www.ojjdp.gov/programs/csec_program.html

you realize that it was written by a 17 year-old girl, but the most revealing thing about it is not the insight into the culture and life, nor is it the documentation of her experience ... it is the level of volition that we can infer and her acceptance of the treatment that she endures. While she may indeed be victimized, these are not the words of a *victim*.

Fifty bucks, it's agreed. (How ironic all my body is worth is fifty. To some, thirty, others a C-note. Doesn't seem like too much for a body, some pride, and a piece of spirit.)

"Come on in, honey *(you sick pervert)*. Let's take care of business first *(gimme the money, bastard.)* Okay, now take off your clothes *(god you're fat.)* Ready sweety? Yes, you have to wear a condom, everybody does. It's for protection and prevention. I know it's like taking a shower with a raincoat or washing your hands with gloves, I've heard it thousands of times *(asshole, put the damn thing on.)* If you don't put it on you'll have to leave. No baby, there ain't no refunds. *(Would you just hurry up before I get my ass kicked for being in the room so long.)*"

So baby puts on the rubber, bitching that he'll never cum with it on. So what, who cares if he gets a nut? He's got fifteen minutes. I'm so drunk that I'm not supposed to notice his rotund bulge bouncing on my stomach as he fucks the shit out of me. I'm not supposed to notice the sweat beading on his face and body, and dripping onto me drip by drip on my face. Or I'm not supposed to notice his saliva dripping on me because he's drooling. Finally I yell, "Honey, time's up. Yes, you made me feel good, didn't you hear me moaning? *(groaning in agony, that pussy's been worn out today. Stupid asshole, get out.)* You got to pay more or leave, *(wouldn't ya' know the dumb fuck trick has another fifty bucks.)* Baby, be gentle *(quit pawing)*. Are you close yet? *(hurry up, I'm sick of you sweating, slobbering, pawing, trying to kiss me and lick my face. Mother fucker, leave the hair alone, I'm going to punch you if you don't hurry.)* You're finished? *(thank god.)* Oh yes I enjoyed it, do come back again. I'll be here."

All this sucking dicks and humping, she's going crazy, she can't take it. Every bastard that touches her, she wishes they'd just die. More alcohol, please, more alcohol. This asshole wants her to take the full condom and drain it in his mouth. That one wants her to get sweaty so he can lick her armpits. This one smells like piss. That one wants to be pissed on. This one hasn't been able to get it up since 1964 and blames it on her. That one wants a shoestring tied around his balls while he's whipped, then he wants a dildoe shoved up his ass. They all argue rubbers. I'm clean, they say. Who would tell you if they did have something? More alcohol, please, more alcohol. This man wants to buttfuck. That one wants to suck her toes. Then there's no-one, only standing out on the rail like a fool. So humiliating and degrading. Everyone drives by knowing you're a whore. What a fucked up name. She ruins the best part of her life on sick perverted fat old men that should be hung by the balls till dead. She wasted her life on chicken-shit, good for nothing niggers that only care about themselves.

They wouldn't lift a finger for a thousand dollars. They can't even carry their own luggage. They don't provide support. They wouldn't know the truth if it knocked them down. They send a bitch to work, yell a lot, lie, collect money, and get together and brag and show off. Besides harassing other girls, that's all they do. They act like they're god and the world owes them and should bow down and kiss their $1600.00 snake skin boots. The nigger is so lazy he can't even take off his boots, she has to. He makes her start work at 8:00 am, and quit around 11:00 pm. After you've humped all day -- between fifteen and twenty-five tricks on any given day -- then this man wants you to take two showers, eat with him (like you've got an appetite) then fuck him. Then he has the nerve to get angry because you want to sleep instead of sit and watch television. Nigger pimps aren't worth the ink it takes to write about them.

Seems like my brain is deteriorating. It's so hard to think, I'm so homesick. I know I have to go home, but I'm scared. I don't know how I'll deal with taking on responsibility. I don't know how people will act toward me now that I've left and try to return. I don't want people to be nice to me because they're supposed to or because they feel sorry for me. I just want them to treat me like a person, even though I don't feel like much of a person. I'm scared to leave this again because this is what I know. I'm also scared to keep doing it because I know what it's doing to me. All the physical of not sleeping right, not eating right. Also with tricks going off on me. Broken bones, bruises, cuts. Then there's the brain. I think I'm gonna have a nervous breakdown, from the stress. Also trying to hide from the police. It's so stupid.

This fucking idiot, fucking, fucking, idiot. He makes me so mad. He knows my phone doesn't work and he calls me to come to his room, so I go and walk into a policeman. The bastard never told me they were there. 'm scared to go to jail in [State] again cause I know he can't bail me out. All I want to do is go to court and fly home. I try to call someone from home every day, it makes me feel like I'm closer to them. I talked to Jerry, but I felt bad 'cause I kept crying and he couldn't understand me. I miss everyone, more alcohol I wonder if I have an alcohol problem? I think about wanting a drink all the time. I stand working and I don't even try to catch a trick. I know it will hurt, and I can't deal with that right now. I wish I didn't have a pimp. One way I feel like I love him and need him and the rest of me hates him so much, I don't understand it. I wish I could understand it. I asked Jerry and he said I wouldn't understand it over the phone or overnight. I'm so sick of this life. I wish I could die and get it over with.

I try to think on why I started, or what it has that I need. I really can't come up with any answers. Maybe it's because subconsciously I enjoy being miserable. One of my dates told me that I hate sex but I enjoy watching men have sex. Maybe it's just the attention I get, like some ego trip. Maybe I like being ordered around. But I hate it too. Maybe I just feel important when I give him the money and see him happy, like he really needs me and I done something good. I guess maybe I'll never understand.

This asshole tells me to keep working. I tell him that there's no traffic, only police. Asshole says stay down. So the police talk to me and tell me to stay in. I'm so afraid of jail, you only got to tell me once. He says stay down. You got it - I went to jail.

Jails make me feel like a criminal, like some real low life. They treat you like you're not human. They make you wish you had a pistol so you could blow your brains out. Life's not worth living if you have to worry about jails or if you go to jail. During booking you get harassment from all the male officers and rough treatment from the females. It's hell, and in some way it makes you feel safe. As long as you're in jail you know some trick isn't going to kill you that night. You eat and sleep and no-one yells at you. As much as you hate the streets you'd rather be on them than in jail. Better yet, you'd like to be six years old and have Mommy tuck you in bed and say it was all a bad dream. Oh, reality really hurts.

I'm so confused. I've been trying to define love, I really can't. I thought it was sharing dreams, mutual understanding. I thought it was standing by and helping the partner no matter if it's good times or bad. I thought love was based on trust, communication and compatibility -- the foundation of the pyramid of love, topped by caring and understanding and the final block being determination. Determined to make it work through thick and thin. I thought love was unconditional and couldn't be priced. I thought it was a commitment, a judgment, and a promise. I was so wrong. Love is how well you obey, how good you play the rules, and how much money you make. It's bark, bow, lay down, and play dead. Fuck it. All this love on terms is a pain in the ass and I really don't need any of it.

Jail again! I didn't even do anything this time. I can understand it if I solicit a policeman or get caught in the act, but all I did was walk down for M&M's and this asshole took me in. Baby got me out. Jails are so solitary and you feel like you're all alone in the world with no-one who cares. Happy Birthday to me! I spent that morning in court. Then I'm supposed to have the day off, so every time he sees a regular he makes me get on it. This was supposed to be our day together and he's out running around with people he claims he don't like. Then he has the nerve to fuck me to make up. Anyway, back to now.

Anyway, I get out of jail, he doesn't have a way for me to get back to the motel. So I have to hitch-hike, yea! I'm completely lost now, I don't even know which street to get on. I'm in a pair of shorts and no shoes and it's 58 degrees. Finally I catch a ride with some total lunatic. He drives like a maniac. He's high, makes a bunk drug deal and we get shot at. I'm terrified. I get to the motel, tell this lunatic I have VD, and hurry to the room where my man that loves me has a roomful of people. He says "hi" and they all leave. In a few minutes he tells me to get ready to go to work. The first trick I get goes off, like I'm not already upset and scared enough. Second trick goes off. This man runs to the room yelling he'll kill the bastard, but of course he doesn't do anything, they're only talk. So I wish he'd hold me or at least give me some comfort, something. But he has to get back to the people I'm told he doesn't like. Later I call him and he passes out on the phone. I go in his room and another nigger is passed out with his arm on him. At least they had their clothes on. I took his ring and left them that way. I sleep in the trick room. He hurts me so much and I still stick by him. When I need him most he's never around. Like I believe he loves me, but he's so busy trying to prove he's a better pimp than everyone else that he forgets to care. I just wish he could take time out once in a while and talk to me about what I feel instead of what is happening between the other girls and their men. He's always so sure he knows what's going on with them that he doesn't notice us. "How do I love thee, let me count the ways." There aren't too many things to count. I don't love him anymore. I'm sure I never did. I just wanted to love someone. I used to like the excitement or challenge or whatever, now I hate it and I hate him for making me do it. I was wrong in thinking that a pimp and a prostitute could make a relationship. He still wants me to marry him. I guess I will. At least I'll always have someone there, even if I hate him. Who said you were supposed to be happy? I really am sick of all his shit. Do this, do that. I keep making up excuses for why I like him, but they're all lies. I don't know why I can't just kick him out. I try everything I can to get him to leave me and nothing works. When he kicks me out I leave and then he comes and gets me and like a fool I always go with him. I've never threatened to leave him, I don't know what he'd do. I'm so tired. I wish this sucker would let me sleep sometime. He makes me get up at 8:00 am every day, but he doesn't get up till noon and expects two or three hundred waiting for him. He makes me work till ten or eleven, but then he makes me stay awake till four or five. Or else he wakes me up to get him something to eat.

So confused about everything. All my feelings contradict themselves. My brain is so cluttered and yet it seems empty. I still care so much but feel like I'm cold. I trust and don't trust. I'm square and not square both and I don't feel like I'll ever fit in anywhere. I'm stuck between two worlds and divided between two worlds. I can't get in. I can't get out. I hate him for what he stands for and I really do miss parts of him. I get so mad cause no-one will listen then I don't speak when they do. It seems like I want bad things to happen to me. That's stupid. He was so affectionate and was always there. He gave me anything (almost) and pampered me, then I want to be left alone -- I'm terrified of being alone. I want to move. I want to stay. My insides hurt so bad I could die. Birds aren't as pretty as they used to be. I hurt and I don't know why. My whole life is a lie. I lie to the people I care about most. I don't mean to. "Oh yeah, I'm fine, I'm alright, I'm trooping." I really wish someone would just blow my fucking brains out, I don't want to die. I'm sick of all those sick fucking perverts. They're sick, sick, all of them, sick. How could they do that to me? I never hurt anyone. I never did anything to anyone. How could they do it? How? I'm sick of *not having anything to do. I'm sick of nightmares, why can't they leave me alone? Everyone: "Oh, I was so worried, oh we care." Mother fucker, don't care about me. You can't even spell my name right. About your being so worried, this is the first time you ever met me. BS you care, fuck you. I'm not impressed so why pretend? I'm tired of people fucking with my mind. At least with the tricks I know where I stand.*

There is so much besides the current point I'm making that is contained in this writing, much of which supports many of the concepts contained in this book, as well as many of the issues that we see in young people who have been sexually abused or are involved with commercialized sex. For example, those of us who work with this population know all too well the level of disassociation that youth experience in order to perform sexual acts, often reporting that they are not present during the act, but go "somewhere else." Notice how in this writing she talks about herself in the first person, except when she is reflecting on her "work" where she speaks in the third person, as though she is narrating someone else's life. She also ends with the statement "*at least with the tricks I know where I stand*," which is a point I made earlier as well as in a later chapter when I'm talking about why young people may prefer to stay with abusers rather than accept the help of non-abusers; because they are clear about the motives of the abusers and confused by the motives of the helpers. But my purpose in using this writing is to underscore the point that her involvement in the life is to some degree by volition, and if she has the power to choose involvement, she also has the power to choose to leave (which she eventually did).

Do not misconstrue what I'm saying as a "blame the victim" stance. Certainly within the broad population of CSEC youth there are those who are truly physically coerced and restrained, but I don't believe that they represent the majority of the population, or at least do not explain that segment of the population who *could* leave, but *do not*. Additionally, I am not denying that their "choice" is not the result of limited options and learned behavior. The psychological term for this is "learned helplessness," and it is often exemplified by a method of training elephants. The method involves tying the elephant to a stake with a heavy chain while they are young. The elephant struggles and pulls in an attempt to get free, but never can. Eventually, the elephant gives up even trying, at which point they can be secured with the most flimsy of ropes and stakes. Even though the elephant could now easily pull free, it still *believes* that it can't, so it no longer even tries. So my point is not that it is the youth's fault or an objective decision. My point is simply that they have the power and skill to free themselves if they *want to*, but to want to involves a change in self-image and identity. I simply believe that we do young people a greater service by helping them to *discover their power*, rather than teaching them to accept that they are *victims*. If we want to help them to break out of the trap of learned helplessness, they should not learn from us that they are helpless.

There is a final lesson that I'd like to draw from this young woman's writing that has to do with an *"aside"* I spoke to in the original text. I identified it as a *"small digression"* and dedicated a whole two paragraphs to it, focusing it mostly on a dark humor coping skill. I referred to it as the issue of Vicarious Traumatization (or VT, so labeled by Pearlman & Saakvitne), but it is also known by several other names[37]. Regardless of what it is called, it deserves much greater attention than I previously dedicated to it; both for our own health and for our ability to remain effective and helpful to the young people we serve.

Charles Wilson of the Chadwick Center for Children and Families stated that *"STS (Secondary Traumatic Stress) is one of the most pervasive and influential factors in child welfare, and yet few recognize its impact on the nature of the work, the ability of people to stay and prosper in the field, and the world view of the people who labor every day to serve this nation's children."* I absolutely agree with his perspective on the impact of STS on helpers and those being helped, its pervasiveness within the field, and … the point that makes us most at risk … how little STS is recognized and addressed among youth workers. Yet STS is and should be considered a serious occupational hazard with real and consequential impact upon the work that we do. No human being can work with a population of children who day in and day out expose you to realities of their lives on par with those related in this young woman's writing and not be psycho-emotionally impacted by that experience. And once impacted, it absolutely affects our work with young people depending upon the coping strategies that we have in place. In a best case scenario, good people may burn out and leave the field with unresolved traumas. Moving to the worst case side of the spectrum, our work may become more about our own trauma than the young person's, or we may cope by becoming so jaded and desensitized that we are of little help to the young people who need our compassion and support.

Secondary Traumatic Stress (STS) is defined as experiencing trauma-related effects caused by closely working with trauma-affected populations. The most important thing to realize is that you *will* experience STS if you work with any population that has experienced trauma. This is not a sign of weakness or a psycho-emotional deficit on your part, it is simply a fact. You cannot work with a trauma-affected population and not experience STS. Additionally, while I have no research-based evidence for this, my personal opinion is that the risk of STS is even greater in youth work than it is when working with some adult populations. The reason for this is two-fold. First, I think the risk is greater when working with populations that are *currently*

---

[37] Soul Sadness (Chessick); Compassion Fatigue (Figley); and, in most common use today, Secondary Traumatic Stress, or STS (Stamm).

experiencing trauma than it is with those who are dealing with the long-term *effects* of trauma. Most populations of at-risk youth are still dealing with trauma in their lives. Much as the impact of STS may be greater when working with *recently* traumatized adults (victims of natural disasters or persons who are coping with recent death or disease), the experience of working with young people who are still *experiencing* childhood trauma may be more impactful than that of working with adults who are dealing with the *aftermath* of childhood trauma. But the second reason has to do with the attraction of youth work. It is certainly not the pay or working conditions that draws people to the field. While this may not be the attraction for all youth workers, many are drawn to the field for *empathic* reasons, as they have survived their own childhood traumas. Depending on their personal level of self-awareness on this issue, they may be extremely vulnerable to STS when working with young people.

So it's important to realize that if you are in the youth work field STS is a clear and present occupational hazard. Regardless of how well or poorly adjusted you are, STS cannot be avoided or eliminated. It is much like being a deployed soldier; you cannot avoid or eliminate the stress of deployment. If you are in the youth work field, you cannot avoid or eliminate STS. So that's the bad news. Here's the good news. You can *minimize* and *mitigate* the negative effects of STS. Minimizing STS involves ensuring a work environment that does not contribute to or aggravate worker stress and trauma. Mitigating STS involves skills and supports that enhance worker effectiveness and reduce the secondary effects of working with trauma-affected populations. Both of these protections, however, begin with recognizing that STS is real and exists and employing intentional strategies to counter its impact.

While a detailed perspective on coping with STS is beyond the scope of this book, some of the best work in this area has been done by Laurie Anne Pearlman and Karen W. Saakvitne. Their work has identified four specific areas important to the management of STS. Two of these areas are strategies that should be adopted organizationally to support a youth work agency's workforce, and two are strategies that individual youth workers should focus on as part of their own personal safety plan.

The two organizational strategies are labeled Professional Strategies and Agency Strategies. Professional Strategies focus on providing your workers the structure that they need to accomplish their tasks in an environment in which they are exposed to STS. It involves providing the necessary training and preparation for them to do their jobs, as well as a safe and clear structure within which to work, adequate supervision and feedback, and assurance that job duties are balanced and manageable. If the working environment suffers from inadequate or ineffective training, structure and/or supervision, or a lack of clarity around job expectations and boundaries, the risk of STS upon your workforce will be greater. Similarly, Agency Strategies refers to the supports that are in place for your work force such as ensuring safe work environments, adequate resources, access to employee assistance, and recognition/appreciation including adequate compensation. When agency supports are inadequate, ineffective, or simply not attend to, you increase your workers vulnerability to STS.

Unfortunately, many agencies today have little or no recognition of STS and intentional strategies to protect their workers from STS are inadequate at best. This is particularly remarkable in that trauma-informed care is a growing focus within the youth work field, but such focus is almost exclusively on understanding the effects of trauma on the *client*, with little or no attention to the effects of STS on the *worker*. Until that dynamic changes it is critical that workers create a personal safety plan to protect themselves from the impact of STS.

The two strategies that should be part of every youth worker's personal safety plan[38] include Personal Strategies and General Coping Strategies. Personal strategies refers to self-awareness/self-care, including knowing and respecting your own limits, seeking assistance when needed, and personal techniques that help you keep yourself emotionally safe in an STS environment. Your vulnerability to STS is increased when you have inadequate or ineffective boundaries, do not create and utilize personal care techniques[39], and/or over-identification with young people and their trauma. Similarly, General Coping Strategies refers to your non-work related self-nurturing and connection to others. Your vulnerability to STS increases when you have inadequate or ineffective social and familial supports, and inadequate recreational and non-work related outlets. Basically, and to put it bluntly, *you need to have a life* outside of work and maintain appropriate boundaries between the two. Youth work is what you do and, to do it well, it cannot be all that you are.

---

[38] And ensuring that your workforce is utilizing these strategies should be part of your organization's Professional Strategies.

[39] Examples may include breathing exercises, 5 minute "vacations," or regular debriefing with co-workers.

The streets aren't under your feet; they're under your scalp.

Economic Concepts

We don't often consider the economics of street culture, though we are often confused by it. The fact is that a large percentage of the population we work with is involved in prostitution; with some of our youth committed to prostitution as a way of life. It is also true that, through prostitution, some of our youth have an immediate earning potential greater than many of us. It is possible to work the streets and, in a single night, make 3, 4, or 500 dollars. It begs the question; if they can make 500 bucks a night, what they hell do they need us for? Even with weekends off and vacations we're talking well over $100,000.00 a year, tax free. Why don't they just save their money for a couple of years, buy a Mercedes and a condo and retire?

To begin to understand this, you have to first understand that you can't buy your way off the streets, because we're not dealing with a socio-economic condition. We're dealing with a conceptual condition. The streets aren't under your feet; they're under your scalp. There is no amount of money or material possessions that are in and of themselves going to change street-developed concepts. But even if you understand this, it is a legitimate question to ask; where does their money go? Because the same youth who is capable of making a few hundred dollars a night through prostitution always seems to be broke. They're trying to bum money off of you to buy a pack of cigarettes, and they come to our programs for food and shelter. So what did they do with their money? If you or I had that earning ability without a mortgage or utility bills, we'd probably have something left in our pockets, yet street-dependent youth rarely seem to.

The Expense of Street Life
We have two misunderstandings that make it difficult for us to comprehend this issue. The first is our conception of how much money can be made through prostitution. While it's true that it is possible to make hundreds of dollars each night, it's also true that it is very rare that a young person actually makes that much. More often than not, they will pull dates until they have enough money to meet immediate needs, and then they'll quit. There may have been a time when they made $500, and from that point forward they will relate that they can make "up to 500 bucks a night." Literally speaking, that's true, although what isn't stated is that most nights

they're lucky if they make 50 bucks. The youth who is actually pulling in a steady income in the hundreds is usually the youth who is working for a pimp. In that case, they're not making a dime, since all of the money is turned over to the pimp.

But in addition to these factors, a second misunderstanding that we have when we attempt to confront this dilemma is that we underestimate the sheer expense of street life. It is not true that you can be poor in terms of cash flow and survive on the streets. Let's itemize some expenses. If you are going to seek shelter you have several options: a shelter program, a squat (or trespassing in an abandoned building), or a flea bag hotel. A prostitution-involved youth is often not ready for a shelter program, and, even if they are, most are filled beyond capacity anyway. This leaves a squat or a flea bag hotel; neither one of which is an acceptable option to a youth with money in his or her pocket. The next option, and the first acceptable one from their viewpoint, is a standard motel, where a room can easily cost you about $35.00 a night. You'll be buying your meals in restaurants, because you don't have a stove or refrigerator, which will run you at least $20.00 a day; and that's eating sparingly at fast food joints. And, while this is not a training specific to street drugs, accept for the moment the premise that drugs have a medicinal role within this culture. The fact is that after you've done what you need to do to get food in your stomach and a place to stay, you need help to dull the pain and numb the trauma. Drugs are tremendously helpful in achieving this goal. Even for a comparatively light user of pot and alcohol, keeping yourself adequately medicated can easily run you another $25.00 a day.

So let's total it up. All we've done is paid for shelter, had something to eat, and purchased a small quantity of drugs to help us cope, and we're already up to $80.00 a day to survive. We would need an annual, after tax income of $29,200.00, or a job paying more than $14.00 an hour after taxes, to maintain this lifestyle. And within these figures we haven't even considered money for transportation, or clothes, or any expenses beyond food, shelter, and drugs. Even if you are unwilling or unable to accept drugs into this calculation, they would still need an after tax income greater than $20,000.00 per year just for minimal food and shelter. Contrary to popular belief, survival on the streets is really quite expensive, and one of the primary reasons why their cash flow does not leave reservoirs in their pockets.

Economics as a Social Science

Another misunderstood factor has to do with economics as a science. The fact is that very few people actually understand how the economy works, and I would include many economists in this category. Personally, I'm fascinated by economics, and enjoy the study of it as a pastime. I believe that most people fail to enjoy economics because they believe it to be a dry, boring, physical science. I enjoy economics, however, because I've learned that it is not a physical science at all, and I enjoy it for the same reason that I enjoy the work I do with young people. Because the fact is that economics is a social science. We all have psychological and emotional needs that affect our economic decisions and a nation's economy is strongly governed by the psychology of its citizens.

Even many economists fail to understand this and tend to treat economics as if it were a physical science. One of my favorite diversions is paying attention to economic forecasts by professional economists. They sound extremely knowledgeable, and back up their predications with charts and graphs of various economic indicators. If you are able to remember their predictions, however, and see how they play out over time, you'll come to realize just how many economic predictions by supposedly learned professionals turn out to be wrong. The reason for this is that they fail to account for one of the most critical factors affecting their predictions, and that factor is people; their psychology, emotions, and the choices that they make in the face of changing circumstances.

The 1992 presidential election provides a good case study of what I mean. If you remember, the primary issue in that campaign was the economy. The Democrats were making the case that the economy was in trouble and getting worse. They had made it their rallying cry, and even posted *"It's the economy, stupid"* on the walls of their campaign strategy headquarters. It worked. Bill Clinton won the election on the public's belief that the economy was broken and Bill Clinton could fix it. That was November 1992. On January 12th, 1993, I watched a news report on the economic turn-around we were experiencing. The lead-in to the story was; *"Since the election of Bill Clinton the economy has begun to show improvement in almost every area."* I don't argue the truth of that statement. The economy was indeed improving since the election. The important thing to realize, however, is that Bill Clinton was not sworn into office to assume the presidency until January 20th, 1993; more than a week *after* that report. Yes, the economy was getting better, but Bill Clinton and the Democrats hadn't done a damn thing! The economy was improving because the American people believed that if Bill Clinton was elected the economy would improve. It was our belief, which in turn governed our actions, and not government economic policy that was responsible for the improvement.

Economics and Psycho-emotional Needs

The fact is that economics and psychology are inseparably connected, and we all have psycho-emotional needs that we meet through economics. If I have a bad day at work I can make myself feel better by spending money on myself. This is how many people get into extreme debt. Economics can be like drugs and alcohol in that respect and, if abused, can have similar devastating effects. On the positive side, economics can also be used for self-reward for accomplishments, and your economic status can make a difference in your ability to cope with stress. If I have a few dollars in my pocket, it's easier to deal with that difficult phone call knowing that I can go out and get a cup of coffee afterwards. Stress relief through impulse spending can actually get quite expensive. I remember a time when I was making efforts to get my own spending under control and I began by paying attention to what my spending habits were. For two weeks I tracked every penny I spent. I asked for and saved receipts from every purchase and, if I couldn't get a receipt, wrote the expenditure down in a book that I carried. At the end of two weeks I totaled up the money I had spent on impulse; a little here for coffee, a little there for a snack, a quarter for a phone call; to learn how much money I was just pissing away on small purchases. I was both shocked and appalled at how much money it was. It was no wonder I was having trouble making ends meet, my finances were hemorrhaging in purchases of less than a dollar each! It inspired me to action, and I immediately stopped getting receipts.

For whatever reason, the vast majority of people face challenges in the area of spending and budgeting. And right now I'm talking about regular, average people who are fairly well adjusted and manage to establish secure and steady lives with their basic needs reasonably met. When you move the psychology of economics out onto the streets, you are now looking at adolescents with little experience with money, who have little or no future concept, little or no incentive to budget, and the psychological and emotional needs they have that can be met through economics are far more desperate than that of the average person. They are a population characterized by poor self-image and low self-esteem, who survive in an environment where they feel disrespected, shunned, and abandoned by the society in which they live. But when they walk up to a cash register with a ten dollar bill in their hand, suddenly people acknowledge them, address them as "sir" or "ma'am," and ask if there's anything else that they'll be needing. Economics is the way in which they can literally buy respect, and having money in their pocket gives them the power to do this.

Economics and Power

Buying respect is just one of the power associations to money. The reality is that in our society today money is power. For the purpose of our discussion here it's not even relevant whether that's good or bad, it just is and we should acknowledge the fact of it. When you have money, you have the ability to make things happen, and the more money you have, the more power to make things happen you possess. When a street-dependent youth has money you will often see them use it in a way that exercises immediate power to affect change. A young man I worked with received a $75.00 check one day. I don't recall where the check came from, and it's really not important, anyway. What is important is that this youth had nothing. He was sleeping under a bridge and his worldly possessions were limited to the clothes on his back. Even though $75.00 wouldn't do much to improve his situation, it's still revealing what he decided to do with it. He gathered up several of his friends and took them out for a steak dinner at Sizzler. Two hours later he was completely broke again, but for those two hours he had the power to make his life and other people's lives a little bit better.

The street culture exists in part as a result of powerless people trying to capture some measure of power and control in their lives, yet compared to the society around them they remain in a powerless position. The fact that everybody but them seems to have power would be almost unbearable to a street-dependent youth if it weren't for one thing; they have learned that they need not be as powerless as we may think. In some respects they can be far more powerful because they've learned that they have the power to get our power. How? All they have to do is climb into a car and engage in an act of prostitution. Through that act, they can capture the power of people who ordinarily wouldn't give them the time of day. The actual exchange is money, but that money represents the power we have and, through prostitution, they can take it away from us. In many ways, power, not economics, is the issue in adolescent prostitution. You will see that in the fact that once the money has been acquired it has often served its purpose. After that, the only thing it's good for is buying respect, helping them to help their friends (remember the "*my friend needs help*" syndrome) or for one other purpose. This last one may be difficult to understand, but they are able to use money to "cleanse" themselves, that is, to pass on the degradation of the lifestyle so that it doesn't cling to them.

Psychological Attachments to Money

In order to understand this final point all we have to do is to realize that we all have psychological attachments to our money. Money represents ideas, concepts, and feelings to us, and it is not uncommon for us to receive a certain amount of validation through money. I know that when I pull a dollar out of my wallet, that dollar makes me feel good about myself. It represents the programs I create, the work I do with young people, and the trainings and presentations I give. I feel that I've made a contribution and made the world a slightly better place, and that dollar is my concrete validation of these ideas. I feel good about myself, and I feel good about that dollar. When a street-dependent youth, earning money through prostitution, takes a dollar out of their pocket, they see a blow job, or an ass fuck. It's degrading, and disgusting, and they can be overwhelmed with the need to get rid of it, to pass it on and, with it, to pass on the feeling of disgust that they attach to it.

I once ran a support group for female adolescents involved in prostitution. At some point they learned that I did trainings for staff and they asked if I would do one for them to give them the opportunity to see what kind of information staff was operating with. I agreed to do it, and picked this presentation as the one I would do for them. It was a fascinating experience that promoted much discussion for weeks, but the presentation itself stopped at this point and was never finished. When I started talking about psychological attachments to money the presentation broke down into group counseling as everyone in the group started sharing experiences and their attitudes about money. It was like I had turned on a light bulb in everybody's head. One girl shared that her pattern was to immediately give her money away, stating that she would get out of the car, walk down the street, and simply pass the money out. In her words, she said:

"*I used to just get rid of it just as quickly as I got it. I didn't understand why I was doing that, 'cause I wouldn't have no money. But I'd pull a date, and then I'd just give the money away.*"

The reason why she did it was that it helped to cleanse her. By giving away the money, she was giving away the degradation that it represented.

Money obtained through street-survival activities; prostitution, drugs, petty theft; is viewed by street-dependent youth as somehow different from the money that you and I have. It is tainted by the manner in which it is obtained. There was a time early in my career when I was working with a youth who had a legitimate immediate need for $40.00. This was long before there was the level of support services that exists today, and the reality was that if she was going to get $40.00 to meet this need, it meant that I was going to give it to her out of my own pocket. I have a personal policy that I never, ever, lend youth money. I never personally lend them anything. There have been situations, however, when a program was not able to provide for a legitimate need, that I have given them things. I refuse to make it a loan because I don't ever want money or property to be a factor in our relationship, or for a youth to not come to see me because they feel guilty about $10.00. So if I ever make a decision to allow a youth to have anything that is mine, I have to first decide that I am absolutely OK with never seeing it again.

Anyway, I made the decision to give her $40.00. Even though I was clear that this was a gift, not a loan, she still insisted that she was going to return it someday. About a month later things began to fall apart for her again and she went back to prostitution. This particular girl was pretty professional in her prostitution activities and was generating quite a large cash flow. I continued to have regular contact with her through this period and, despite the fact that she was rather flamboyant with her resources, she never once attempted to pay back the $40.00. This, of course, was not an issue with me, as I had forgotten it as soon as I had given her the money. But after almost a year she was making another attempt to get off the streets and out of prostitution. She got a job at McDonalds and she came to me with her very first paycheck, which was not for very much, and wanted to pay the money back. The difference was that the money in this paycheck was "good" money, clean and untainted, and therefore equal in value to the money I had given her. But she never of dreamed of trying to pay me back with "whore" money. That money was dirty, and of lesser value than the money that she had received from me.

Summary

Taking all of these factors into consideration you can begin to get an idea of why street-dependent youth seem to be able to get by, but lack the ability to get ahead. It's a mistake to believe that before we provided shelter for youth they weren't able to find a place to sleep. It's a mistake to believe that before we had programs to feed them they weren't able to find a way to eat. Certainly the manner in which they met these basic needs on their own is often unhealthy for both them and the community. But they can survive without us; they don't need us to get by. They desperately need us to get ahead, however, because the economics of the streets is a spider web that keeps you trapped in a downward spiral.

Key Points - Economic Concepts

- You can't buy your way off of the streets. Financial status alone will not transition youth out of street life, and living on the streets is often more expensive than a stable lifestyle.
- Economics is a social science, and we all have psychological and emotional needs that are met through economics.
- Street-dependent youth use economics to meet needs for respect and power, and to "cleanse" themselves from the degradation of the street lifestyle.

2.0 Commentary:

What jumped out at me most when I reread this chapter on economics is the change in our language and the value of our money since the original writing. As I've referenced elsewhere, the term "prostitution" related to youth has been replaced with references to "commercial sexual exploitation." The dollar values I mention seem almost nostalgic, as what I could purchase for one dollar when this book was first issued (1998) would cost me $1.41 in today's (2013) dollars, and every time the government prints money ("Quantitative Easing") the value of the dollar falls. This, in fact, is the true definition of inflation, which most people mistakenly understand as the *cost* of items going *up*. Inflation actually represents the *value* of your dollar going *down*. What I could buy for a dollar when I was born (1952) now costs $8.66. In some cases, what we think of as "higher" costs is actually goods and services becoming *cheaper*. If I'm paying $5.00 for a hamburger that cost me $1.00 when I was born, I can complain that it's $4.00 more expensive … when actually it should have cost me $3.66 *more* than that to represent the same dollar value, so its cost has actually gone *down*.

This is one of the main causes of people struggling and poverty rates growing, particularly among the working. If you were making $40,000.00 annually when this book first came out and you received a 2% COLA[40] every year, today you would be making $54,911.00. However, to equal the *spending power* of your original $40,000.00 salary you would need to be making $56,400.00. In other words, steady, 2% increases in salary since 1998 has *reduced* your spending power by about $100.00 per year, simply because the *value* of the dollars you are earning has *decreased*.

But this is not a book about politics or economics, except as it relates to the psychology of street-dependent youth. And while the economy has changed the landscape of our markets as we are still impacted by the effects of the recession that consensus believes began in December of 2007, the different landscape doesn't change many of the underlying premises of the original text. Economics is still a *social* science, and our ability to come out of this recession has been strongly influenced by people's *beliefs* and *emotions*. There is a tremendous amount of capital being held in reserve due to the fact that people are uncertain about future tax rates and other government actions. This money is not being spent, which would go a long way to digging us out of the recession, due solely to the fact that people are *uncertain*. The reason the money is not being released is not due to "the economy," it is due to people's fear and uncertainty about the future. That's a *social psychology*, not an *economic*, reason.

Where the original text discusses the psychology of a youth's reaction to different economic circumstances, particularly related to how a youth gets their money, the points made remain valid. What is different from the original text are some of the economic circumstances described.

Again, this is not a book about politics or economics, so the particular psycho-social relationship to an economic stimulus that I would like to highlight in this new edition has to do with a condition that has developed

---

[40] Cost Of Living Adjustment. Federal COLA's were 2-3% throughout the '90's. In 2013 the federal COLA is 1.7%.

over the years that, while on many levels could be considered a positive, has created some negative unintended consequences -- consequences that, as is so often the case, are too easily dismissed as a problem with the *young people*. The truth, however, is that they are reacting to economic circumstances that *we* have created, and they are simply exhibiting rational and predictable responses to the environments that we create for them.

Here's the good side of the equation. Many areas have developed comprehensive continuums of care for street-dependent youth. Running the spectrum of services from street outreach, to drop-in, to shelter, to transitional and independent living, and including wrap-around services from case management to physical and mental health care; these services often also include high levels of incentives and subsidies as a basis for engagement and retention. In the most developed systems a youth can get everything they need with little or no requirements or commitments on their part. As long as they are willing to receive the services, the system is willing to offer those services. Here are the complaints I hear from people working in such systems: so many of the "kids today" appear ungrateful and entitled, and many seem disinterested in changing their lives or getting off of the streets, often simply aging out of the youth systems and into the adult systems. These complaints, of course, are presented as "problems" with the *young people*. To some degree, however, it may be problems with *our systems* to which the young people are naturally adapting.

Let me use an analogy. The United States Nation Park Service bans feeding wildlife in all national parks, partly to protect visitors by ensuring that wildlife does not get too "comfortable" around humans. But it is not simply to protect the human visitors; it is to protect the animals themselves. The following is a direct quote from The National Park Service website[41]:

"Animals that are fed by people become dependent on human food, and may lose their natural fear of humans and their ability to forage for natural foods. There is a lot of truth to the saying, "a fed animal is a dead animal."

The website goes on to say that they have had to euthanize animals, including deer, coyotes, and rock squirrels because they have become aggressive toward humans or *"completely dependent on food handouts."*

Street-dependent youth are not wildlife, and I am not insinuating that we treat them as such. But we are all animals in the strictest sense, and as such we react and adapt to our environment. When we give too much and ask too little in return we create *dependency* at best and we perpetuate their circumstance at worst. It should come as no surprise to us that a system that subsidizes and provides everything sees many young people exiting the youth system for the adult system with little change in their ability to provide for themselves[42].

---

[41] http://www.nps.gov/grca/naturescience/wildlife_alert.htm

Of course, these concepts are not new. 250 years ago Benjamin Franklin made similar observations when he wrote:

"I am for doing good to the poor, but I differ in opinion of the means. I think the best way of doing good to the poor, is not making them easy in poverty, but leading or driving them out of it. In my youth I travelled much, and I observed in different countries, that the more public provisions were made for the poor, the less they provided for themselves, and of course became poorer. And, on the contrary, the less was done for them, the more they did for themselves, and became richer[43]."

Even before Franklin made that observation there was the Chinese proverb attributed to Lao Tzu some 6,000 years ago:

"Give a man a fish and you feed him for a day. Teach a man to fish and you feed him for a lifetime[44]."

One of my former adolescent clients, now in her 40's, was reflecting on what was helpful and what was unhelpful about the service system when she was on the streets. One of the main services being offered was a drop-in service that provided for basic needs with absolutely no strings attached. As long as you didn't create problems in the center, you could access it for as long as you wished, years even, for food, clothing, and other basic needs. She told me that, in retrospect, the *least* helpful thing to her were those unlimited, no strings attached basic needs, because it made it so that she could survive on the streets without having to make any changes in her life. It was only when she went to another city where such services were not available that she had to make efforts to meet those needs herself, and living on the streets became extremely challenging. She didn't get off of the streets because her basic needs were being met; she got off the streets when she lost her unrestricted access to basic needs.

Of course, we are talking shades of gray here, not black and white principles. I am not saying that we should do away with services for youth or that no youth have been helped by the services we have created. I'm simply saying that good intentions do not always correlate with good results, and it is incumbent upon us to constantly consider and review the means by which services are provided in order to reduce negative unintended consequences. Provision of basic needs in and of itself is not a bad thing, but it is not enough and needs to be offered in support of other efforts. Our indicator should be when we see behaviors in young people that we find distasteful, such as a preference for remaining involved in street life or a sense of ingratitude and entitlement. It is inaccurate and

---

[42] I mentioned a similar concern in an earlier chapter when I talked about our approach being one of "homelessness" sometimes resulting in youth accepting a "homeless" identity.

[43] Ben Franklin; Relating to Prices and the Poor, 1766

[44] This quote is sometimes misattributed to Jesus, but it actually appears nowhere in the Bible. Its first appearance in western culture was in 1885 in *Mrs. Dymond*, a novel by Anne Isabella Thackeray Ritchie, when one of her characters stated *"if you give a man a fish he is hungry again in an hour. If you teach him to catch a fish you do him a good turn."*

counter-productive to blame young people for these behaviors. It is only helpful when we use these observations as flags for us to examine our own practice.

For example, much of the entitled attitude that we find so offensive can be directly related to an over-reliance on or misapplication of incentives and subsidies. I wrote about this in an article I published in 2007. Instead of saying the same all over again, I'll simply reprint the article here.

Carrot Pro's and Con's
A reflection on the use of incentives in youth programs

Let me ask you a question. Are knives good or bad? The answer, of course, is; it depends. Cut me a slice of bread, and knives are good. Cut my throat ... not so good. This is my attitude toward the use of incentives in youth programs. Whether they are helpful or harmful depends a great deal on why and how they are being used. Yet in my experience, youth programs are often unaware of the fact that incentives have the potential for harm and, therefore, incentives are sometimes implemented with insufficient thought given to the impact they may have. Programs should always be aware that incentives, when used inappropriately, can go well beyond benign ineffectiveness and enter into the realm of doing harm. Before implementing incentives in your program, you may wish to consider the following potential pitfalls.

Pitfall #1: Incentives may treat the symptom rather than the disease.

Usually when incentives are being discussed it is because young people are not doing something that we want them to do. They are not showing up, or they are not participating adequately from our perspective, or they are not accomplishing the goals we wish them to accomplish. So we seek to encourage their efforts by offering monetary rewards, goods, or services. While this often alleviates to some degree the issues of lack of attendance, participation, or accomplishment, it doesn't address in any way the problem(s) responsible for these issues.

Basic Youth Development practice asserts that young people can and will be involved, participatory, and accomplished if they are given legitimate and relevant opportunities. If you accept this assertion (as I do), then where issues with attendance, participation, or accomplishment exist, the problem is a lack of legitimacy or relevance with the opportunity. Offering incentives does not address this problem. Instead, when incentives work, they allow us to avoid addressing the problem by substituting entitlement for legitimacy or relevance. While this may solve the issue, it doesn't solve the problem, and it relieves us of the responsibility for designing opportunities that are legitimate and relevant to a young person's needs. We may see an increase in attendance, participation, or accomplishment, but are we really doing a service for the young person? Do the increases that we see really mean anything to the young person's life?

I once interviewed a young woman who explained to me in very precise detail the *minimum* efforts she needed to make in order to collect the equivalent of $350.00 per month from various youth program incentives. This was the extent of the benefit of these various involvements, from her perspective. If the goal of these programs is to ensure that this young woman has access to $350.00 per month, and knows what hoops she needs to jump through to collect it, then these incentive programs are working well. I suspect, however, that the programs have different goals in mind, in which case the incentives may be more problematic than they are productive.

Using incentives to substitute for the challenging work of addressing a program's legitimacy and relevance to the young people it serves is a lazy way of providing service, and can end up being more of a disservice than anything else.

Pitfall #2: Incentives may act as a form of exploitation.
The main focus of my work is with street-dependent youth. Many of these youth fall prey to adults through prostitution and other forms of exploitation. While no population of young people should ever be exploited by adults, this population is particularly impacted by exploitation, requiring programs and care givers who accept the responsibility for interacting with them to be vigilant against any activities that may be exploitive.

Let me put forth a premise, as my position on this is grounded in this premise. A program that doesn't teach young people new skills and new coping mechanisms fails the young people it serves by reinforcing street-developed concepts rather than teaching new ones. This is my problem with programs that are based on removing choice and control from young people, despite any short-term results they may achieve. Mandate a young person to a staff-controlled environment where they are told what to do and when to do it, and you will probably see accomplishment and progress, at least while the young person is in the program. Such programs, however, have notoriously high recidivism rates, and most street outreach programs can talk about the successful graduates from mandated, structured programs who end up back on the streets after their successful "graduation." Why? Because the program is doing the same thing the pimp is doing -- taking control of the young person's life and making their choices and decisions for them. It works for the pimp, and it works for the program, at least in terms of getting the young person's compliance with what you want them to do. The difference, of course, is that the pimp wants compliance with negative behaviors and the program wants compliance with positive behaviors, but the lesson learned by the young person in both cases is that someone else is responsible for their choices and decisions, and when the structure is removed (they graduate) all they know is how to do is what someone tells them to do -- so they gravitate towards that same dynamic, which usually means a return to the streets.

But is it really fair to compare incentives to exploitation? Yes, if exploitation is the basis of the exchange. When we speak of exploitation, we are talking about a situation where a young person is facing a choice that serves needs other than theirs. On the streets this usually takes the form of some kind of transaction. In order to meet an adult's need for power, sex, or opportunity, something the young person desires is offered, such as money, shelter, or relative safety. This is how the street economy operates. I give you my body (service, sex, whatever), and you give me my survival (money, food, shelter, protection). Street-dependent youth understand and accept this basis of exchange. They are comfortable with it -- but it is not a good deal for them. It is exploitation, and they need to learn how to survive differently and be given opportunities to do so.

Now, let's look at the basis of many youth program incentives. We have a need (meeting contract or self-imposed goals for attendance, participation, or accomplishment) and we offer money, goods, or services to meet these needs. The young people offer their body (by showing up, participating, and/or meeting goals), and we, in exchange, offer them survival (by providing the incentive). What is the difference between this exchange and those that they engage in on the streets? It is the same as the difference between a pimp and a mandated program -- one exploits for negative motivation and one exploits for positive motivation. But the principle involved is the same and we end up perpetuating negative concepts and behaviors rather than changing them. Look at any youth service system that has a high reliance on incentives, and I guarantee you that staff will be complaining about the attitude of entitlement that the young people exhibit. But this attitude of entitlement is not due to something "wrong" with them; it is a result of us relying on exploitive manipulations to meet our program's needs. Incentive programs run the risk of creating the very attitudes and behaviors that we claim to dislike. In a very real sense, we get what we pay for. But far worse is the danger that we reinforce beliefs and behaviors that need to be challenged for a young person to successfully exit street life.

Pitfall #3: Incentives may reinforce negative beliefs about young people.

Much of my point here is an extension of what has already been said above, but as our beliefs about the young people we serve have a direct impact on our success with them, this point deserves its own attention. I've already talked about how incentives may breed entitlement and we can end up blaming the young person for an attitude and behavior that we've perpetuated. But an even greater danger lies in the beliefs that may be created when incentives don't work. And, contrary to conventional wisdom, they often don't.

There are two major ways that incentives can fail. Either they don't resolve the issue (e.g., they don't increase attendance, participation, or accomplishment) or they resolve the issue unsatisfactorily (e.g., attendance is sporadic, participation is limited, or accomplishments are half-hearted). In both cases the problem is one of a basic cost/benefit analysis on the part of the young person. Is the benefit (incentive) equal to or greater than the cost (what I have to give up or do to receive the incentive)? Note that nowhere in this equation is the legitimacy or relevance of the opportunity, we are simply competing with what it is worth to the young person to sell us their body instead of doing something else (hanging with their friends, engaging in street drama, earning money illegally). Since most programs have limited resources for incentives the question often becomes -- do I make a bunch of money selling drugs, prostituting, or stealing, or do I show up at this program thing for some secondhand clothes, a movie pass, or some McDonald's coupons? Hmmm, that's a tough choice. In fact, if this is the quality of the incentives we have to offer, we rarely can compete with simply hanging with friends.

The bottom line is that most programs cannot afford to offer incentives that rise to the level where they can win in a cost/benefit analysis, which means that incentives often fail to result in satisfactory resolution of the attendance, participation, and accomplishment problems we are attempting to address. At the same time incentives may directly impact beliefs and behaviors that we don't like to see. The result is that we begin to blame the young people for their lack of commitment and enthusiasm, if not outright dislike them for their unpleasant attitudes. Once we arrive there, we're really not in a position to be much help at all.

Pitfall #4: Incentives may be insulting.

A young woman I knew was involved in a community committee looking at services for homeless youth. The adults involved, outside of the committee and without consulting her, decided that it was unfair that the adults were attending as part of their paid time while she was attending essentially as a volunteer. To correct this injustice they decided that she would be given $20.00 every time she attended and, at the next meeting, she was informed of their decision. That was the last meeting she attended.

The fact is that it was important to her to be attending as a volunteer. She felt that the services had done so much for her that she wanted to give back. When she was told that she was, in effect, no longer a volunteer, she no longer had the reason she was attending.

This is a subtle form of insult; to make assumptions about the participant's motivations without their input and to reduce something that is priceless (a motivation to give back to your community) to something as valueless as 20 bucks. Now consider that 20 bucks is probably considerably more than most programs offer as an incentive and try to imagine the impact that has on the receiver. How much value am I going to place on my attendance, participation, or accomplishments if the value you place on them is a coupon for a Big Mac? Rather than a reward or compensation it can feel like an insult, and instead of gratitude we see resentment. This brings us back to Pitfall #3. Since we don't understand why our magnanimous efforts are being received with resentment, we conclude that we must be working with ungrateful little snots.

The good news about incentives.

This is not to say that incentives are all bad and never have a place in youth services. One of the best programs I know has incentives as a major component of its design. But I am trying to make the point that incentives can be a double-edged sword and that they can be as harmful as they can be helpful. Recognizing this means that programs have a responsibility to use incentives in a considered, careful manner, and to ensure that any incentive offered is based on the positive potential of incentives while avoiding the negative pitfalls described above.

A positive application of incentives assures that they are being used to *alleviate barriers* rather than to substitute for legitimacy and relevance. Things like offering child care to support attendance, reimbursement for costs of transportation, or even services such as food or shelter to relieve a need to seek them elsewhere may be justifiable uses for incentives. The key is that the incentive is related to the *barrier* and in support of a young person's *desire for the opportunity*, rather than being tied to the program's needs or an attempt to *create* a desire for the opportunity. Instead of "I will pay you for doing this for me" the offer becomes "If you wish to do this, I will compensate your costs."

In Conclusion
If you are thinking about incentives realize that you are playing with an idea that has potential for harm. Incentives can be very helpful if they are compensating for the cost of a young person's desire to do something, but very dangerous if they are being used to create the desire. Ensure that the incentive is a reasonable and justified compensation that removes a barrier preventing a young person from doing something that they wish to do and you have a positive incentive program. Use the incentive as a way of bribing the young person to do something that you want and the incentive program may end up creating more problems than it solves.

The most important point to remember from all of this, old text and new text alike, is that when looking at the issues related to "homeless" and often simply at-risk youth, our greatest challenge is not socio-economic conditions, it is the youth's conceptual view of themselves and their world. As I've said many times, the streets are not under your feet, they're under your scalp. Anything we do in the provision of goods and services should be viewed less through the lens of how it affects them economically and more through the lens of how it affects them psychologically. To paraphrase that old Chinese proverb; meet a youth's basic needs and they survive for a day ... teach a youth to meet their own needs and they survive for a lifetime. This is one of the reasons why I am such an advocate for Positive Youth Development principles and practices in youth programming. In its most simplistic form, PYD is about reducing that which we do *to* or *for* young people and replacing it with things that are done *by* young people *with* our guidance and support. It is a "teaching people to fish" approach that avoids many of the unintended consequences of a "rescue the victims" design that permeates many of today's youth programs.

If a person's concept of ownership does not include their own body and life, you can forget about talking to them about shoplifting.

Concepts of Property & Ownership

Concepts of property and ownership are often responsible for the more challenging aspects of working with street-dependent youth. One of the innocent behaviors related to property and ownership concepts that many find confusing is a youth's apparent inability to hold on to possessions. You'll often see youth gathering large amounts of possessions and then abandoning them all, or simply not having them the next day without good explanation, or even seeming to care.

At our emergency shelter program it's not uncommon for guests to fill their lockers with as much stuff as they can get their hands on, and then leave it all behind (we recently removed 1,640 pounds of abandoned possessions!). We saw this behavior at the drop-in center as well, where our original philosophy was to have clothes available for youth and, if they needed them, to let them have unlimited access. It was only a matter of days before we saw that, under this policy, a youth would be coming in and getting 8 or 9 complete outfits, literally as much as they could carry, and returning the next day in need of clothes again. Staff was left scratching their heads trying to figure out what had happened to the wardrobe they had picked up yesterday. In less than a week we were putting a limit on how often they could access clothes and how many they could take.

Property and ownership concepts are also responsible for less innocent behaviors. Many of the criminal activities in which street-dependent youth participate, including the lack of respect that they can show for private property, and the ease with which they justify shoplifting, vandalism, and other forms of theft, are directly a result of their concept of property and ownership.

"Getting Your Buttons Pushed"

To momentarily get off of the point, I'd like to caution you that you have some specific values and beliefs that will be challenged in your work with street-dependent youth. I don't know what yours are, but I know that you have them. We all do. There are things that you feel strongly about that street-dependent youth will challenge, either intentionally or as a consequence of their behaviors. The official term for this is *"getting your buttons pushed."* I guarantee you that, regardless of what your particular issue is, you *will* get your buttons pushed. When that happens, unless you have trained yourself to realize that this is your issue, not theirs, you will stop *responding* to their needs and begin *reacting* from yours.

I speak from experience on this. I have very strong beliefs about property rights, and yet I work with a criminalized population that breaks into cars, vandalizes, and shoplifts. For me, early in my career, these behaviors became the issue. My work wasn't about their survival or their histories of abuse, or their need for support and working with their self-esteem; it wasn't even about helping them to transition off of the streets and to create a safe, stable, healthy life; *it was about getting the little bastards to stop fuckin' stealing!* I made a lot of mistakes, and was forced to confront the issue only when it became apparent that what I was doing wasn't working. The young people I was working with weren't getting better, and they kept failing to live up to my belief system.

I once heard a definition that described insanity as continuing to do what hasn't worked in the past with the expectation of different results. So, when I got tired of wishing that they were different, and decided that I wasn't willing to dismiss them simply because they weren't living up to my standards, I resolved to understand why they acted the way they did and learn what I could change in *my* behavior that would help them. You will go through the same process. It doesn't matter what your issue is; drugs, domestic violence, sexism, prostitution, parental control; whatever it is, be prepared to face the same choice I did. If you want to be successful, you'll have to eventually examine *your* behavior as closely as you do theirs.

So, to get back on track, opening myself to learning about how street-dependent youth understood property and ownership was an incredible learning experience. One of the things that I learned is that all property and ownership concepts, yours, mine, and street-dependent youth's, are based upon a core belief system. Unless and until you work with this core belief system, you can talk to people about property rights, you can talk to people about the immorality of stealing, and you can send people to all the little anti-theft and "thinking error" programs you can find. None of it on its own will have any effect on their behavior. The change must take place in their core belief system before you will see any change in their choices, decisions, and actions.

Basis of Property/Ownership Beliefs

The core belief I am referring to has to do with how you answer this question; *Do you believe that you have absolute control and ownership over your own body and your own life?* The closer you get to an absolute "YES" with no hesitation; to a firm, unquestioned belief in control and ownership of your body and life; the more firmly you will respect property rights and refrain from stealing, cheating, vandalism, and other dishonest or criminal behaviors. The closer you come to answering this question "NO," the more you will disrespect and de-value property rights. You, of course, are encouraged to think about this and reach your own conclusions, but for the moment I ask that you accept this premise as true, because if it is true it explains much of the property related behavior you will see with street-dependent youth. The fact is that when you're dealing with young people with histories of sexual and physical abuse, who are surviving on the streets through prostitution, and who believe the world is random and out of their control, you are dealing with a human being whose concept of ownership does not apply to their own body or their own life. Your body is simply a commodity, a resource for other people to use and exploit. If a person's concept of ownership does not include their own body and life, you can forget about talking to them about shoplifting. You may have heard the saying; *never try to teach a pig to sing, it will only frustrate you and irritate the pig*. Well, that's what you're doing when you try to educate street-dependent youth on the value of property. It makes no sense to them, and you're simply wasting your breath.

That doesn't mean that it's hopeless and there is nothing we can do. Rather, it means that the way to address these issues is to clearly understand how property and ownership concepts function within the culture of the streets, and to begin to address behavior issues by working with the core belief system. In other words, if you want them to stop stealing, teach them how to set personal boundaries and to take charge of their lives.

Street Property/Ownership Concepts

A street-dependent youth's concept of ownership can be captured in the expression *"possession is 9/10s of the law."* That's an expression that could easily have been developed on the streets. It is a simple explanation for how ownership feels in the street culture. If you possess it, it's yours. As simplistic as that sounds, it truly does come down to *possession equals ownership*. A youth will be in a department store, pick up an object that they like, walk around with it a bit, and then attempt to leave the store with it, sometimes making little effort to hide the fact that they're walking out with it. When they are confronted by security for shoplifting, if you pay attention to the youth's behavior it will often seem as though the guard is attempting to take something from *them*. Even though they may be able to realize that they are stealing, there is also a part of them really feels that since they possess the object, it does, or should, belong to them.

The Issue of Touch

If we are to influence their concept of property and ownership to where we can begin to see new behaviors, we have to start at the root of these concepts. We will not be successful by discussing the morality of stealing or property rights. We first must help them to learn that they have absolute control and ownership over their own bodies and lives. One of the primary ways that we do this is by ensuring that we respect their right to exercise that control and ownership by setting boundaries, and one of the first things to consider is the issue of touch. I want to be clear that I am an advocate of "touch therapy." I strongly believe that street-dependent youth, like all adolescents, need and benefit from healthy and appropriate physical contact with adults. But I also strongly believe that all such contact must be unquestionably on their terms, and with their conscious permission. Our behavior around issues of touch must model and communicate that they have absolute, unquestioned authority over who touches them, when, where, and how.

This area in particular is where I often see good people with the best of intentions, people who have nothing but love and concern for young people and want only the best for them, make horrible mistakes without realizing it. I see it in people who care about youth and just want them to know that they are loved and accepted, and they show that by walking up to them and hugging them, or taking them by the hand, or touching their shoulders. It makes me cringe, because I know that their sincere efforts to help are doing harm. They may be trying to communicate love, acceptance, and concern, but they are also communicating; "*I decide when to touch you, I decide how to touch you, and my touching you is not your choice or decision.*" Programs I operate have clear policies that any and all physical contact must unquestionably be on the youth's terms and with the youth's permission. And I'm serious when I say that you have to *ask*.

This can be new and difficult for us. When a youth approaches our streetwork teams asking if they have a fever, it's our natural reaction to place our hand on their forehead. But we have to ignore our natural reaction, and train ourselves to ask permission through statements such as; "*I would need to put my hand on your forehead to tell, is that OK with you?*" And this can also be new and difficult for the youth. They're not used to giving permission to touch, and they can react confused or frustrated. "*Well, fucking yeah you can touch my forehead, duh! How else you gonna tell if I have a temperature?*" But you still go through the process of getting permission, because the new concept you are trying to communicate to them is that you would *never* assume that you have any right to touch them in any way without their consent.

This can be hard to do sometimes. One of my programs is an emergency overnight shelter. We have 30 youth who are crashed out sound asleep, sometimes coming off of drugs, and we have to wake them up and get them out by 9:00 in the morning when the program closes. Yet staff is not allowed to touch them. You can't put your hand on their shoulder and shake them a little bit to help wake them up, because you can't ask somebody who is sleeping for permission to touch them. So you have to be a little more creative than physically waking them. I would add as an aside here that there are other reasons to wake youth non-physically. Sleep can be terrifying for street-dependent youth. Nightmares and night frights are common occurrences. Youth may wake up aggressively, and with physical contact they may wake up lashing out. It's best for everyone if your morning intervention is done from arm's length.

Power and Touch

There are power issues that also play a role in the issue of touch. Remember that power is a core issue with street-dependent youth. When you look at how touch is initiated between people, you learn that the general rule is that touch is initiated by the person with greater power. You don't walk into the Board Room as an employee and go around touching all the Board Members, but it's not uncommon for a Board Member to walk into your work environment and pat people on the back, put a hand on their shoulder, and initiate other small contacts. Every time you initiate touch with a street-dependent youth without gaining their permission, you not only communicate that it is you who decides when and how they are touched, you also communicate that you get to make that decision because you are the more powerful person. Many people have attempted touch out of love, and received a reaction as though they had just tried to exercise authority over the youth. In fact, without knowing or intending it, they had.

The Right of Refusal

Being clear about permission involves more than simply asking. It also involves the manner in which you ask. Asking permission must be done in a way that the youth can refuse the permission without personally refusing you. Street-dependent youth will rarely consider their feelings on touch if it means rejecting you. And if they are giving permission to take care of you it's almost as bad as not being asked for permission. If I see a youth who is upset and I ask *"may I give you a hug"* technically I'm asking permission. But there is no way that they can say no without rejecting me. Instead of communicating respect for their needs, I've placed them in a position to have to decide between their needs and mine. If, on the other hand, I ask *"do you need a hug,"* then they can give or deny permission based on what they need, instead of based on what I want to do. They can say *"no, I'm fine,"* and it has nothing to do with me. This also helps me to avoid taking it personally if I am refused.

As you develop stronger relationships with specific youth, it may not be necessary to ask for permission each and every time that you touch them. Certain forms of touch, such as a platonic hug at greeting, may become accepted norms within the relationship. The key, however, is to make certain that the norm develops with the youth's knowledge and consent, and that you then remain alert to clues that indicate any discomfort that the youth may begin to have with the norm. It is also important that you don't communicate that you are *afraid* to touch them. Accepted social touching; such as a handshake upon greeting or agreement; is both acceptable and encouraged, as long as it is kept to its simplest form. Handshakes that do not end, but rather extend into a period of holding the hand, or double-clasp handshakes should be avoided.

The Value of Objects

When you begin to understand how the concept of ownership translates to the streets, you begin to realize that on the streets you never feel that you really own anything. Every piece of property becomes subject to someone else possessing it, and, as a result, the property will transfer ownership to the other person. The inability to establish a feeling of ownership is a terribly powerless feeling, and not something that a person to whom power is an issue will be comfortable with. As a result, street-dependent youth compensate, and, in this case, they compensate by developing strong and often unreasonable attachments to specific objects; for example, the AC/DC shirt that I talked about earlier. It may be an article of clothing, or a pocket knife, or some other small object that they can carry with them at all times, but it's something that they have somehow managed to make a connection with and over which they have been able to establish a sense of ownership. Concerning this particular object, youth will be willing to fight and die for it. It's often something that is easily replaced, but that doesn't matter. Their sense of ownership is intense, and can provoke extreme reactions.

This sense of ownership can develop very quickly. We once received a donation of 100 teddy bears at our emergency shelter program. Each bear was identical, without any difference what-so-ever in size, color, or construction. We gave one to a girl who subsequently set it down for a moment. A second girl picked it up and began to hug it. It nearly came to a physical confrontation over who owned that bear. Staff thought that the solution would be pretty simple. After all, we had 99 more just like that one. But it wasn't as simple as giving out a second bear. Neither girl was willing to accept an identical bear, they both wanted *that* bear.

Another object-related behavior is a tendency to connect to people through objects. One of the things that used to drive me crazy when I first started doing on-going counseling with street-dependent youth is that I would notice that after they had left my office, I didn't always have everything that was in my office before they arrived. The thing that kept me from reacting to this as simply dishonest, kleptomaniac behavior was that I became intrigued by *what* was disappearing. I had some fairly nice things in my office that I was quite attached to, and those objects were never touched. What was disappearing were paper clips, or pencils, or message pads. I began to realize that either street-dependent youth were fencing things on the office supply black market, or there was something else going on. As I began to learn about and understand the emotional attachment that street-dependent youth develop with objects, I realized that what was happening was that they were attempting to leave with a little piece of me. This behavior was not an aggressive act towards me, or an attempt to rip me off somehow. In fact, it was more of a compliment and a sign that we were connecting than anything else. So I began to intentionally fill my office with objects, little SuperBalls or other small, inexpensive toys. Instead of having to steal things, objects were available for the taking. After I did that, nothing ever disappeared from my office again.

I did see a new behavior, however. Things would sometimes appear in my office. I would suddenly notice a small object, sometimes hand-made, sitting on my desk or inconspicuously left elsewhere in the room. I never saw when the object was left there, and there was rarely anything with it to identify who had left it. It would just suddenly be there, and my interpretation was that they were leaving a piece of themselves for me. I put up a special shelf in my office to display these objects when I came across them. Rarely would a youth claim credit for leaving the item, but I would notice that youth would quickly scan the shelf when they came back.

The Time Factor

Like all other behaviors, property and ownership can be affected by the youth's sense of time. In this case, time explains the tendency to abandon property and leave possessions when they change circumstances. Youth at our emergency shelter are given lockers when they enter the program and it doesn't take long for them to fill these lockers virtually to the top with as much clothing and other items as they can get their hands on. It also doesn't take much for them to simply abandon this collection. Staff at our program routinely cleans out lockers and stores possessions in our basement when youth leave the program, and we have a policy that we donate to other agencies, such as Goodwill, anything that is not claimed within 7 days. Without that policy, our basement would be overflowing with abandoned items in less than a month.

The root cause of this behavior is the youth's sense of the past. They have a conditional sense of ownership to begin with; everything, after all, is owned only until someone else possesses it; and when the possessions are no longer with them their concept of owning these possessions slips into their concept of the past. Even though they may have been at the program as recently as that morning, their locker contents can quickly cease to be things that they own, and instead become things that they _used_ to own.

None of us have much incentive to care about or recover things that we have owned in the past. Replace them, maybe. Recover them, no.

"Turf"

The concept of "turf" or behavior associated with specific geographic areas is also related to property and ownership. Street-dependent youth tend to congregate in specific areas, and even go as far as to personalize those areas by assigning "street names" to them. I had an experience showing a friend from out of town around Portland, and I was identifying places as "Paranoid Park[45]," and "Tweeker's Park," and "Vaseline Alley." It wasn't until I noticed the perplexed look on my friend's face that I realized that I no longer knew what these areas were really called, and that the names I was using were the street names that they had been given.

Street-dependent youth identify with these areas. They virtually live there, and their flesh and their blood are invested there. Yet the strong attachments that they have to these areas are constantly challenged by messages that this is just one more thing that they don't own and have no right to. Despite the fact that they literally have no place else to go, they see us as coming there from our warm, comfortable homes and, using the power of the police as protection, usurping the only little square inch of the planet that they feel an attachment to; looking at them with disdain, and acting as though they have no right to be there. If you can put yourself in their shoes for a moment and comprehend how they feel, it goes a long way toward explaining the aggressive, obnoxious, and disrespectful behavior that street-dependent youth exhibit in public.

Self-protective Behaviors

There is another, perhaps deeper, reason for this negative public behavior as well. That reason is that street-dependent youth know something about us before they even meet us, and they know it simply because we're adults. What they know about us is that, if they let us get close, sooner or later we're going to use them, abuse them, exploit them, hurt them, lie to them, abandon them, or diminish their lives in some way. Now, you and I may know that that's not true. You and I may know that we care about them and want to help them live safe and healthy lives. But they don't know that. It hasn't been their experience with adults so far. So, regardless of how tough they act, the fact is that they're scared of us. They're scared of opening up to us and becoming close and being vulnerable. And if they're out on the streets being loud, obnoxious, and aggressive, they're not going to have to deal with that because we're going to walk on the other side of

---

[45] Actually named O'Bryant Square, Paranoid Park is also the name of Gus Van Sant's 2007 movie focused on a skateboarding teen in Portland … though the film is set mostly at the Burnside Skatepark rather than the real Paranoid Park.

the street. And from the other side of the street, we can't hurt them.

You'll see that behavior when you're on their turf. There will be pockets of street-dependent youth and the public stays away from them. It's one of the ways that they keep themselves safe, and it works, at least in terms of alienating people and keeping them at a distance. It doesn't work at keeping them safe from public authority, however, and the behavior is often viewed as an aggression against the community, resulting in crackdowns and other public responses. But the worst thing that we can do as advocates is to allow that behavior to work. It's generally not the sweet, polite, and pleasant to work with youth who really needs our help. They're probably going to be OK without us. It's the deeply hurt youth; and you can estimate the depth of their hurt by the level of aggressive, anti-social behavior that they exhibit; that really needs us to get through to them. And the factor that makes it possible for us to break through this behavior is that, despite its appearance, the behavior is not offensive, it's defensive.

I once did a training for a downtown citizens patrol who told me that one problem that they were having is that they would encounter groups of street-dependent youth who would be blocking the sidewalk, requiring the patrol to cross the street in order to avoid them. In response to their question of what they should do about it, I suggested that they might want to try not crossing the street. Instead walk up to the youth and politely, respectfully, ask the youth if they would mind letting them walk by. They took my advice and reported later that the youth were very cooperative, allowed them to pass, and that they were now on a first name basis with many of the young people that they had previously been in fear of.

It is far too easy to fall into the trap of seeing these kids as tough, worldly, aggressive, sophisticated, and street-wise, but what you have to remind yourself is that this public image is a defense. It's a suit of armor that protects a small, scared, vulnerable, wounded child who is desperately trying to not take up too much room in this world. Your job is to see past the armor. To see beyond the behavior to the person that the behavior protects, and that often is not easy. Because as you begin to break through the defenses, you can be assured that the youth will be terrified by the bond that is developing. Initially you may not see a decrease in negative behavior; you may even see an increase as the youth tries to push you away. Hang in there with them. Do not let the behavior work. The minute you do, the minute you decide that this particular youth just isn't worth it, both of you have lost. It's good to keep in mind the words of Johann Wolfgang von Goethe[46] who said; *"If we take people as we find them, we may make them worse, but if we treat them as though they are what they should be, we help them to become what they are capable of becoming."*

---

[46] Also sometimes attributed to Haim Ginott.

Anger

One of the more common defensive behaviors that you will encounter, and it's one that appears extremely offensive, is anger. I've referenced anger at several points in this manual, and will only take a moment to remind you that it can be unlike any anger that you may have experienced in the past. Rage may be a better word, and it can be exhibited with a level of intensity that can affect you physically, and is often customized for your specific weaknesses. There are several things that are important to understand about anger in addition to the responses I've discussed earlier in the manual. One of them is that street-dependent youth have survived by developing the ability to disassociate themselves from feelings and emotions. When I say that, I'm speaking very literally. It is common for youth involved in prostitution to report that they leave their bodies during the act, and that they go "somewhere else" until it's over. You will see youth walking around in the dead of winter wearing just an undershirt because they are so disconnected that they can't feel the cold, even though their bodies may be reacting to the cold. You'll see youth who will self-mutilate, cutting on themselves or burning themselves with cigarettes. It's not self-mutilation with traditional mental health causes. They're not trying to disfigure or attack themselves; they're simply trying to see if they can feel anything.

This is probably the least revealing part of this manual. Counselors, therapists, and youth workers have long been aware of this disassociation and the youth's ability to cut themselves off from feelings and emotions. As professionals we make many efforts to help young people realize their need to reconnect with feelings, and we spend much of our time with them working on this issue. What we sometimes forget or don't realize, however, is that if we are successful, if the young person we are working with does begin to reconnect with their feelings and emotions, the first feelings that they're going to connect to are rage and anger. And it will often appear as a sudden, intense, outburst.

This is where we can make a huge mistake and give them a mixed message that only drives them deeper into disassociation. After months, sometimes years, of encouraging them to reconnect with their feelings, constantly driving home the message *feel, feel, feel,* they suddenly explode and start turning furniture over in our office. We then respond: *wait a minute, don't feel that!* Instead of helping to further open them up to their feelings, our fear of their anger results in responses that simply shuts them down again.

Not only do we need to learn to be comfortable with their anger, I would suggest that providing street-dependent youth with a safe place to express anger is one of the things that they need from us. There are limits on it, of course. Verbal and physical violence needs to be contained and responded to appropriately. But anger itself will often require validation, not repression, and in all cases we need to learn how to not take a youth's anger personally. It's not about you; it's always about the youth and is often a sign that progress is being made. What they're feeling may not be pretty or fun to be a part of, but at least they're beginning to *feel* again.

I met a 15 year old girl one day in the following manner. At about 4:00 in the afternoon she stormed through my office door, yelled at me for a minute, and stormed out. I probably would have remembered that as simply another unusual, unexplained experience with a youth, except that she did it again the next day at about the same time. She repeated this behavior several times per week, for several weeks. It literally got to the point where I started setting my schedule around the expectation that I was going to be yelled at around 4:00. The day finally came when, as she was storming back out, she paused in the doorway and, half looking over her shoulder, said in a quiet voice, "*thanks.*" The next time she came in she sat down after yelling. She left without saying anything, but after a few more visits she stopped yelling and would just come in, fume a little bit, and then sit down for a minute or two. All total it was nearly two months before we actually started talking. This youth held so much rage and anger that she could barely contain herself. She had choices, though. She could explode on the street, and somebody would clean her clock. She could lash out aggressively, probably assaulting and hurting someone, and deal with the guilt and legal consequences. Or, she could storm into my office and blow up where she would be safe, and the only thing in danger of getting hurt would be my ego if I decided to take it personally.

Even if the anger is directed at you, realize that it's not about you and don't take it personally. Certainly anger needs to be expressed within the limits of the program, and it's necessary to have guidelines and procedures that keep everyone safe. But that doesn't mean the young people you're working with have to always be pleasant. In some cases the best service you can provide is to let them get the rage out. Our transitional living program has a punching bag in the basement. While we have agreements against violence and verbal abuse, we have no agreement that says that you can't be angry, and residents who *are* angry are permitted and *encouraged* to go beat the hell out of the punching bag.

Experiencing a youth's anger is not an easy thing to do, and I'm not going to pretend that it is. A success lecturer named Jim Rohn was once asked by an audience member how he personally was at doing all the things that he was admonishing his audience to do. His answer was that the best advice he could give them was to listen to him very carefully, but don't watch him too close. I'll give you the same advice. It is always easier to tell people how to do something than it is to actually do it. Will you always remember in the face of an angry youth who is lashing out at you that the anger is about them, and that this could be a healthy situation, and that your personal feelings and ego aren't even a part of this picture? I know I don't. My first inclination is to react personally; with anger, fear, embarrassment, defensiveness, and a whole range of other, very personal, emotions. But the key to successful work with street-dependent youth is to train yourself to skillfully *respond*, regardless of how you emotionally *react*. It may not be easy, but it is what *works*.

Key Points - Concepts of Property & Ownership

- Behaviors such as vandalism, theft, and difficulty with holding on to possessions are the result of a youth's inability to develop concepts of property and ownership.
- Property and ownership concepts are ultimately based on our belief in our ownership and control over our own bodies and our own lives. Sexually abused, prostituting, and neglected youth do not have a concept of ownership that extends to their own bodies and lives.
- One of the most vital lessons that we must model is that youth have absolute control over their bodies and personal space. Physical contact should never be initiated without asking permission.
- Aggressive, obnoxious public behaviors are defensive, not offensive. They are designed to keep us at a distance, and the worst thing that we can do is to allow the behavior to succeed.
- Expressions of anger are often a sign that progress is being made, and allowing anger to be expressed appropriately is one of the most valuable services we can offer.

2.0 Commentary:

I may have reworded some things differently in this section for better clarity, but this remains one of the most important concepts to understand, and how we implement our practice with an awareness of these issues is critical to effective youth work. About the only thing that I would have changed is that I would have de-emphasized the focus on street-dependent youth. In the years since this was written I've had the opportunity to work with other populations of youth through my Positive Youth Development consulting practice, including juvenile justice involved youth, the multiple populations that attend Job Corps Centers, and youth struggling with addiction. It has been my experience that an understanding of these concepts is just as important with these populations as they are with street-dependent youth.

It makes sense that they would be. After all, the basic premise is that the problematic behaviors referred to have their roots in a youth's inability to believe in their ownership over their own life and body. Such beliefs are often exasperated on the streets, but they are not usually created there. For the most part they start at home through a lack of opportunity to create healthy bonds through various forms of abuse and neglect, traumatically impacted family systems, and/or through involvement with systems that make decisions for youth and subject them to mandates. You do not have to be on the streets to be afflicted with a sense that you are not the owner of your body and life, you simply have to have grown up in environments where that has been the lesson.

The challenge is that it takes time, tolerance, and patience to address these issues. A young person who can barely keep their anger and rage in check (and often does not) is not going to learn how to do so overnight, nor are they going to experience some kind of epiphany that suddenly changes their attitudes toward vandalism and graffiti[47]. But the truly challenging thing for us as youth workers is that the most effective way to help young people through this is to change *our* behavior, not *theirs*. It is not what we ask them to do that will make the difference; it is what we do differently in our practice and responses.

One of the primary developmental tasks of the adolescent is the development of a stable sense of identity. While such development actually occurs throughout one's life, it is in adolescence that we first begin to relate our identity to our lives. The fact that an adolescent's task is to develop a stable identity means that, prior to doing so, their identity is *unstable* and constantly changing, which is why you will see youth who identify with one subculture one day and a different subculture the next, and they will exhibit different behaviors and even beliefs depending upon the environment that they are in and the people that they are around. An adolescent is more conscious of, and self-conscious about, their changing identity than they are at any other time in their life.

This focus on "who they are" is often viewed by adults as narcissistic[48], but it's really exactly the opposite. Because the adolescent has not yet developed a stable sense of identity, they mostly have an external locus of self-definition. They define who they are by their environment and by their perception of the way they are being treated. That being the case, the way to help them understand that they are the masters of their life and body is to treat them as though they are. This requires a focus on *our* behavior, not theirs.

This, by the way, is the theory behind the Positive Youth Development

---

[47] This is particularly true where such actions represent a bond or sense of belonging, such as with gang tagging.
[48] One of my personal pet peeves is the adult tendency to regard what should be considered normal adolescent development through the lens of pathology.

Protective Factor of High Expectations. When you believe certain things about people and act towards them based on your beliefs, they will eventual adapt their behavior to conform to your beliefs. The Pygmalion Effect, or the Self-fulfilling Prophesy, originally hypothesized by the Rosenthal-Jacobson study in 1968, is widely recognized in both education and business. It states that people will act or behave in the way that others expect them to act or behave. This is what makes High Expectations, or positive regard for and belief about a young person, a Protective Factor, because they will conform to the beliefs that you have about them. In the same way, low expectations can be considered a risk factor, because young people will also conform to negative beliefs. If you are working with young people through a negative, deficit-based belief system, you are doing worse than simply not helping ... you become a risk factor in their lives.

This underscores the importance of healthy and appropriate boundaries in youth work, and it is our responsibility to set and maintain the boundaries. Nowhere is this more important than in dealing with a youth's sense of property and ownership, as you are often in the realm of *emotional connection* when doing so. Take, for example, when I was discussing the value of objects and talked about youth using objects to take a piece of me with them, or to leave a piece of themselves with me. That's not an object exchange, that's an *emotional* exchange and the establishment of an emotional bond. Without an awareness of and scrupulous attention to appropriate boundaries it would be easy to exploit those emotions, or allow the behavior to turn into something inappropriate for a professional relationship. Another area where boundaries are a concern is when I talk about healthy touch. I make the statement that all such contact must be unquestionably on their terms, and with their conscious permission, but what I should have clarified is that touch should also only be offered and accepted within the confines of boundaries that are *appropriate to the relationship*. Young people may offer or accept touch that is completely inappropriate to the relationship that technically meets the standard of "on their terms with conscious permission." It is *our* responsibility to also consider whether the touch meets professional boundaries.

How we communicate is also critical. While it is true that much (if not most) of how we communicate is non-verbal, we tend to consciously rely on verbal communication to a greater degree than we do on non-verbal communication. This can be problematic from the standpoint of translation and intent, as young people may not always assign the same meaning to the words we use as we do, and therefore may receive different messages than we attempted to send. But it can be equally problematic in the area of helping youth develop their sense of ownership. Take, for example, a tendency shown by many youth workers to express approval of a youth's accomplishments or improvements through statements like "I'm proud of you." This seemingly innocent and, in fact, intended to be a supportive and acknowledging statement, may actually have a negative impact on a youth struggling with their sense of ownership. When we say something like "I'm proud of you," we make the issue about us and our feelings rather than about the young person and their growth or accomplishment. In a professional relationship it really doesn't matter whether we are proud of them or not. They are not in our lives to make us proud, and whether or not we take pride in their accomplishments is irrelevant. In fact, it can be counter-productive, as we don't want them looking to how they make us feel to be a measurement of their success or effort. It also may place an undue emotional burden on the youth, because if they can make us proud and we express that as an accomplishment of theirs, then they can also disappoint us and, by so doing, "fail" in their own eyes based on their read of our personal feelings. They may then base their choices and actions not on how they feel, but on how they perceive that we feel.

But even more important to the issue of ownership is that saying things like "I'm proud of you" may feel to them as though we are robbing them of their accomplishment. Why should we be proud? We didn't do anything noteworthy, the young person did. When you take pride in other people's accomplishments in a therapeutic relationship, it can be perceived by the client as a form of emotional theft. The truth is, no matter how good you are at the work you do with young people, any success they have is *their* success, not yours[49]. We may be really good at providing the path, the guidance, and the structure, but it is the young person who has to walk the path, accept the guidance, and utilize the structure. For us to take personal pride when they do so is like saying that the car won the race. Yes, the better the car, the more the driver has to work with ... but it's the *driver* that gets the trophy.

It's okay to bring pride into interventions, but to address their sense of ownership we need to be careful to ensure that it is *their* pride we are inserting, not ours. There is nothing wrong with saying (and, in fact, it is helpful to say) something like; "You've done really well, *you should be very proud of yourself.*" Statements like that are much more motivating and relevant to a young person's needs, particularly in the area of their sense of ownership, than any statement of personal pride.

---

[49] How many counselors does it take to change a light bulb? Only one, but the light bulb has to really *want* to change.

*Adolescent prostitution can only exist in a community
where there are adults who are willing to pay for sex with children.*

Inter-cultural Relationships

The premise of this book has been that when working with street-dependent youth we are doing cross-cultural work. I maintain the truth of that premise, but I'd like to qualify it now with the clarification that street-dependent youth do not truly belong to a separate culture. Rather, they belong to a subculture of our dominant culture. This fact adds new elements to the relationship in that street culture does not exist separately and distinctly from our own. In fact, the culture of the streets not only has the challenge of co-existing with ours; it is actually derived from and wholly enmeshed with our dominant culture, adding new dynamics to the conflicts that exist between the two.

Relationship between Sub and Dominant Cultures

When subcultures are created within a dominant culture it is the result of large groups of people becoming disenfranchised from and failing to fit the norms and mores of the culture that is dominant. They share a common belief system that doesn't fit with the mainstream. As a result, the dominant culture will tend to distance itself from the subculture. It will be viewed by the dominants as their "dark side," and the focus will be on the differences between "those people" and "us." The view from the subculture, however, will be one that is constantly confronted with cross-overs and similarities. While our dominant culture may hold the belief that street-dependent youth exist outside of our society, the truth is that they are a consequence and a reflection of who we are.

If you work with street-dependent youth in the long-term, and you are successful at building trust and understanding their lives and experiences, a result will be that you will get to know who their dates are; the people who are abusing and exploiting them sexually. You'll learn that we're not talking about drooling troglodytes from Transylvania. We're talking about doctors, lawyers, police, politicians, businessmen, family men, pillars of our communities, and, yes, even youth care workers.

I once had the experience of referring a youth to an agency, and when she walked in the door she was greeted by a person whom she had dated. That was the day I stopped making blanket referrals to agencies. I now either qualify my referral with an explanation that I have no personal knowledge of what that agency may actually be like, or I refer to a specific person that I know.

The result is that even though street-dependent youth live within a culture that takes a vocal stand against sexual abuse, prostitution and child exploitation, they are also dealing on a daily basis with the evidence that our culture actually supports and tolerates those activities. They're getting into the cars with the same people who speak out against them and how they survive.

Self-alienation

It is this reality that creates one of the most difficult barriers to our efforts to re-integrate street-dependent youth with our culture. The level of hypocrisy that they are forced to deal with sets up a self-alienation dynamic where, despite how willing they may be to give up life on the streets, they are not willing to be like us. They see all adults as hypocrites, phonies, and selfish exploiters. As already stated, integrity may be somewhat different on the streets, but it remains one of a street-dependent youth's most highly valued concepts. You end up with a young person who will hold their head high and with pride make statements like the following, which was made during a group session: *"I may be nothin' more than a sleazy little street walking whore, but by God at least I'm honest about it!"*

The implication is, of course, that we are not honest about ourselves, and that who we are is no better than who they are; in many ways, we may even be worse. And the truth is, based on their experience with adults, they're right. I wouldn't want them to be the adults they've known either! This perspective may seem in conflict with earlier parts of this manual where it was stated that street-dependent youth see us as "good" and "untainted." Several of their behaviors, such as their cocky attitude, were explained by their feeling dirty or diminished in our presence. But there is a difference in how they perceive adults one-on-one, and how they perceive us as a group. In individual encounters they see us as having everything they want, and their only explanation is that somehow we are deserving of good things and they are not. But as a group, as a society of adults, we are hypocritical and phony. We are the ones who exploit them, and then blame them for our own failings. Even when they become convinced that some of us are not hypocritical and phony, they will still be repulsed by us as a group; feeling toward us in many ways the way a sexually abused child would feel towards a parent who refuses to see or believe what the other parent is doing.

So they don't want to be like adults, or more accurately, who they believe adults to be. But that doesn't mean that they can't find a way to do good in the world; to justify what has happened to them, and to fill a need in our society. Many do it by not getting off of the streets; by instead continuing to prostitute themselves. When youth speak to us in a manner that implies that they are doing something good through prostitution, we sometimes misinterpret their message as a pro-prostitution stance; that they are performing needed sexual services. I would encourage you to listen more closely, because the true reason goes much deeper than that. Youth involved in prostitution see themselves as tainted, ruined, and dirty. They believe that there's nothing more that can happen to them and that they are irreversibly damaged. But they can still be a good person, and turn what has happened to them into a positive thing by protecting other youth. They do that by continuing to stay on the streets and to stay involved in prostitution, because they believe that if they weren't in the car pulling a date with this guy he'd be home raping his own children.

Unfortunately this isn't such a wacky theory on their part. One of the more common requests I've heard from young people who have regular, or repeat, customers is that the john likes to have them dress and act like one of his own children; often even calling them by his child's name. It doesn't take a very creative youth to imagine what this guy might be doing at home if they weren't available. In fact one of the youth I worked with had the experience of getting into a car, only to discover that the driver was her father, whom she hadn't seen in over five years. Even after both realized who they were, her father still went through with the date.

So there is plenty of evidence to support their theories about adults and, realizing what they believe about us, it is probably a good sign that they don't want to leave the streets and become who we are. The challenge is to show them that being an adult does not necessarily mean being an adult like the ones they've known. Yes, there are people like that in the world, and they have had the sad misfortune of meeting most of them in their lives. But there is another world where people are good, honest, healthy, and caring. And they can still become a part of that world, they're not too damaged or tainted, and the challenge is to get them to believe that. We do it by being completely honest and aware of how our dominant culture is influencing them, and consistently providing a different influence.

Direct and Indirect Relationships

There are two primary ways in which street-dependent youth are influenced by our dominant culture, which I will call direct and indirect influences. Direct influences are those derived from interpersonal relationships; the adults that they have contact with during the course of their day. Since these are the influences that have the greatest impact, I will deal with them first and discuss the indirect influences later.

Living in a constant state of survival consciousness teaches you to make extremely quick decisions about people. If you are getting into a car and have only a few seconds to determine if this person is going to beat, rape, or kill you, you develop the ability to gather quick information and make snap judgments. A youth involved in prostitution will scan the car and the driver even as they are climbing in, looking for warning signs like visible weapons or missing door handles. They use the same pattern of snap decision in every encounter they have, believing it is better to reject somebody who may be of help, than to trust someone who ends up hurting. While each situation they find themselves in is unique, and differing environments result in differing judgments, there tends to be three broad categories that they have for adults. These categories may not be conscious, and the names I have given them are not street terms, but rather terms that I have placed on the descriptions of adults that I've heard from young people. It won't take long for you, however, to see the evidence of these attitudes toward adults, or for you to be categorized as one of these three if you do not consciously act to avoid it.

The "Users"

The first and largest category is the "users." A user is anybody who involves themselves with the youth because they want something from them. They often will have and be willing to provide things that the youth wants and needs, but there is always a price to pay, and more often than not, the youth expects to be overcharged. A user can be anyone; from families, to dates, to pimps, to politicians.

Reporters and other media representatives often fall into this category. For some reason, stories about street-dependent and homeless youth will be popular, and reporters will be paying attention to the youth and getting their stories and pictures. The next day the story is over, the reporters and attention are gone; yet the youth's life is unchanged, or changed in that the experience has been a negative one for them. We often have difficulty with media wanting to do stories on our transitional living program. They always want to interview the young people in the program, but their questions are rarely about the youth's goals and successes. What sells are the stories from the street. They want to hear and write about the youth's pain, and their experiences with drugs and prostitution. Once again the message that the young person receives is that they are valued for their aberrant behavior. The difficult path of transition captures no attention, but their activities on the street lands them in the news.

Youth involved in prostitution often go through a natural stage of transition where they may deny that they have ever pulled dates. One of our female residents was at this point in her life, where she wouldn't acknowledge in any way, shape, or form, her prostitution activities. A reporter came to the program to do a story on us at a time when we really needed some publicity to raise community support. This particular resident was very invested in the program and wanted to help out with the publicity and to have an opportunity to share how much she had benefited by being in the program. The first question that the reporter asked her was whether or not she had ever prostituted herself. When she answered "no," the reporter asked if there was another resident he could interview instead, one who had been involved in prostitution. You don't have to have a Ph.D. to understand what kind of message that sends to a young person.

These are the types of experiences street-dependent youth have always had with adults, and as a result they've learned that there's always a price. Every adult who pays attention to them wants something in return, so they're always looking for the payoff. And here's the key; they are far more comfortable when the payoff is clear and up front then they are when they don't know what the price will be. This is why service providers are often in such awkward and tenuous relationships with street-dependent youth. Our interest is in the youth's needs, and our goal is their success. That's our only payoff. From the youth's perspective, however, they don't see that as a payoff for us, and it leaves them wondering why we're being nice to them. They can't figure out what we really want and they're constantly waiting for the other shoe to drop. This becomes a source of incredible anxiety that makes it difficult for them to be around us.

I once responded to a crisis call from a girl who had been beaten and raped by a john. I went to the hotel and took her to the hospital, stayed while she talked to a rape advocate, and then took her back to the crisis line where we let her stay the rest of the night on a cot in the back. The nicer we were to her, and the more we tried to make her comfortable, the more agitated she became. It finally reached a point where she literally screamed out: *"What the Hell do you want from me? Do you want my ass, or what?"* The idea that we could be doing this for no reason other than that she's a human being who deserves nothing less simply did not occur to her.

This is the answer to the question that many youth workers have struggled with for years, that question being: *We meet their needs, we care about them, and we treat them well; so why do they decide to give all of that up and go back to their pimps?*

The answer is: *They know what the pimps want.*

The "Authoritarians"

The second category of adults is authoritarians. Authoritarians are the police, the juvenile justice system, and various institutions and programs that exercise some sort of legal mandate or authority that the youth is subject to, or act in a manner as though they have the right to exercise authority. Their contact with authoritarians results in a very clear message; street-dependent youth are bad or incapable and they need to be punished or controlled.

My personal opinion is that, generally speaking, we are not dealing with young people who are bad or incapable. Street-dependent youth are basically good people who are in a terribly bad situation. As a result, they may engage in some actions and behaviors that we consider bad. But these behaviors are not caused by the youth's inherent "badness;" rather they are rational and predictable behaviors in response to their life experience and circumstances. And the fact that they are able to survive on the streets proves how capable they are. But as I said, that's my personal opinion, and it's an opinion that is not shared by most street-dependent youth themselves. They see themselves as bad, and they have grown quite comfortable with the belief that they are somehow damaged, and twisted, perhaps even evil. This is another attraction to the occult and Satanism that many youth toy with, although I'll remind you that the real attraction in supernatural phenomenon is an attempt to gain power and control over their lives. They also see themselves as incapable, which is what makes them prime targets for pimps and other adult exploiters. They're more than willing to let someone tell them what to do, as long as it's their choice about who does the telling. This belief about themselves often manifests itself in youth who go out of their way to be "bad" and take pride in the "bad" things that they do. This is simply an inside-out version of our basic human instinct to be good at what we do best. If you truly believe that what you are is a bad and incapable person, then you will strive to be the best bad and incapable person you can possibly be.

So, street-dependent youth can actually be quite comfortable with authoritarians. They often know what authoritarians want, they agree with the message that they are bad and incapable and need to be punished or controlled; in fact, they spend a good deal of their time punishing themselves by placing themselves in situations where they will get hurt; and they understand structure and authority; it's how the pimps deal with them and they've learned that the world works by the weaker doing what the more powerful command. But their problem with authoritarians has to do with the hypocrisy they see. To begin with, many authoritarians hold street-dependent youth to a higher standard than they hold themselves, and it is not uncommon for youth to feel like they are being expected to behave in ways that most adults don't behave. Additionally, some adults in positions of power abuse that power; and street-dependent youth, because they are so disenfranchised and those who would abuse often see them as a victim nobody cares about, seem particularly vulnerable to being beaten and raped by abusers in the system. But the real hypocrisy is that street-dependent youth feel as though they are being unfairly singled out and punished for the failures of our society. It's important to remind ourselves of something that street-dependent youth know all too well, and that is that adolescent prostitution can only exist in a community where there are adults who are willing to pay for sex with children. Most communities, however, blame and punish the children for the act, and the adults involved are dealt with much less severely.

Even in areas that have customer laws, that is, where the buyer of prostitution services is also considered a prostitute, street-dependent youth are treated differently in often very subtle ways. A few years ago the manager of a city in Oregon was arrested for paying for sex with a 16 year old girl on the streets, and he was charged with prostitution. But here's a question for you to consider. Why was the charge prostitution? This was a 16 year old girl. Wouldn't a more appropriate charge be child sexual abuse, or statutory rape? If the girl involved had been a 16 year old cheerleader, I doubt that it would have resulted in a simple charge of prostitution. But it wasn't a cheerleader; it was just a girl on the streets. And if you're on the streets you can expect to be viewed and treated differently in our society.

The "Rescuers"

The final category from the street-dependent youth's perspective is the rescuers. This is the category that many of us who work with street-dependent youth are in danger of slipping into. Rescuers tend to be representatives of non-authoritarian systems composed of a variety of well-intentioned groups and individuals who want to help youth on the streets and want to make their lives better. The danger here lies in the message that youth often interpret from our efforts, that being, that there's something wrong with them and they need to be changed. There are two problems with this message. The first is that street-dependent youth are all too willing to agree that there's something wrong with them. They already believe that they are bad, tainted, and damaged human beings. The message we send often not only doesn't help, it may actually confirm their belief system and further alienate them. But the second impact of that message is that it again feels hypocritical to them. They wonder why they should trust representatives of a society that obviously has something seriously wrong with it or they wouldn't be in the situation that they're in. As we communicate that there's something wrong with them, their life experience with hurtful and exploitive adults confirms that there's also something very wrong with us. The economies of the culture that they are surviving in are supported by adults in our community, and often these are known and respected adults. Even as our culture overtly speaks out against street economies and passes laws to combat them, we also covertly participate in and support those activities. Without adults paying for sex with children, there isn't a child on this planet who could survive through prostitution. This fact results in the youth believing that if there's any "making better" to be done maybe we should start with *our* behavior, not theirs.

Another danger with this category is that there's a very narrow line between rescuers and users. Many people are attracted to working with this population without a clear consideration of what their motivation is. As a result, they often find themselves in the position of wanting something from the youth that meets a personal need; the very definition of a user. Since they haven't clearly examined their motivation themselves they are often not conscious of what they're using the kids for, setting up a very uncomfortable and confusing dynamic that street-dependent youth will feel and react to with distrust. One example may be somebody who is not skilled at developing a personal social life so they work with youth in order to meet their needs for social contact. People may enter this work in order to help with their own healing process, such as a person recently clean from drugs who now has a mission to impose their new sobriety on every young person they meet. My own time in this category was spent trying to get street-dependent youth to stop stealing; not necessarily to help them, but to satisfy my own personal standards around property rights.

I do believe that we all act in our own self-interest at all times even when we appear to be altruistic. We don't help others out of self-sacrifice, and I don't believe self-sacrifice to be either noble or helpful. But it's important that we consciously examine what our self-interests are around working with this population and make sure that our reasons for doing this work are able to be satisfied from the work itself and the service that we are providing, not from or at the expense of the young people that we work with. This is a danger not only for individuals and their motivations, but for a program focus as well which can also result in exploitation. While I have seen excellent programs that have a specific issue focus; such as a religious or anti-drug orientation; I have also seen programs such as these that result in exploitation. The specific anti-drug program, for example, may focus on your weaknesses or failures as a human being while holding former drug users up as examples of people who are now good. Meanwhile, the youth exposed to that message may choose to kill the emotional pain from pulling dates that night by using drugs, and the program's message serves to further confirm how worthless they are. A religiously based program may tailor its message to saving street-dependent youth from their sins, forgetting that the youth may need to sin tonight in order to survive. In both of these situations the short-term result is that representatives of the program feel good proclaiming their success or ministering to their religion, and the youth on the streets feels worse, absorbing more shame and more degradation. This is a form of exploitation.

One of the young people I worked with had an appointment with her pastor just prior to an appointment with me. After she had left him, her pastor gave me a call to tell me that she was on her way. He was incredibly jubilant about the meeting he had just had with her and happily relayed that they had just had a great conversation and how he felt he had really gotten through to her. You could tell from his attitude that this conversation had literally made his day, because he felt so good about the interaction. I was expecting an equally happy youth to arrive at my office, but a little while later she showed up in tears. In discussing the conversation with her, the only thing that she could remember was the pastor's message that Jesus had died for her sins. Her statement to me was; *"If he was trying to die for my sins then he fucked up, because my sins are still here."*

The short-term result of her conversation with her pastor was that he felt better, and she felt worse. This is one of the greatest challenges of our work; to ensure that we are not the ones being helped at the expense of the youth that we are serving.

The Fourth Category

There is a fourth category of adults. It consists of adults clear with themselves and honest about their involvement with street-dependent youth. Their only agenda is to provide street-dependent youth with the respect they deserve and the assistance they need to make the positive changes that they've chosen to make in their lives. These adults neither exploit nor abuse the youth they work with. It's likely that you and your organization are members of this category. But it's equally likely that this is a category of adults that the young people you meet will not have had much experience with. You're going to be someone who they can't understand and, as a result, they're going to be desperately trying to lump you into one of the other three categories as their anxiety skyrockets trying to figure out what the hell you want from them. Their behavior towards you will flip flop between who they think you are; a user, an authoritarian, or a rescuer; and every time you fail to fit into these categories you will become more threatening to them.

When they finally begin to believe that you really are different, that is often the time when they will do everything in their power to drive you away. They will become more challenging, more obnoxious, and negative behaviors will increase. The reason for this is that as they begin to accept the fact that you really are the type of person that they've only imagined could exist, and they realize that you actually enjoy and care about them, they begin to feel bad. Their belief is that the only way you could possibly care about them is if you don't understand who they really are. Their own self-image is that they are so horribly tainted and bad that a good person like you couldn't possibly feel that way if you really knew them. So, rather than continue to fool you; which they don't want to do to someone as nice as you; they begin to actively demonstrate just how unworthy they are of your attention. It can be a very unpleasant time in your relationship with a youth, but it's extremely important to realize that increased negative behavior is not an aggressive stance towards you, or a sign of failure. It's actually an attempt to protect you from them and a sign that you're starting to get through. It is part of the process that youth may need to go through as they learn to trust and to let people get close to them, because letting people get close is an extremely threatening thing for them to do. The worst thing you can do is to allow their behavior to work, to take the negative acts personally, and to let yourself get to the point where you feel that this particular youth just isn't worth the effort. Regardless of how successful they are at demonstrating that they just don't deserve to be cared about, care about them anyway. If you can hang in there with them through this period you will eventually see the protective armor begin to drop away.

Indirect Relationships

Indirect relationships to our culture are mainly the result of contact with mass media and social attitudes. Don't let the image of these youth as homeless and living on the streets delude you into believing that they don't have much contact with radio and television. It's often surprising how much opportunity they have and they can be extremely media oriented. The biggest problem with this comes from the fact that they are so literal in their communication styles. This results in very little critical thinking and they tend not to question what they hear and see in the media. I've often heard repeated things that they've heard on TV as though the information was some sort of irrefutable natural law, and it really doesn't matter whether the source was a news program, sitcom, or soap opera. If it was on TV, it's a fact.

In light of this, consider that most aspects of the street culture lifestyle, including prostitution, drugs, and the criminal underworld, makes for really good media. Start paying attention to how many books, movies, and TV shows have parts of this culture as either a backdrop or a focus. In fact, many TV shows have had specific plots concerning youth who have run away and become involved in living on the streets. Now imagine what it would be like to be actually living that lifestyle and see it portrayed through a medium that you interpret as fact. Especially when you consider the standard canned plot line that is generally used in these shows.

Most of the "youth on the streets" theme shows that I've seen generally go like this; young person leaves a warm, loving, good home and ends up on the streets, either for some inexplicable reason, or because of something bad that they've done, or due to the influence of some evil other person. The show's hero is contacted by the family to go out into the seedy world of prostitution and drugs and find this poor, misguided kid. He or she locates the kid and rescues them in the nick of time from some conflict that threatens their life, and saves them from the horrible people out on the streets. They put a quarter in the phone, call home in tears and beg to be allowed to come back. Family, of course, welcomes them back with open arms and they all live happily ever after.

Real street-dependent youth watch this and their reaction is; *Well, that's not me. Nobody's out to rescue me, and I have no home to go back to. So I must be one of those other people. I must be one of those hopelessly tainted evil people that the hero rescues the good kids from.* And we all feel the need to be good at what we are. So if you believe that you are bad and hopelessly tainted, and you see media images that reinforce that belief, then you're going to be the best bad, hopelessly tainted person you can be. And the images that they receive from the media helps to reinforce and lock them into that lifestyle because they encounter those images already believing that they are bad, and the media simply confirms that for them.

Even when TV gets it right, there seems to be something about our image of street-dependent youth that just doesn't let us believe the reality of their lives. In the fall season of 1997 I saw an episode of "Touched by an Angel" that, at first, was absolutely different from the standard plot that I previously described. There was still the main kid needing rescuing, and the hero; the angels in this case; in the roll of rescuers. But other than that it was an amazingly accurate and caring portrayal of youth on the streets. That is, right up to the end. In the final wrap up, as the focus youth was saved from the streets, all she had to do was *apologize to her father for hurting him, and ask if she could come home*. It was so close, but, in the end we still believe, and communicate to youth on the streets, that it's their fault, they're to blame, and they're the ones who are hurting us.

Summary and Conclusion

When you study the interaction between our dominant culture and the subculture of the streets, you begin to realize that all inter-cultural relationships, both direct and indirect, tend to be exploitive and degrading towards street-dependent youth. You learn that, in many ways, street culture is created and supported by adults in our society. When we begin to understand the process that resulted in youth living on our streets, we realize that there aren't many options for young people in our culture. The narrow path we allow young people to follow begins with dependency in a nuclear family supported by compulsory government education, and then is followed by attending college and entering the work force; with the option for military service allowed. If, for any reason, you fall off of that path, the only existing options are incarceration or the streets. Those two options are supported by our culture. Incarceration is supported through our tax dollars and government regulations, and the culture of the streets is supported through direct cash donations to youth by the adults in our community who are paying them for sex. When we pass judgment on the choices, actions, and behaviors of street-dependent youth, we are also passing judgment on ourselves. We share the responsibility, and the situation we condemn was not created by the youth. They are simply trying to survive by choosing among the alternatives that we allow.

In closing, I'd like to share a final thought from the essay that I've been quoting. It's from a section where she was describing the positive things that she's experienced on the streets. We sometimes forget that there's good and bad in everything and that there are positive aspects to the streets as well. At this point she was referring to the different types of services that she's encountered on the streets, and she was specifically referring to a drop-in center. The remarks she makes, however, are broadly applicable to any type of service, and demonstrate exactly what street-dependent youth really need from a program:

"We also have the drop-in center, which helps out much more than some kids realize. Not only do they give out food, but clothes and advice. They know how we live and they don't act too good for us. They accept us for who we are, not how we live. It makes me feel good when I go in there and one of the staff asks me how I'm doing and I'll say oh good and I'll tell them about some time I spent with my family and they like to hear about it and ask questions and share things about themselves with me. I know that helps a lot of us, that they are there to help us and they are sincere. We know they're not just there to feed us and hurry us out so they can go home. And that's what we need, is more people like them. It shows me that there are people with different lifestyles who do care."

Key Points - Inter-cultural Relationships

- Youth on the streets do not form a separate and distinct culture, but rather a sub-culture of our dominant culture. As such, there is a natural polarization that exists between the two.
- From the streets the dominant culture is viewed as being hypocritical and phony. This sets up a self-alienation dynamic where street-dependent youth don't want to be like adults.
- Street-dependent youth survive by quickly categorizing people. They will try to categorize you in order to understand what you want from them.
- Street-dependent youth have both direct and indirect relationships with our dominant culture. Almost all of these relationships are degrading, or exploit youth in some form.
- Youth need to experience non-exploitive relationships with adults who can influence a different perspective on life beyond the streets.

2.0 *Commentary:*

The more things change, the more they stay the same. That was the feeling I got when I reviewed this final section of Street Culture. Sure, there are a lot of dated references, but in many ways it feels like things are exactly the same, only different. Some of the external trappings of street life have changed, and being on the streets as a young person, at least in the United States, looks a little different due to changes in service systems, the influence of technology, and the fact that our dominant culture has experienced its own changes and shifts over the years. I'm also pleased to report that I see less fictional exploitation of street-dependent youth. I'm not sure to what it's attributed, but "kids on the street" just doesn't seem to be fodder for television shows and literature as much as it once was. Where there are exceptions to this, there seems to be greater attention to avoiding exploitation and misrepresentation. An example would be Shelly Fredman's "No Such Thing as a Free Ride[50];" book #4 in her *No Such Thing As; Brandy Alexander Mystery series*. While not a book about street-dependent youth, and a totally fictional tale, the book did have the culture of the streets as a plot element. But the author took the time to engage me as a consultant to ensure that whatever fictional representation she created was at least an accurate image of the young people.

But where things haven't changed, and where they may have even gotten worse, is in the area of infotainment; shows that package news and information in an entertainment format. Such shows fall on a spectrum ranging from news "special reports" to reality-type shows documenting the cases of various counselors or therapists as they solve the problems of "troubled youth" on the screen in your living room in a half-hour. These types of shows continue to be seen by young people themselves, with the same possible negative impact on a youth's identity and self-image.

But I think that an even greater concern, and one with which the creators of such shows seem unconcerned, is the "frozen in time" aspect of highlighting specific negative characteristics of a young person in the media. Some of these shows give so little thought to the impact of media exposure on a young person that I personally find them difficult to watch, having a similar reaction as I do when I see a parent smacking their kid out in public. As an example, ABC's 20/20 aired a show in early 2011 that I thought was so exploitive that it moved me to write a newsletter article, which I share below as a way of making my point. This article appeared in Issue 143 of The Youth Networker on February 4, 2011.

Homeless Youth and the Media
Some thoughts on unintended consequences

---

[50] Available in paperback and a Kindle edition through Amazon.com

Last week, ABC's 20/20 aired a program highlighting the plight of homeless youth, focusing on 4 youth who they followed for 14 months. If you missed the show, you can watch the entire episode here[51].

I've been hesitant to write this article, as I'm sure much good may result from this program. But when we are dealing with the lives of young people, we owe it to them to consider the unintended consequences of being identifiably depicted in the media. The reality of these unintended consequences was the catalyst for most youth-serving agencies back in the 80's and 90's, at least those with which I was associated, developing Media Policies in an attempt to protect young people from media identification. I was reminded of the need for such policies when I watched the 20/20 special. Many people will point out the positive aspects of the show ... I'd like to take a moment to consider the other side of the picture.

I was extremely uncomfortable with several depictions of the life of 17-year-old Rebekah from Falls City, Oregon. In one scene, 20/20 cameras recorded her and some friends partying and chugging down vodka. This is an image that is now recorded for all time and aired nationally ... can any of us predict how that scene might affect Rebekah 5, 10 or 20 years from now? Not to mention the fact that if I recorded under-aged kids drinking and posted it on YouTube, I might be subject to arrest ... I have to wonder why 20/20 gets a pass. But even more disturbing to me was the way that they depicted a 59 year old man who was providing Rebekah with housing. Granted, I know nothing about this situation, but 20/20 was unable to document *any* evidence that the situation was anything other than what he and Rebekah claimed it was. However, 20/20's agenda on this was evident in the scene where they kept asking leading questions until Rebekah finally conceded that *"maybe he looks at me,"* and then they cut to an out of context question where a youth worker stated that she had never heard of a situation like that being innocent. But without any evidence to the contrary, is it fair to present a man who may only be providing something that Rebekah's own parents are unable to provide as a predator to a national audience? And did the media consider what might result when the man views the program, only to see that his act of charity has him nationally disgraced? Did the media consider what that might do to Rebekah's ability to continue to be housed?

And what about the story of June? Only 14 and obviously dealing

---

[51] When I last checked the video was still available at: http://abc.go.com/watch/2020/SH559026/VD55108764/2020-128-homeless-youth , which makes my "frozen in time" point, as it originally aired over 2 years ago.

with major issues, did the media consider how exposing her sexual activities and emotional struggles might affect her later in life? Even more difficult for me was watching the segment when June begins to tell the camera about her suicidal thoughts. Maybe it's just me, but when a young teen begins to consider suicide, that's when you *turn the cameras off* ... something the media rarely considers doing.

Please understand that this is not a criticism of the programs highlighted in this show. My concern is with how identifiable media exposure may affect the young people exposed. The show begins by stating that they are about to open our eyes to something that is going on all around us, and yet most of us are unaware. I had to ask myself, why is that? I personally was involved with several of these national media shows over 30 years ago, and the media sporadically dips into the street subculture from time to time. They have never been hesitant to expose these kid's lives ... and then they go away, until there is some new reason to expose them. But when they leave, the kids are still there, with their pain frozen in time and preserved in a way that may make it harder for them to leave those lives behind. Kids who have never received attention for anything get on national TV for being homeless, in pain, sexually active, and abusing drugs. What does that teach them, and what impact will that have on them in the future?

I don't have the answer to those questions. Until I do, I will remain cautious and concerned anytime the media wishes to identifiably expose young people.

I speak about this exact same media behavior when I talk about the "users" in the original text, and I'm saddened by how little has changed over the years.

But my greatest regret in reviewing the changes over the past few decades is not in how little we've impacted the media exploitation of youth, but that we have had little success in changing the public image of young people in general. The two are probably related, as the media is no small influence on public opinion, but today young people are still viewed as "less than" and they remain the one segment of our society against whom it is acceptable and condoned to disparage, dismiss, and discriminate. I'm not intending to be political here or to come across as some naïve, theoretical child rights advocate. I'm not even saying that young people aren't different from adults ... in fact, I think the differences between young people and adults are often under-recognized, which is why I harp on the fact that adults working with young people are by definition engaged in cross-cultural work. I'm just saying that differences are the basis of all interpersonal relationships and, if we claim to value diversity, we should ensure that all people are respected for their differences. When it comes to adult attitudes toward young people, respect is often not present. And in my opinion, it is this lack of respect that may underlie the reason why so many young people are subject to abuse and exploitation in the first place.

I am a voracious follower of news reports concerning street youth around the globe, and I am always fascinated (and appalled) by how the existence of street-dependent youth knows no borders. I even sometimes learn things about geography ... for example, when I read an article about youth homelessness in Warrnambool[52]. Yeah, I know ... I never heard of it either, but that's exactly my point. I regularly run across stories about street youth from every country and continent on earth. Regardless of a nation's wealth or poverty; regardless of its form of government ... you cannot find a location on this planet that does not have children living on its streets.

I've heard some advocates blame capitalism or American culture for youth homelessness. If that were the case it would be a uniquely American phenomenon ... it is not. Whatever the underlying causes of youth homelessness are, they are global circumstances unrelated to most social, economic, or political factors. My personal journey has brought me to a point where I believe that one of the underlying causes of the exploitation and abuse of young people may be widespread and socially accepted disrespect for and marginalization of the young.

This attitude is so ingrained that we don't even hear it most of the time. Take for example a radio discussion I was listening to when LeBron James decided to go with the Miami Heat. One guy thought that, for a whole list of reasons, the decision was the result of "stupidity" on James' part, and then made the statement -- unchallenged by the other hosts -- *"this is an example of why we don't let 25-year-olds run the world."*

25-year-olds aren't even adolescents, but they are still considered "young" -- and this is an example of our attitude toward youth. When Bernie Madoff got busted, did anyone say "this is an example of why 71-year-olds shouldn't be in the financial business?" No, of course not ... that would have been considered a ridiculous association and disrespectful to all senior citizens. Yet it seems to be OK to be disrespectful to the young.

Youth is the only class of people that it is still socially acceptable to discriminate against and disparage. They are routinely denied rights and privileges that would result in rioting in the streets if we tried to deny to any adult population. More importantly, even if you can make a situational case to rationalize the denial of certain rights and privileges, it becomes more challenging to defend the dismissive and disrespectful manner in which these rights and privileges are often denied, justified by the fact that they're "just kids."

---

[52] Turns out that Warrnambool is in Australia. Who knew?

We live in a society where the prevailing image of young people is predominately negative, ranging from young people being incompetent, lazy, and disrespectful, to young people as manipulative, violent, and predators. Certainly, within the youth service field, particularly the segments of the field that have been influenced by Positive Youth Development, we focus on High Expectations and our view of young people is changing. But our desire to demonstrate High Expectations is constantly undermined by our exposure to the low expectations of young people held by the general population. Not only do I believe that this sets young people up for exploitation and abuse, but it is even more shameful in that our negative attitudes toward the young are generally *not true*. History is filled with examples of young people who achieved greatness. From the Marquis de Lafayette, who came to the aid of the American revolutionary cause and was commissioned as a major general by the United States Congress at the age of 19; to Sacagawea, a near-legendary figure in the history of the American West who played an indispensable role on the Lewis and Clark Expedition at the age of 14 (while a teen mom, no less); to Anne Frank, who wrote one of the most moving diaries in world history between the ages of 13 and 15, young people have a long and documented history of demonstrating their capacity and the contributions they can make if they are afforded the opportunities to make them.

But the telepathic side of me is picking up on some thoughts out there. Yeah, but I'm working with street kids (or gang members, or school behavior problems, or insert about a dozen other negative categories we've created for young people). Trust me, Jerry, not every kid I'm working with is a Lafayette, a Sacagawea, or a Frank. OK, I'll give you that … if you give me that not all of the people working with those kids is an Albert Einstein, a Harvey Milk, or a Martin Luther King. We're not talking about human behavior or accomplishment, we're talking about human capacity … it's about a belief in what young people are capable of, rather than a focus on what an individual youth may actually be doing. Even the most alienated, issue-laden, behavioral problem youth has human capacity underneath all that surface crap … the question is are you going to believe in and respond to the crap or the capacity, because whichever one you chose will be the one that you nourish.

And in any case, even if you don't believe in a young person's capacity, you cannot deny their humanity. As a human being, young people, like any other human group on earth, have the right to be treated with respect and honored for their differences. No age or other status should ever be a justification for dismissing or disparaging a group of people. Throughout history, whenever we have allowed any group of people to be treated as "less than" it has resulted in exploitation and abuse at best, and atrocities at worst. It should come as no surprise that we live on a planet where young people are exploited and abused in every culture and in every society. Until we are willing to address how we think about and act towards young people, we are likely to see the same issues generation after generation.

The starting point is the belief that every youth has innate resilience.
~ Bonnie Benard

APPENDIX

An Introduction to the Positive Youth Development Approach

What is Youth Development?

Youth Development[53] is the name given to an approach to working with young people that focuses on psychological, emotional, and social development rather than problems or deficits. Based on research into human resilience, the principles and practices of the Youth Development approach have become a recognized best practice for youth programs and an approach required by many public and private funding sources.

The Youth Development approach (hereafter referred to as PYD) is still in its own infancy in terms of universally agreed upon structures and definitions and I have borrowed from a range of perspectives in presenting this version of PYD. However, the term "youth development" refers not only to a youth work practice, it is also used to describe a process of growth in which all young people are seeking ways to meet their physical and social needs and build competencies. PYD as a practice is grounded in the belief that all choices and decisions made by young people are a result of this process of development, and that by supporting young people's developmental process we have greater positive impact than we do by focusing on their problems or deficits.

Resilience and Protective Factors

PYD is grounded in decades of research into human resilience. Just as human beings are "hard wired" with a will to survive, it is also our nature to overcome and grow from the challenges we face. Yet research indicates that there are environmental factors that tend to inhibit our ability to face and surmount challenges. These inhibiting environmental factors are called Risk Factors, and refer to such things as neglect, poverty, domestic violence, physical/sexual abuse, family separation and conflict, alcohol and drug use/abuse, school performance problems, and so on. But another category of environmental factors tends to have the opposite effect, fostering and supporting innate resilience and enabling people to be more successful

---

[53] Also known as Positive Youth Development (PYD), or the Youth Development approach.

when dealing with their personal challenges. These fostering environmental factors are called Protective Factors and, where they exist, they are able to compensate for Risk Factors in a person's environment and foster the innate resilience within each individual.

Protective Factors is an area of PYD that may be presented in different ways depending on the source, but the lack of uniform presentation does not represent a lack of consistency between the sources. Regardless of how Protective Factors are presented, the presentations tend to be saying the same things in slightly different ways, and all presentations can generally be represented by a focus on 3 specific Protective Factors: Caring, Supportive Relationships; High Expectations, and Meaningful Participation (sometimes referred to as "Opportunities for Participation").

Relationships in and of themselves do not constitute a Protective Factor. In fact, many relationships may actually be risk factors in a young person's life, which is why an understanding of the qualifiers "caring and supportive" is critical. Caring and Supportive Relationships are those that demonstrate care in the sense of being genuinely concerned about or interested in knowing and understanding who a young person is as an individual. From the youth's point of view, the interest must be in as they are *now*, not solely in what they may become or what problems they may be facing. Again, from the youth's perspective, they perceive *support* based upon your willingness to act as a resource for them without it impacting your interest in them. Regardless of what negatives they may perceive about themselves, they do not perceive a change in the care you are showing when they reveal those negatives to you.

In order to maintain the Protective Factor qualities of a relationship, it is also important to view relationships through the lens of a defined association. Any type of relationship can actually have Protective Factor qualities, provided that both parties have the same understanding of what the relationship is. It ceases to be a Protective Factor and may in fact become a risk factor if there is not a mutual understanding; for example if one party perceives a counseling relationship, while the other party sees a friendship.

When we speak of High Expectations in the PYD sense of the term we are not referring to goal accomplishment or "hoops" to jump through, but rather a belief in a young person's competence, worth, and ability. As young people tend to have an external locus of self-definition, what we believe about them helps them to define who they are. When they perceive positive messages about themselves from our High Expectations, they will tend to develop and demonstrate beliefs and behaviors that are congruent with their perception. The reverse is also true, and as young people will live up to High Expectations, they will also live down to low expectations. In a very real sense, how young people behave in our presence is a mirror reflection of how we believe they will behave.

Meaningful Participation, the final Protective Factor, is simply ensuring that young people are active participants in their environment and take an active role in the choices, decisions, and activities in their lives. It is direct involvement and active participation; a direct connection between what they do and what they experience; that fosters innate resilience and serves as a Protective factor.

Developmental Outcomes

The "bottom line" of all youth work is the outcomes that are produced. Outcomes are generally measured in terms of an increase in observable accomplishments (Achievement Outcomes; such as jobs, diploma's, housing, etc.) or a decrease in future undesirable choices (Prevention Outcomes; such as pregnancy, drug use/abuse, recidivist behaviors, etc). PYD differs from other youth work disciplines in that Achievement and Prevention outcomes are not the primary focus. Instead, PYD focuses on Developmental Outcomes (referred to as "DO's" as a reminder that this is what we are trying to "do"). DO's are beliefs, behaviors, knowledge, and skills that result in a healthy and accomplished adolescence and adulthood. PYD does not say that Achievement and Prevention Outcomes are unimportant or unnecessary. Rather, it postulates that the best way to obtain Achievement and Prevention Outcomes in a meaningful and lasting way is to focus on DO's, for if a young person successfully develops positive beliefs, behaviors, knowledge, and skills, the result will be that they begin to accomplish Achievement and Prevention Outcomes as a natural consequence of healthy development.

DO's are also presented differently by different sources. One of the earliest presentations was created by Dr. Maria Montessori in the early part of the 20th century. Montessori defined outcomes in 4 "dimensions" (emotional, moral, cognitive, and social) across 4 "planes" of development (birth-6, 6-puberty, puberty-18, and 18-24). As PYD came into practice as a recognized approach, many researchers described DO's as "The 5 C's" (Competence [academic, social, and vocational]; Confidence [positive self-concept]; Connections [to community, family, and peers]; Character [positive values, integrity and moral values]; and Contributions [active, meaningful roles in decision making and facilitating change]). Some researchers substitute Caring (positive regard for others) for Contributions, while others add it to the list as a 6th "C." Dr. Kenneth Ginsburg, in developing a model of resilience for the American Academy of Pediatrics, identified *seven* "C's" -- adding Coping (positive coping strategies), and Control (an internal locus of control) to the original 5.

One of the better known presentations is the Search Institute's 40 Developmental Assets. As with Protective Factors, different sources are not contradictory, but are simply different presentations of similar concepts. Regardless of the way DO's are described, the idea is to focus on *who a young person is becoming*, as opposed to *what* a young person is *doing*.

I have personally found one of the better presentations of DO's to be that which was developed for the Advancing Youth Development curriculum, which based on application and practice I have slightly modified over the years from its original source[54]. In this presentation, DO's are described as 2 categories of 6 outcomes each. The first category, Aspects of Identity, contains outcomes representing beliefs and behaviors demonstrating a sense of personal well-being and a connection and commitment to others, and includes the following outcomes:

Self-Worth:
 I am "good" and I contribute to others and myself.
Mastery and Future:
 I am "making it" and will succeed.
Safety and Structure:
 I am safe in the world and daily events are somewhat predictable.
Belonging and Membership:
 I value and am valued by others in my family and in the community.
Responsibility and Autonomy:
 I have some control over daily events and am accountable for my actions and their consequences.
Self-Awareness and Spirituality:
 I am unique while attached to families, communities, & higher beliefs or principles.

The second category, Areas of Ability, contains outcomes representing knowledge and skills that provide the ability and motivation for current and future success, and includes the following outcomes:

Employability:
 I have the ability and motivation ... to gain the skills necessary for employment.
Mental Health:
 I have the ability and motivation ... to cope with situations and to engage in leisure and fun.
Cultural Ability:
 I have the ability and motivation ... to respect differences among

[54] Advancing Youth Development; A Curriculum for Training Youth Workers, developed by the AED/Center for Youth Development and Policy Research in collaboration with the National Network for Youth.

groups and individuals.
Physical Health:
I have the ability and motivation ... to ensure current and future physical health.
Intellectual Ability:
I have the ability and motivation ... to learn, think, problem-solve, and study independently.
Civic and Social Ability:
I have the ability and motivation ... to work collaboratively and to sustain relationships

Note that Areas of Ability refers to *capabilities* and *skills*, not accomplishments. Getting a job is an Achievement Outcome; having the *ability* and *motivation* to get a job is a Developmental Outcome.

(s)OS: A Framework for Youth Development

Implementing a PYD approach is about focusing on DO's while building an environment of Protective Factors. As such, PYD is not so much *what you do* as it is *how you do it*. Different programs can all be PYD programs based not on similarity of program *model*, but rather on similarity of program *framework*. That framework is called (s)OS, or (services), Opportunities & Supports, which is 2 (not 3) different frames.

The first frame is (services), which is set in parentheses' and not capitalized to indicate that it is often an important foundation for, but is *not*, PYD. Services are things that we do *to* or *for* young people, such as providing them with shelter and meeting other basic needs. When we do to or for, we do not assist with someone's development or foster their innate resilience; we simply provide for their needs. A PYD approach *minimizes* (services) and *maximizes* the second frame; Opportunities & Supports.

Opportunities and Supports should be considered a single frame as they are two sides of the same coin, and successful implementation requires that they are inextricably connected. An Opportunity is anything that is done *by* youth; that is, they are in the driver's seat and have a direct link to the responsibility for the action. The other side of the coin is the Support, or things that we do *with* youth. While they are in the driver's seat, we are on the passenger side providing encouragement, knowledge, and resources. An Opportunity without a Support is a set up for failure, and a Support without an Opportunity is simply adult-directed activity. The framework for PYD is to turn as many (services) into Opportunities & Supports as possible -- thus addressing the Protective Factor of offering young people opportunities for Meaningful Participation.

This is where the PYD emphasis on *youth participation* comes from and why the creation of successful youth/adult partnerships is so critical to the successful implementation of the PYD approach. Most traditional youth programs are structured to provide services that target Achievement and/or Prevention Outcomes. A PYD program will create opportunities and provide supports that assist young people with their growth and development.

A Note on Youth Participation

In my consulting work I have found that PYD implementation is often weakened by 3 specific misunderstandings of the proper role of youth participation.

1. Youth participation is PYD

    No. Youth participation is a component of the PYD approach as it represents 1 of the 3 primary Protective Factors. But the other 2 Protective Factors are equally important. Youth participation in the absence of Caring, Supportive Relationships and High Expectations will not be as effective at promoting Developmental Outcomes and fostering resilience.

2. Youth participation is important because it improves programs by considering youth input and perspectives

    Well, yes -- but that's missing the point. It's true that programs will benefit by including youth as partners, so strategies such as youth advisory boards and youth seats on Boards of Directors are highly recommended. But improving your program is not the reason why you implement strategies of youth participation -- that's just a fortunate additional result. The reason to implement participation is that Meaningful Participation is one of the Protective Factors necessary to promote a young person's development and foster their resilience. Therefore, youth advisory boards and youth on your Board of Directors are excellent opportunities for the small number of youth serving on those boards; but what about everyone else? Planning for youth participation requires strategies that provide opportunities for *all young people* to participate at some level, at least in the decisions and actions that directly affect them.

3. Youth participation means giving the power for decisions to young people

    No. To think this way is to create Opportunities without corresponding Supports. Youth participation is about sharing power *with*, not giving power *to*. Adults maintain legitimate and relevant roles in youth participation strategies, but young people also have legitimate and relevant roles. Youth participation does not refer to youth acting *in the absence* of adults, but rather to youth and adults working in partnership.

Specific strategies related to youth participation are another area of varied perspectives within the PYD community, however the common thread is that that to promote development, young people must be active participants in programs.

Core Competencies and Basic Skills

The success of any effort or discipline will be directly affected by your mastery of between 5 and 7 core competencies related to that discipline. PYD is not an exception to this rule, and there have been many efforts to identify the core competencies required by PYD. While I have recognized that many aspects of PYD are presented differently, I've pointed out that the different presentations do not represent contradiction or disagreement. Different presentations of core competencies, however, are sometimes conflicting and contradictory. My theory on why this is the case is because PYD is an *approach*, not a *model*. The core competencies I need to be a PYD vocational education teacher will be different from the core competencies I need to be a PYD street outreach worker. While I support the identification of the core competencies needed within whatever *model* you are implementing, I discuss core competencies related to the PYD *approach* as 4 specific "basic" skills.

> Active Listening:
> The ability to listen and respond in a way that improves understanding.
> Information Sharing:
> The ability to provide complete and relevant data.
> Negotiation, specifically, Win/Win Negotiation:
> The ability to negotiate for mutually beneficial outcomes.
> Delegation:
> The ability to entrust authority.

These basic skills are critical to relationship development, the demonstration of High Expectations, and the implementation of strategies for youth participation regardless of the *model* in which you are working. They should be utilized in addition to the core competencies required by your program's model, and when so utilized they enable you to use a PYD *approach* within your model.

Summary and Credits

PYD focuses on promoting adolescent development and fostering innate resilience. It does so by targeting Developmental Outcomes through a framework that minimizes services (to or for) and maximizes Opportunities & Supports (by and with). The goal is not to change or "fix" the young person, but to increase the amount of Protective Factors to which the young person is exposed in their environment.

While there is no universally accepted "template" for implementation, all PYD literature tends to share common themes. The information contained in this introduction is a composite of those themes, with much influence from the Advancing Youth Development curriculum created by the Academy for Educational Development/Center for Youth Development and Policy Research, in collaboration with the National Network for Youth, which was the product of a 3-year project funded by the Office of Juvenile Justice and Delinquency Prevention (OJJDP) at the U.S. Department of Justice. Information from that curriculum has been significantly modified and merged with other resources and original work by JT (Jerry) Fest and is presented here with grateful acknowledgement to everyone who has contributed to the PYD body of knowledge.

About the Author

JT (Jerry) Fest has worked with street-dependent youth for over four decades. He founded Janus Youth Program's Willamette Bridge -- a continuum of services that includes streetwork, emergency shelter, transitional living, independent living, case management, and youth business and partnership programs. He developed the "self-government" model of residential services, one of the earliest program models based on the principles of Positive Youth Development.

Mr. Fest trains and consults with programs nation-wide. He has served on the Board of Directors of the Northwest Network for Youth, the National Network for Youth, and is the creator of the InterNetwork for Youth. He served 2 terms as the Region Ten representative to the National Council for Youth Policy, representing youth services in Alaska, Idaho, Oregon, and Washington. In 1996 he was selected as Citizen of the Year by the Oregon Child and Youth Care Association for his work with street-dependent youth, and is the recipient of the year 2000 Helen Reser Bakkensen award for "Exemplary Leadership, Service, and Advocacy on behalf of Homeless Youth."

Made in the USA
San Bernardino, CA
18 November 2014